TARGETED
PUBLIC
RELATIONS

ALSO BY ROBERT W. BLY

Selling Your Services

The Copywriter's Handbook

Secrets of a Freelance Writer

Business-to-Business Direct Marketing

The Elements of Business Writing

The Elements of Technical Writing

The Advertising Manager's Handbook

How to Promote Your Own Business

Direct Mail Profits

Ads That Sell

Creative Careers

Dream Jobs

Create the Perfect Sales Piece

Keeping Clients Satisfied

TARGETED PUBLIC RELATIONS

*How to Get Thousands of Dollars
of Free Publicity For Your Product,
Service, Organization, or Idea*

ROBERT W. BLY

HENRY HOLT AND COMPANY   NEW YORK

Henry Holt and Company, Inc.
Publishers since 1866
115 West 18th Street, New York, New York 10011
Henry Holt® is a registered trademark of Henry Holt and Company, Inc.
Copyright © 1993 by Robert W. Bly
All rights reserved.
Published in Canada by Fitzhenry & Whiteside Ltd.,
91 Granton Drive, Richmond Hill,Ontario L4B 2N5.

Library of Congress Cataloging-in-Publication Data
Bly, Robert W.
Targeted public relations : how to get thousands of dollars of free publicity
for your product, service, organization, or idea / Robert W. Bly.—1st ed.
    p.   cm.
1. Public relations. 2. Industrial publicity. 3. Advertising media planning. I.
Title.
HD59.B58   1993   92-33432
659.2—dc20   CIP
ISBN 0-8050-1975-8 (alk. paper)

First Edition—1993

Designed by Paula R. Szafranski

Printed in the United States of America
All first editions are printed on acid-free paper.⊗

10   9   8   7   6   5   4   3   2   1

*This book is dedicated
to my sons, Alex
and Stephen*

CONTENTS

ACKNOWLEDGMENTS

I'm indebted to Dr. Jeffrey Lant, David Yale, Dr. Andrew Linick, Pete Silver, Don Levin, Alan Caruba, and the other authorities on public relations mentioned throughout this book. You learn by doing and watching, and I've certainly benefited from watching them in action.

Thanks also to Lynn Gorman, Bruce Berman, Steve Davis, Corinne Shane, Garrard Stoddard, Don Libey, Dottie Walters, and everyone else who contributed time, ideas, or material for use in this book. If you're one of the group and I left you out, my apologies for the accidental omission.

There are many other people I've come in contact with over the years who have helped me develop and refine the techniques presented in this book. I won't name them all here. But they know who they are. Thanks, folks!

And a special thanks to my longtime editor, Cynthia Vartan, for her support and dedication.

And thanks to my wife, Amy, who took care of the baby while I wrote this book.

PREFACE

As advertising costs increase and marketing budgets get slashed in today's competitive business environment, businesspeople need alternatives to costly print, radio, TV, and direct-mail advertising for generating new leads and sales. While publicity costs less, for many companies it has not been as effective as print advertising or direct mail in generating immediate, direct responses.

This book is written to correct that situation and help you generate inquiries, increase sales, and gain visibility in the marketplace through low-cost/no-cost public relations techniques that *work*.

It is based on a powerful but underused concept in publicity: Targeted Public Relations. Targeted Public Relations is different from conventional public relations in a number of ways:

- Like direct mail, it is targeted toward specific audiences rather than taking conventional PR's "shotgun" approach in targeting mass media.

- It generates not just coverage and visibility but an immediate, tangible, measurable *response* (inquiries, orders, and so on)—again, much like direct mail or print advertising, but at a small fraction of the cost.
- Because it appears in the free media, it gains you the same third-party validation and endorsement that conventional PR does.

Therefore, Targeted Public Relations will be the new "secret weapon" of small and medium-size businesses throughout the United States, giving them a tool that *increases* the effectiveness and results of their marketing programs while *reducing* the cost.

It works regardless of the economy. In a soft or recessionary economy, Targeted Public Relations maintains a steady flow of profitable sales leads, exposure, and new business. Companies forced to cut back on expensive print and broadcast ad schedules can still afford to do Targeted Public Relations, because it is so inexpensive.

In a healthy economy, Targeted Public Relations serves as an *adjunct* to other marketing communications activities; use of Targeted Public Relations in conjunction with traditional marketing tools (radio commercials, Yellow Pages ads, direct mail, sales promotion, and the like) generates more and better results than any of these methods used alone.

Targeted Public Relations is a concise, practical handbook, packed with examples of publicity materials, such as model press releases, pitch letters, query letters, bios, articles, resource boxes, and checklists. Examples, in most cases, are not made up; I have used publicity materials that were successful in the "real world"—and, when available (not always), I give specific details on the actual results achieved along with an analysis of why each promotion worked.

I do have one favor to ask. If you create press releases,

publicity campaigns, or other PR promotions using *Targeted
Public Relations* that are successful, please send copies to me
so I can share them with readers of the next edition. You will
receive full credit, of course.

Bob Bly
Copywriter/Consultant
22 E.Quakenbush Avenue
Dumont, NJ 07628
201 385-1220

TARGETED
PUBLIC
RELATIONS

CHAPTER 1

An Introduction to Targeted Public Relations

PUBLIC RELATIONS MADE SIMPLE

A great many books have been written on public relations, most of them more sophisticated than this one. They report on an array of impressive, big-league public relations techniques—techniques that, unfortunately, are just not right or practical for 99.9 percent of small and medium-size businesses . . . including (I suspect) *yours*.

I have twelve years experience in public relations, but that's probably no more or less than the authors of those other PR books. The difference is that I think I know *you*—my audience—better than they do, and I have written this book with *your* marketing objectives, *your* budget, *your* available resources, and *your* plans, objectives, hopes, and dreams firmly in mind.

1

REALITY IN PUBLIC RELATIONS

Much of what is heralded as new and innovative and exciting in public relations is, unfortunately, geared toward Fortune 500–type companies and major PR firms—and therefore not doable within the budget or resources available to most small businesses.

By comparison, the public relations strategies and techniques outlined in this book are designed to be doable by the *average* business owner or manager who is not a public relations expert and has limited time, money, and other resources to devote to PR activities.

As a result, the public relations activities and tasks outlined in this book have the following in common:

1. They don't require an investment in high technology such as a fax machine with broadcasting capability, voice mail, and so on. Most can be done from start to finish with a typewriter, some typing paper, a photocopying machine, and a roll of stamps.

2. They don't require a huge investment. The average budget to do most of what is outlined in this book is a few hundred dollars; many can be done for under $500. A few, such as the newsletter discussed in chapter 9, may run slightly more, depending on your volume.

   But nothing here comes close to what you would spend running even a single full-page ad in an consumer magazine or large-circulation daily newspaper.

3. To succeed at marketing requires an expenditure of both time and money in varying amounts. You can elect to spend more money and less time, or more time and less money, but you can't get results if you are unwilling to invest in either one.

   Because most of the promotions outlined here require minimal money, they necessarily require some investment of your time. The time investment is not excessive, however, and can be tailored to fit your schedule, depending on how much publicity you seek and what your sales and marketing goals are.

4. Although retaining a professional PR counselor, freelance PR writer, or PR agency is a good investment if you select the outside professional properly, the promotions in this book are explained in enough detail and with sufficient examples so you can "copy" what I've done and do it yourself—even if you are not a professional writer or publicist—without professional assistance.

    This is truly a "do-it-yourself" how-to business book, not just theory or background. By following the examples, formulas, and "recipes" in *Targeted Public Relations*, you will be able to create successful PR campaigns, on your own—quickly, easily, effectively.

5. I realize that small and medium-size businesses today are cutting back on personnel and budget, and your resources for doing marketing activities may be more limited than in previous years. So wherever possible, I give you shortcuts and resources that enable you to get more done with *minimal* expenditure of time and effort on the part of you and your staff. For example, instead of taking your secretary away from his or her work to stuff press releases in envelopes, the "Publicity Distribution/Outlets" section of the appendix lists resources that can do it for you cheaper than you can do it in-house.

6. Finally, everything in this book is designed to generate one thing: results. Specifically, Targeted Public Relations gives you a results-to-expenditures ratio unmatched by any other promotion or marketing tool available. For an investment of a few days' time and a

few hundred dollars in a Targeted Public Relations campaign, you can achieve results comparable to what an ad agency might charge you $10,000 to $20,000 or more for and take weeks to implement.

Now, I'm not saying that Targeted Public Relations is *better* than advertising, or that you should do this *instead* of having an ad agency; in fact, chapter 12 discusses how you can maximize results by integrating public relations with your other marketing activities. I *am* saying that of all the marketing activities you do, public relations is likely to get you the best results at the least cost. As a result, it is an excellent *supplement* to advertising and promotion in good times . . . and in bad times, it can maintain your visibility and marketing success when you are forced to cut back on paid advertising and other, more costly promotions.

WHAT IS "PUBLIC RELATIONS"?

The *Dictionary of Advertising Terms* defines public relations as

(1) activities of persons or organizations intended to promote understanding of and good will toward themselves or their products or services, (2) the degree to which such entities have obtained understanding and good will from their publics, (3) a management staff function which seeks to assess and favorably influence public opinion of a person, good, or organization by delivering messages to such publics without incurring direct media costs.

In his book *How to Promote Your Own Business* (NAL), communications consultant Gary Blake and I wrote, "Publicity is a kind of free advertising. By providing editors and program directors with news and other information, you can get your business coverage in the media. You do not pay for the coverage, and are not identified as the source of the story."

PUBLIC RELATIONS VERSUS ADVERTISING: A COMPARISON

How does public relations differ from advertising?

- Advertising is paid; public relations is free. When you run an ad, you pay for the space; when a newspaper writes an article about your company, you don't pay for it.
- Advertising is clearly identified in the media as a paid promotion. Readers and viewers know it is a promotional message paid for by a sponsor.

  Publicity is not identified as a paid promotion. Even though a story about a product or organization may have resulted from a publicity campaign, the article or report never acknowledges that fact. (For instance, you almost never see an article in a newspaper or a magazine say "According to a press release sent by the PR department of So-and-So Corporation. . . .")
- When you advertise, you have almost total control over the contents, format, timing, and size of your message. You specify how big your ad is and when it runs. You write the copy and design the layout, and your material appears exactly as you created it.

  When you do public relations, you have almost no control over the content, format, timing, and size of your message as it appears in the media. That is, you can write whatever you want in your press release, but you can't dictate to the newspaper how it is printed or used, nor can you review or approve any changes made. You provide the press with written materials that they use (or don't use) in any way they see fit. Your press release may appear word for word in one magazine but be rewritten almost beyond recognition in another. One industry trade journal may write a cover story based on your material; another may not publish it at all.

- Advertising is "repeatable"; PR is not. The same advertisement can be repeated as many times as you wish in a given publication; the same TV commercial can be broadcast night after night. But a media source is going to run a given press release or cover a publicity event only *once*. To get covered again, you're going to have to provide the media with a new story, or at least come up with a different angle or new spin on the old topic.

- People are skeptical of advertising. They tend not to believe the claims made in advertising. Many believe that if your service was any good, you wouldn't need to advertise.

  On the other hand, people tend to take what they hear on radio, see on TV, and read in the paper at face value: They believe that if the newspaper printed it, it must be true.

  Because publicity is promotion in the guise of editorial, feature, or news material, people do not identify it as promotion and are therefore not skeptical of it; indeed, they believe it.

- In many instances media coverage of your event or story can appear to the public to be media endorsement of your organization or product—for example, a favorable story about your charity on the evening news, or a good review of your software package in a computer magazine. What's more, things that would sound conceited, self-serving, and not credible if *you* said them about yourself in an ad seem complimentary, flattering, and impressive when the media say them about you.

- Advertising is relatively expensive; PR is relatively inexpensive. Many small and medium-size businesses that can afford only limited advertising (with limited results) can do much more PR—and get better results—on a fraction of the budget they'd spend on paid advertising.

- Publicity must have an "angle"—that is, a hook or theme that engages an editor's attention—in order for it to have a decent chance of being noticed, read, and used. Therefore, it must appeal to editors and program managers as well as to the consumers (your prospects and the people who read the magazine or listen to the radio show).

An ad has to appeal to only one audience: your prospects. You don't care whether the media like or are interested in the ad, because they have already agreed to run it in exchange for a given amount of money.

COMMON MYTHS ABOUT PR

Right up front, I'd like to address head-on some common myths about public relations.

THE MYTH: *Press releases don't work anymore.*
THE REALITY: *Press releases DO work—and they are the most cost-effective and least time-consuming form of PR.*

At least once a week I hear a talk or read an article by a public relations agency executive, industry guru, or consultant proclaiming the death of the press release. "Press releases don't work anymore," they say. "Editors are deluged with press releases, get too many of them. You have to do something different. Fax your material to editors; call them with story ideas; send out fact sheets or fliers—not press releases."

Baloney. The fact is, no PR tool is simpler to use or as effective as a basic, well-written, short press release based on a strong hook or angle. Press releases still work. They work well. They're easy to produce. And inexpensive to distribute.

I agree that done *wrong* (as many people do them), press releases can be a waste of time and money. But done *right* (as explained in detail in chapter 5), they are one of the most hardworking, result-getting marketing tools going: Nothing beats them.

Examples? I am a marketing consultant. During the height of the recession of the early 1990s, I saw that small businesses needed help coping with the sluggish economy. So I wrote a booklet of fourteen sales and marketing strategies they could use to prosper in bad times. I mailed a press release announcing the availability of the booklet to several hundred business editors at magazines and newspapers; dozens reprinted the release or used it as the basis of an article on marketing in a recession, and more than 3,000 people sent in $7 each to purchase the booklet from me.

So don't tell me press releases don't work. They do.

THE MYTH: *The "legitimate" media snub and do not use PR.*

THE REALITY: *Much of the "news" you read in the newspaper, hear on radio, and see on TV has its origins in PR materials sent to the media by organizations and corporations looking to promote their cause, product, or service.*

Most businesspeople I've talked to tell me, "I know my industry publications will print my press releases, because they want me to advertise with them. But I want to get my name on the front page of the *Wall Street Journal* and the *Harvard Business Review*, and the 'better' publications don't use PR materials. What should I do?"

The simple answer is that prestigious and well-respected publications such as the *Wall Street Journal, Forbes, Fortune,* and the *New York Times* are interested in and will use good stories, regardless of whether they uncovered the story through intensive investigative reporting or a press release sent to them by a company or group like yours.

Editors are busy and always on the lookout for good material. If your PR materials contain news or information that's of interest or genuine use to their readers, they'll print it. In fact, much of what you read in respected journals, important business magazines, popular consumer magazines, and the nation's largest and most-respected daily newspapers has its origins as PR materials sent by marketers in the hopes of promoting an event, cause, product, or service.

Proof? *The Columbia Journalism Review* surveyed one issue of the *Wall Street Journal* to find out how many of the stories were generated by press releases. The survey revealed that 111 stories on the inside pages were taken from press releases, either word for word or paraphrased. In only 30 percent of the stories did reporters put in additional facts not contained in the original release.

Virtually any media outlet you're seeking publicity from can be swayed to give you some coverage, provided your materials are on-target and you can offer or create a story of genuine interest to its audience. And doing so is relatively easy, since there are only seven basic themes or hooks for news and feature stories that will interest editors and program directors. (These are discussed in chapter 2.)

THE MYTH: *Printed PR promotions do not work without follow-up.*

THE REALITY: *Follow-up can help increase results, but well-written material will "sell itself" and generate lots of publicity without a single follow-up call or letter.*

To get you to hire them, some PR firms or consultants will try to sell you on the idea of follow-up.

"Sure, you know your product best, and maybe you write well enough to put out some releases," the PR agency tells you, "but the releases won't get printed unless you follow-up with the editors.

"When you hire us, our account executive will spend a good part of his or her time following up by telephone with the publications and programs to which we send your material. This follow-up will ensure that they review and use your material; without it, your release will end up in the round file."

This statement is partially true. What's true is that follow-up is valuable, does increase results, and can get some editors who missed your material to give it consideration. What's more, hiring a PR agency is a good way to ensure this follow-up, because you are too busy to do it yourself.

What's not true is the notion that, without follow-up, printed PR materials are not effective and have little or no chance of getting published.

In reality, a press release, if it is well written and contains information of interest, can get wide coverage from a significant number of media outlets without follow-up phone calls to even a single editor.

An example is the Koch Engineering "DRY SCRUBBER" press release shown in chapter 5. This press release, mailed to fifty or sixty technical and trade journals in pollution, chemical processing, pulp and paper, and related industries, generated more than eighteen published stories resulting in 2,500 inquiries to the company . . . without a single follow-up call.

So while follow-up can't hurt and is usually beneficial, it is not necessary, and the lack of time to follow-up press release mailings should not stop you from distributing press releases or from handling your own PR.

It's much the same with query letters used to interest editors in running articles by or about you. Many of the successful query letters shown in chapter 6 generated acceptance and publication of the article—without a follow-up letter or call to the editor. If the copy is written according to the guidelines spelled out in the chapter, the letter will get the editors to respond to you without you having to contact them.

The bottom line: PR works even if your time and resources for editorial contact are limited. Follow-up is helpful but far from essential. Well-written materials "make their own case" with editors and get printed without your help.

THE MYTH: *You need "contacts" to get publicity.*

THE REALITY: *Contacts do help, but you can succeed beautifully without them.*

Another argument many PR agencies use in selling their services to you is that they have "contacts" in the media and you do not.

Many PR firms present media contacts—editors, program directors, and other media people they know and have a working relationship with—as an advantage they use in getting publicity placement. When these PR firms pitch their services to you, they'll push this as a selling point.

Do you need contacts to get your name into the papers? Some PR agencies would have you believe the answer is "Yes, definitely—it's the most important thing." My belief is that contacts, while of some benefit, are not needed, and the non-PR professional can obtain profitable results without knowing a single editor personally or "doing lunch" with producers and program directors.

One advantage full-time PR professionals have over you, a person for whom PR is just one of many job functions, is that they have the time to spend building media contacts. This investment will pay out over time: For example, an account executive at a PR firm handling half a dozen computer accounts can get to know the important editors at the top half-dozen or so computer publications. The "investment" in time and energy spent in establishing these relationships is "amortized" (spread out) over the half-dozen clients—and so it becomes cost-effective.

On the other hand, the small business owner who has total responsibility for all facets of her operation—research, product development, manufacturing, management, finance, marketing, distribution, sales, promotion—can perhaps devote one-twentieth of her time or less to public relations. For the little PR she does—a press release this month, a feature article in June, a press conference in October—she simply cannot afford to spend the time getting to know and cultivate editorial contacts in the same manner the full-time PR professional can.

Instead, the business owner or manager who has part-time responsibility for public relations can, and should, build up a list of media contacts slowly, over time. You do this by creating and maintaining a list or database of any media contact or outlet that runs a story or short item about you based on PR materials you sent. Your "media contact list" consists of the names, titles, publications or stations, addresses, phone numbers, and fax numbers of editors, writers, reporters, program directors, hosts, and other media people who have previously given coverage to your PR efforts. How do you build it?

Every time you get media coverage, you should immediately do two things.

First, send a thank-you note to the reporter or editor who used your material. Your note should thank the person for taking the time to write about you, while also giving brief mention of one or two other story ideas that might be right for the publication and that you could help with by providing more information. The letter should be short and primarily focus on a sincere thank you; the mention of new ideas should be a soft-sell and take only one or two lines.

Second, enter the media person's name, publication, and other contact information (address, phone, and so on) into a card file, your Rolodex, or a computer database. Whenever you get coverage from a media source that hasn't written about you before, add that name to your database.

In a short time, you will have a contact database of media people who have covered you or used your PR materials in some way, and therefore have some familiarity with you and your company.

Just as in direct mail, sending letters to your "house" list of existing customers will almost always produce a greater response than mailing the same letter to a rented list of "cold" names. Sending PR materials to your house list of media contacts will result in greater use of your materials than mailing the same press releases to a list of editors or program directors taken from one of the media directories listed in the appendix.

Does this mean you send your PR materials only to your house media contact list and not to other sources? No. Any release you distribute should go to your house list as well as all other appropriate publicity outlets listed in whatever media directories you are using.

The purpose of maintaining a media contact database is to ensure that these people get *all* your materials and are not accidentally left out. Make sure your media contacts get *all* your PR mailings, because these are the people most likely to give you coverage.

To sum up: For the small and part-time PR practitioner, it is not cost-effective to "court" the press for purposes of making personal connections to increase the odds of media placement. The better strategy is simply to keep track of and maintain constant contact with every media source who *does* cover you, based on the assumption that any editor or program director who has featured you once is likely to want to do so again if you present a story or angle of interest.

■ ■ ■

THE MYTH: *Editors want to be wined and dined.*
THE REALITY: *Editors don't have time to be wined and dined.*

This is an extension of the myth that close personal contact with media people is necessary to getting media coverage. The intent is to get preferential treatment from editors and reporters by getting to know them personally and establishing a close relationship with them, and also by giving them perks—such as taking them out to lunch in a posh restaurant or giving tickets to a basketball game.

While editors are human and a minority may respond favorably to such treatment, my experience is that most don't want it—and would rather you do not try to monopolize their time with small talk and three-martini lunches. The reason is that, like all of us, editors are busy people . . . but in addition to being busy, they constantly face tight deadlines. (Few editors do not feel pressed by looming deadlines for the next issue almost all of the time.)

As a result, most editors prefer to keep PR sources—even good ones—at arm's length. They prefer to receive story ideas and proposals in a letter or press release rather than have the details transmitted in a lengthy conversation. Most editors are print-oriented and so prefer written communication; if they have questions, they'll ask. If a conversation is necessary, they'd rather it be five minutes over the telephone than a two-hour lunch.

So the truth is that it's not necessary to wine and dine editors as you might an important prospect or customer. If you want to, go ahead and do so. Just be aware it's an unnecessary activity.

■ ■ ■

THE MYTH: *To get the media's attention you have to be different, outrageous, crazy, and creative.*

THE REALITY: *Although a creative approach can sometimes yield a publicity windfall, most editors and program directors prefer to be approached through "proper channels" using traditional, standard formats for media contact.*

Neophytes and others not experienced in dealing with the media tend to think along the following lines: "Editors are swamped by a flood of mail from PR firms and publicists daily and receive many more press releases than they can ever hope to use. Mine will get lost in the pile unless I make it stand out by being creative, different, far-out."

Based on this reasoning, these neophytes have, over the years, used a variety of tactics in their efforts to be different—from printing press releases on bright purple paper, to sending out a press release with a set of novelty-store plastic chattering teeth and a cover note that said to editors, "Here's a story you can really sink your teeth into."

Are these people right about editors being swamped with material, and do such tactics work to make your release stand out from the crowd?

It *is* true that virtually every editor is swamped with press releases and receives many more than he or she can possibly use. For example, Pamela Clark, formerly an editor with *Popular Computing*, said her staff received 2,000 press releases a month.

However, *putting real news or information of interest or value* into your press release, not using gimmick tactics such as purple paper and chattering teeth, is what makes your material get read, noticed, and used. While editors do not read or use 99 percent of the releases and article proposals sent to them, most at least *scan* each piece of mail, which means you have about five seconds to get their attention. A headline or opening paragraph that communicates vital news, important information, or other content of interest to the editors and their readers will grab the editor's attention and get him or her to read further.

"But won't a purple press release or set of chattering teeth also help get my stuff noticed?" you ask. Yes, but in a negative, not a positive, fashion. Editors look down on such gimmicks as unprofessional, and such tactics as printing a press release on colored paper or mailing it with a scented letter immediately mark you as an amateur whose material is not worthy of serious consideration. As a result, the editor will probably trash your material as frivolous, not important.

The best way to approach the media is still with the standard tools: query letters, press releases, fact sheets, phone calls. You may fear you won't get noticed because your material looks plain, but what interests editors is content, not appearance. Come up with a strong story idea and write it in a lively, compelling style. Style and substance—not gimmicks—will win the editor's heart.

THE MYTH: *Sending press releases through the mail is an archaic and ineffective way to communicate with the media. Distribution should be via wire, modem, floppy disk, fax, Federal Express, or other rapid-access media.*

THE REALITY: *A photocopied or offset-printed one- or two-page press release, sent to editors via first-class mail, is just as effective as fax or Federal Express—and much, much cheaper.*

A number of distribution services and individual PR practitioners claim that using a fax is a superior method of distributing news than the mail, but that is only partially true. A fax does get your material out much faster than if you print and mail it. However, I see no evidence that editors give faxed materials more consideration than mailed materials.

Similarly, my wife handled a project where the client said, "Mail all the releases Federal Express; that will really get the media's attention." (This occurred before faxes were common.) The cost was tremendous when compared with the cost of regular first-class mail for a one-ounce letter, and we saw no evidence that any editor was duly impressed or took extra notice of the material because it was sent Federal Express. People think such express delivery will work, but keep in mind that editors get many Fedex packages and fax messages daily—so sending your press release in such a manner has minimal added impact.

As for electronic submission, some magazines do welcome longer feature material sent on floppy disk or via modem, but the standard format is still a printed manuscript, and this is accepted by 99.99 percent of the magazines in the United States. If you can provide a floppy disk—fine. But it is not necessary, nor will it usually increase chances of acceptance.

THE MYTH: *You can't buy PR with advertising.*
THE REALITY: *In some publications, you can.*

We've always been taught that advertising and "editorial" are separate. That is, the editorial department of the publication operates separately, independently, and without input from the advertising department. This means the fact that you are an advertiser does not increase your chances of getting your press release run in the publication, any more than the fact that you are not an advertiser means the publication *won't* run your release.

But is this really true? Or can you "buy" some publicity by promising the publication you'll run a lot of ads if it runs your free publicity notice?

With some publications, you can do just that.

Whether a publication's editorial content is influenced by your promise to run an ad depends on the level of the publication. My experience is that at the higher-level, well-known, nationally respected publications (periodicals such as the *Wall Street Journal* and the *New York Times*), you cannot buy editorial space by promising to spend money on advertising, nor do the PR materials of advertisers receive even the slightest extra attention from the editorial staff. The exception might be when the advertising department wants the editorial department not to run a negative story about an advertiser, but unless you're involved in toxic dumping or public scandal, don't worry about this.

In publications that have smaller circulations and are more specialized or regional—that is, local instead of national, or industry-specific ("vertical") publications versus general business ("horizontal") magazines—the plain truth is that advertisers *do* get preferential treatment in some instances. I have seen it many, many times and know it to be a fact beyond dispute.

For example, when I was the public relations manager of a small company manufacturing chemical process equipment, the "space rep" (person selling ad space in the publication) of a Canadian chemical magazine wanted my company to advertise in his journal. I told him that while I was happy to see him, it would be unlikely that we would advertise with him, since most of our business was in the United States.

He paused. "Do you have press releases?" he asked. Of course, I told him, we probably had done six or seven in the last year alone. "Give me one copy of each release," he told me. "Why?" I asked. "You'll see" was his reply.

In about two months, he sent me a follow-up letter with

the latest issue of his magazine. *Every one of our press releases had been reprinted, with product photos, in that single issue!* His letter suggested that we could continue to get such favorable coverage by taking out some ads in the next few issues. Here was a blatant case of unabashed selling of ad space through favorable editorial coverage; obviously the advertising department controlled the editorial department at this magazine.

In another case, a client of mine was approached by the leading trade journal in his industry, which said it would write and publish a feature article about him in exchange for a big order of ad space. What's more, the publisher said, my client could get an even larger article and be featured on the front cover, if he paid a sum of several thousand dollars *in addition to* the cost of the ads. And this was from a highly respected industry publication readers valued for its editorial excellence, reporting, and objectivity. If only they knew!

Another colleague reports that a local business magazine, published by the chamber of commerce, would run a large, positive feature article about his business—an article that he could write and submit, and that would be run as written—if he joined the chamber. In fact, the chamber makes this offer to all potential members.

If you live in a small town, as I do, take a look at the local weekly "shopper" newspapers distributed free to all residents. Such newspapers are not reporting hard "news" per se but are really in the business of disseminating news about people and organizations in the community, including businesses. Send them a press release, and they will publish it. Take an ad, and you get featured in editorial roundups highlighting local businesses and their services.

Since many publications do give editorial favors in exchange for your ad dollars, should you ever take the initiative in suggesting such an arrangement to the media? You should *not*—at least not when communicating with staff writers and editors.

Never say to an editor "Please run my article; I advertise in your publication" or "I may place a lot of ads in your publication if you run my press releases and cover my grand opening." This is likely to infuriate the editor—it demeans the profession of journalism and insults him or her personally—and will kill any chance of that editor using your material now or in the future.

If the media outlet is one that allows advertising sales to influence editorial decisions, you'll find out when someone makes such a suggestion to *you*. It may come from the editor, but typically it comes from the publisher or space rep, who says "Run an ad with me and I'll get your press release published"—or the lesser promise of "Run an ad with me and I'll personally place your press release on top of the editor's desk and try to get him to run it."

If you do decide to broach the subject of getting press coverage in exchange for placing your ad with the publication, bring it up with the publisher or space rep, not the editor. Say something like "If I run these ads with you, what can you do for me editorially?" You'll quickly find out whether—and to what degree—the advertising department can influence the editor in favor of running the PR story of a particular advertiser.

THE MYTH: *Every fact printed in the newspaper or broadcast over the airways is checked and verified.*

THE REALITY: *Most PR materials are picked up and run with almost no verification of any kind.*

As mentioned earlier, a survey of an issue of the *Wall Street Journal* found that in 70 percent of the stories based on PR materials, the reporter did not put in facts other than those found in the press releases. In my own experience, I have found that editors rarely do much interviewing of sources to add to the material in the release and do not challenge claims made or check the accuracy of the information given. Instead, they tend to run PR materials pretty much as is; if they edit, it's usually for style, grammar, and to cut material to fit space limitations, not to add or verify factual content.

I do PR for many software companies and have mailed dozens of releases. I have found that 90 percent of the phone calls my clients get from editors are to verify the *price* of the software before the release is printed; rarely do they question the features listed or the accuracy of claims made.

Many editors are too busy to check the statements in your releases for accuracy, yet they do not want to appear to be endorsing you, nor do they want to take responsibility for claims *you* make about your product in your own materials. So if there is doubt as to the accuracy of information, or if your copy states an opinion or makes a claim that is likely to be challenged, the editor may get out of this dilemma the easy way—by simply not printing your material.

To solve this problem and get editors to run all your material, put controversial statements and claims in quotations and attribute them to an executive from your organization.

For example, if you write in a press release:

AML is currently the only logistics company specializing in the shipment of medical products and materials,

the editor may say, "To print this statement I have to check every business directory in the country to make sure that indeed there is no other firm offering such a shipping service." If she didn't, and in fact there were other firms providing the medical shipping service, she'd be printing inaccurate information. Since the editor cannot conclusively prove through research that AML indeed has no competitors, her most likely move would be not to print the statement.

But when we phrase the same information as an attributed statement,

"As far as we know, AML is the only logistics company currently specializing in the shipment of medical products and
materials," says Norman Freeman, company president,

the editor will readily print it, because she is on safe ground.
By printing it as an attributed quotation, she is not claiming
that AML is in fact offering a one-of-a-kind service; she is
merely reporting that the company president *claims* his service is one-of-a-kind . . . and the fact that Mr. Freeman has
made such a claim is beyond dispute, because it's right there
in his press release.

Should you put falsehoods, exaggerations, or puffery in
your press materials simply because you can get away with it?
No. Your materials should be accurate and newsworthy, giving real information, not advertising puffery.

The reason? Aside from the fact that it's bad business to lie
to your prospects, customers, and the public, lying to editors
is worse. If you trick them into printing something inaccurate,
and a reader points it out to them, they'll be displeased with
you, and they won't use you as an information source again,
because they don't trust you. So you will get no further publicity as long as those editors are working at those publications.

THE MYTH: *When it comes to getting publicity, it's largely
a matter of luck and timing.*

THE REALITY: *Chance favors the prepared mind, and
timing can be controlled.*

People who are unsuccessful at public relations (or anything else, for that matter) view those who are successful with
suspicion and cynicism. "Oh, they are lucky," claims the executive at one company who sees a favorable story about his
competitor in an important industry journal. "They must have
contacted this staff writer with the right story at the right

time. When we mailed our release, the magazine wasn't interested in this topic, so they didn't run it. Now, of course, it's a hot topic, and our competitor must have suggested the story to them just when they were planning to cover it."

Do I disagree that timing is important? No. In public relations, marketing, promotion, new product introductions, and selling, timing is critical: You succeed largely because you reach your media contact, target market, or prospect at just the right time.

However, as noted motivational expert Dr. Rob Gilbert pointed out to me in a conversation as I was writing this chapter, timing can be controlled—and, says Gilbert, "The way you control timing is to be there all the time."

For example, let's say you own a collection agency and are an expert in collections. You can never tell in what month a particular editor at your city's largest business magazine will want to do a story about the collection problems faced by small businesses and how to solve them. But one thing is certain: If you send this editor a press release on collections strategies and tactics every month, eventually your material will wind up in his lap *in the month he decides to do that story.* And when that happens, whom do you think he will interview—you or your competitor whom he's never heard of?

Recently my wife and I took our two-year-old son, Alex, to a town carnival. At one game of chance, you could win a small stuffed animal by placing a quarter on one of ten numbers, then hoping, when the wheel of chance was spun, that the pointer would end up on your number. It occurred to me that if I wanted to be certain of getting a stuffed animal for Alex, I could do so by spending $2.50 and putting a quarter on each of the ten numbers simultaneously: I'd *have* to hit with one of my ten bets. (In fact, we bet normally and won a stuffed animal on the first spin!)

In PR, the same principle applies: Keep putting yourself "out there" in the media—with query letters, pitch letters, press releases—and you will hit the winning number—with the prize being publicity for your company or service. It's inevitable.

Does this mean that a one-shot press release or PR promotion won't work? Not at all. Even a single press release or media appearance on TV or radio can generate scads of press coverage and hundreds or even thousands of inquiries and sales. But on the other hand, your first effort might bring little or nothing. When you treat publicity as a one-shot event, you're gambling. When you have a consistent, ongoing program, with efforts going out monthly or on some other regular basis, it's almost a certainty that you'll get the result you want sooner or later (sooner if you follow the formats in this book).

WHAT IS TARGETED PUBLIC RELATIONS?

I have defined public relations and discussed some of the common misconceptions. But in this book I have introduced the term Targeted Public Relations. What is that? And how does it differ from conventional or ordinary public relations?

As discussed in the preface, two characteristics distinguish Targeted Public Relations from conventional PR campaigns.

First, Targeted Public Relations concentrates on reaching a small, narrow segment of the market—specifically, those people who are prospects for the product or service you are selling.

You'd think this is a given of any public relations campaign, but it isn't. Often the client tells the PR firm: "Get me as much press as possible; I want to see our name in every newspaper every day of the year!" The objective of such a conventional PR campaign is quantity instead of quality: The client wants to generate a fat file folder full of press clippings, rather than increase sales or influence a specific audience in a specific way.

Targeted Public Relations, by comparison, says measuring PR success by counting clippings or the number of column-inches the company gets in the newspaper is folly. Getting a lot of articles about you published, or seeing your picture in the paper, may be flattering and ego-stroking, but if it doesn't get you customers or business, it's largely a waste of money, don't you agree?

Targeted Public Relations says: Concentrate your time, effort, dollars, and other resources on as narrow and tightly focused an audience as possible—one that consists primarily of people who are potential customers for what you are selling.

Example: I could probably get stories and photos of me in my local town newspapers if I did a concentrated PR campaign targeting those two papers, sending them a continual barrage of material; I'm sure they'd print it. However, I sell my consulting and writing services primarily to large corporations, and there are no large corporations in my town.

Therefore, such an effort, while getting me lots of press and giving me clippings I can show off to my relatives and friends, would be a waste of time and effort, since it wouldn't get my name known among potential customers and wouldn't generate any new business for me.

For this reason, I target my self-promotion Targeted Public Relations activities toward a select group of a dozen magazines, half a dozen newsletters, and three or four associations, all of which reach my potential clients with little or no waste. It may not be as ego-gratifying, but it brings me more business than I can possibly handle.

Best of all, my costs are minimal, because the media outlets I want to reach are few and easily identified. Why spend money mailing five hundred press releases a month when only ten publications matter to your marketing success? Targeted Public Relations says: "Don't."

The second major difference between Targeted Public Relations and conventional public relations deals with the goal or objective.

In a conventional PR campaign, the objective may be any one of the following:

- Get the client's name in the paper as much as possible.
- Generate a large file folder full of press clippings.
- Get the client on TV and radio talk shows.
- Generate a certain number of articles or press mentions each month.
- Make the client more visible, famous, well known, or recognized.
- Create a positive public image for the client.
- Create brand awareness for the client's product.

The Targeted PR campaign may also seek to accomplish one or more of these goals, but in addition, it will have as its *primary* mission these objectives:

- Get not only the client's name in the media but also the address and phone number—so the client can be reached easily by potential customers interested in learning more about the product or service.
- Generate inquiries directly from PR items as they are published or broadcast.
- Increase both the quantity and the quality of sales leads generated by PR—that is, get the greatest number of qualified prospects to inquire about the client's product or service as a direct result of the PR coverage.
- Generate, if feasible, direct sales or walk-in trade or traffic from PR items.

THE RESPONSE DIFFERENCE

Although the "targeting" aspect of Targeted Public Relations—the focusing in on a specific, well-defined audience and the media that reaches it—is important (and covered in detail in chapter 3), it is the idea of generating a *direct response* from PR . . . and not just media coverage or "ink" . . . that makes Targeted PR so cost-effective.

Marketers traditionally think of public relations as an image-building, rather than a direct-selling, activity, yet PR is one of the most cost-effective and successful methods for generating large volumes of direct inquiries and sales.

Example: Adrienne Zoble, a marketing consultant and author of the book *The Do-Able Marketing Plan*, did some PR for her book and got a small (approximately one-sixth of a page) article about the book published in *Inc.* magazine. This tiny article, which gave the price of the book and a phone number for placing orders (no address), generated 650 orders at $49.70 each, for a gross of $32,305—proof that PR is effective at generating a measurable and substantial direct response.

Marketing professionals serving clients who seek to generate leads and sales via direct response traditionally recommend such vehicles as direct mail and advertising. While I believe in direct mail and advertising, and use both frequently, the problem with them is that they are expensive.

Consider direct mail. Cost per thousand for a direct-mail package might be $600, including printing, mailing, postage, and lists. If the response rate is 2 percent, then you're getting twenty leads for every thousand pieces mailed, at a cost of $30 per lead.

By comparison, when I was the advertising manager at Koch Engineering, we paid our ad agency $1,000 or so to write, print, and distribute the press release (shown in chapter 5) for the "DRY SCRUBBER." It generated 2,500 leads, at a cost per lead of about 40 *cents* per lead.

The advantage of Targeted Public Relations over direct mail (and direct-response advertising) is that it generates the same type of direct inquiry or order at a fraction of the cost per response.

On the other hand, while a direct-mail package that generates a certain percentage of responses can be "rolled out" to a large number of mailing lists and mailed again and again, a given press release usually can be used only once. (Exceptions? Of course.)

Therefore, Targeted Public Relations does not necessarily replace traditional direct-mail and print advertising as a response-generating tool, but its cost-effectiveness does suggest that a Targeted PR campaign should almost always be used to supplement or augment direct-mail and space advertising—and often, an offer that works well in direct mail and direct-response space ads will work in a targeted public relations campaign. Chapter 12 goes into detail about how to integrate PR with direct mail, print advertising, and other media for maximum results.

EIGHT ADDITIONAL BENEFITS OF GETTING YOUR NAME IN PRINT USING TARGETED PUBLIC RELATIONS

Targeted Public Relations, like any good PR, gets your name into print where prospects and customers can see it. In addition to increasing your visibility and generating immediate leads, it makes sense to keep your name in print for the other benefits that will accrue to you. PR writer David Wood says the following are eight of the most valuable benefits PR offers the average business (this list is reprinted with permission of the author from *New England Real Estate Journal—Advertising and Public Relations Guide*, July 10, 1990, p. 6):

1. *Reinforce who you are and what you do.* You may think everyone knows who you are and the type of product or service you offer. But, observes Wood, chances are there are many people who have never heard of you or aren't exactly sure of what you do, where you're located, and so on. Getting your story into print tells people who you are and what you do, and some of those people could be potential customers.

2. *Let people know you're active.* Knowing you exist and remembering you when your service is required are two entirely different things. Being visible in print reminds people and keeps your name in front of them—so when they need the product or service you're selling, they know who to call. Not being in print is harmful, because "out of sight, out of mind" is probably more true in the business world than anywhere else.

3. *Publicize a specific project or event.* If a tree falls in the middle of the forest and no one is around to hear it, was there really a sound? If you expect people to know what you're up to, you better tell them. Don't depend on someone else, and don't be afraid to promote yourself.

4. *Enhance your company's image and reputation.* This is a natural outgrowth of all positive publicity. People tend to begin thinking of your company as a successful organization when they see your name regularly in respected publications. On a personal level, individuals who have been quoted or have written articles are now positioned as experts or authorities in their field, and don't we all want to do business with experts?

5. *Become an "of course."* What's an "of course"? It's when

a prospect is sitting down to prepare a list of potential vendors or suppliers and says, "Of course I'll have to include XYZ Company." What the prospect is really saying is, "XYZ Company is a major player, and I'd be making a mistake not to at least consider buying from them." One of the key contributors to becoming an "of course" is to constantly remind potential customers of your activities, accomplishments, and capabilities through the printed word. (Selling a quality product or rendering a superior service is another key factor in gaining a reputation as an "of course.")

6. *Impress clients, bankers, and investors*. You may not necessarily be impressed with what you see and read about yourself and your company in the newspapers, business magazines, and trade journals, but you'll be surprised at the effect it has on others. Prospective clients, bankers, investors, and the like often perceive you as a larger, more impressive organization than you may actually be, based on clips and articles about your company (that you or somebody working for you actually wrote).

7. *Gain "brownie points" with others on your team*. Few of us work alone, and our successes usually involve the efforts of other team members, such as coworkers, colleagues, subcontractors, managers, bosses, clients, consultants, and other vendors. By publicly acknowledging their contributions in print, you are not only giving them their just due, but you are building up incalculable goodwill that will come back to you many times over. And it encourages the best people in each field to want to work with you because of your professional attitude.

8. *Recognize and reward your employees*. Don't forget your own people. The same wisdom you use with respect to team members applies equally, if not more so, to your

own employees. Recognition and reward play an important part in employee satisfaction, and public praise goes a long way. (It does not, however, serve as a substitute for more tangible acknowledgments, such as bonuses, pay raises, or comp days.)

Before we can create a successful Targeted Public Relations campaign, we have to know what appeals to editors and their readers. This is covered in chapter 2.

CHAPTER 2

ESI AND RSI: THE KEYS TO A SUCCESSFUL TARGETED PUBLIC RELATIONS CAMPAIGN

WHAT RSI AND ESI ARE

A major difference among advertising, direct mail, and other promotions versus PR is the audience.

An ad or direct-mail package has only *one* audience: It must appeal to your prospects—the people who read the magazine or whose names are on the mailing list you rented—to succeed.

Ad copy is written for them and only them. You don't, for example, care whether the magazine's editor or publisher is intrigued by your ad, just as you don't care whether the mailing list broker is impressed with your mailing. Why should you? You don't have to please these people, since they give you space in their publication or use of their lists in exchange for money.

The PR practitioner, on the other hand, must appeal to *two* audiences . . . and please them both, to be successful.

One audience is your prospects—the people who read the magazine, watch the TV show, tune in to the radio program on which you want to be featured. You have to gain their attention and generate sufficient interest to get them to respond and contact you for further details.

However, the readers and viewers will never even get a chance to receive your message *unless the editors and program directors are convinced* to feature it in their publication or show. Media coverage can't be "bought" with money, gifts, or bribery. It has to be *earned*, by giving editors news, information, and other material good enough for them to use.

The editors and program directors, then, comprise the second audience whom PR practitioners must please. The best press release, with the most fascinating content and greatest offer, won't get a single response unless it is printed. And whether it gets printed is decided *entirely* by the editors at the various publications—not by you.

Therefore, the successful public relations campaign must appeal to what I call RSI, which stands for Reader's Self-Interest, as well as ESI—the Editor's Self-Interest. Importantly, each audience has a different agenda.

RSI

The reader (prospect) wants to be informed, entertained, and educated. He or she is looking for current events, important news, entertaining feature articles, useful information, and helpful advice. Among the strongest RSI appeals are stories that help readers achieve what they want in life. Some of these wants and desires are to:

- Be popular.
- Be appreciated.
- Be right.
- Feel important.
- Feel successful.

- Feel smart.
- Make more money.
- Save money.
- Have financial security.
- Save time.
- Have more leisure time.
- Enjoy leisure time.
- Do a better job at work.
- Find an enjoyable, rewarding career.
- Improve business skills.
- Pursue a hobby.
- Have self-esteem.
- Be secure.
- Be content.
- Be happy.
- Be free and independent.
- Establish a meaningful relationship.
- Be attractive.
- Attract the opposite sex.
- Be sexy.
- Satisfy sex drive.
- Have romance.
- Be comfortable.
- Avoid discomfort.
- Be distinct.
- Have fun.
- Have an easier life.
- Be a good spouse or partner.
- Have children.
- Be a good parent.
- Provide for the children.
- Make the children happy.
- Gain knowledge.
- Find out about others.
- Gratify curiosity.

- Be healthy.
- Lose weight.
- Be fit.
- Feel energetic.
- Avoid effort and work.
- Avoid pain.
- Avoid things that cause fear and anxiety.
- Have more than others do.
- Feel less guilty.
- Have status.
- Be relaxed and rested.
- Have power.
- Fulfill their destiny.
- Be unique.
- Be superior.
- Have self-esteem.
- Have the approval of others.
- Help others.
- Be remembered by others after death.
- Be famous.
- Be part of the "in" crowd.
- Be "in-the-know."

Almost every American spends his or her waking hours in satisfying these desires. And these RSI factors determine, to a large extent, what people choose to watch, listen to, or read.

The stories you provide the media must satisfy these RSI wants and desires; otherwise, people will not read and respond to them.

ESI

Here are five key factors that motivate editors. While many of them are related, I list them separately for simplicity's sake. They include RSI, PSI, ASI, JI, and ESP.

RSI

One of the editor's major responsibilities is to provide sub-scribers, readers, and listeners with a satisfactory product. That is, the editor must know her audience and then create a magazine, paper, or program that contains the type of material this audience needs and wants.

As a result, ESI and RSI are related to some degree; material written to satisfy the reader will probably satisfy the editor as well. However, there are four additional ESI factors that influence editors that readers don't care about: PSI, ASI, JI, and ESP.

PSI (Publisher's Self-Interest)

Every editor or program director has a *boss*, and like any em-ployee, the editor's career advancement depends largely on making the boss happy.

You might say, "Well, the publisher wants to make money, and that means keeping subscribers happy, so PSI equals RSI."

That's rational thinking, but remember: People are not al-ways rational. And that includes publishers.

It takes a lot of money, and guts, to start a magazine or newsletter, or buy and run a newspaper or radio station today.

Publishers, like many self-made entrepreneurs, are an in-dependent lot, with egos. Therefore, they may want to use their publication as a forum for expressing their own political, philosophical, or moral beliefs, ideas, and attitudes.

You see this in many publications and programs (I won't mention examples, for fear of libel) in which the content is obviously "slanted" toward one viewpoint or extreme. Ar-ticles are slanted usually at the dictates of a higher-up, such as a publisher or owner. The editor or program director merely carries out the wishes of the superior, or at least is influenced by them in some way.

So, for example, if you are promoting an organization dedicated to social programs, expect negative treatment from conservative radio shows and publications that are against this type of public assistance.

ASI (Advertiser Self-Interest)

More specifically, ASI stands for the interests of the advertising department, which is responsible for getting people to run paid ads and commercials in the medium. It includes sales reps who sell ad space in magazines as well as sales reps who sell airtime on TV and radio.

The advertising department's primary concern is to generate revenue for the publisher—and commission for itself—by selling as much advertising as it can.

And, as discussed in chapter 1, while in a "perfect world" there would be no mix between editorial and advertising and no pressure or influence of advertisers' needs on editorial content, in the real world such is not always the case.

The fact is, advertisers, and the advertising department, often can and do exert some degree of influence on the press. This tends to happen more in small, local, regional, and specialized media than in large, national, mass media, but nevertheless it does happen.

So, for example, if your press release supports an environmental group and blasts the chemical industry, it probably won't get a positive reception in a trade magazine read by chemical manufacturers.

Or let's say you invent a new type of widget and send out a press release claiming it is ten times better than conventional widgets and it makes every widget now on the market obsolete. If the magazine's income depends on full-page ads from the other ten largest widget manufacturers, it is not going to run a release saying all those widgets stink.

Be aware of who is advertising in your target media and what those ads are saying. Realize you may have difficulty placing stories that threaten, attack, or go against these major advertisers.

Another department whose work is affected by editorial content is the *circulation department* or *promotion department*. The circulation department's job is to get people to subscribe to the magazine or newsletter—primarily through direct mail, but sometimes using space ads or direct response TV commercials. The promotion department's job is to get people to pick up copies of the magazine or newspaper at the newsstand, or tune in to a particular radio or TV station or program. This is done using ads, commercials, and special promotions, such as having a radio show host sign autographs or march in a parade.

Editorial content and quality make the circulation/promotion department's job easy or difficult: It's easier to sell a good publication that people like; more difficult to get people to subscribe to something that's inadequate or off base for the intended audience.

Therefore, for circulation/promotion people, the ideal editorial content is "promotional" in nature—that is, stories and programs they can use to gain attention and induce people to watch the program, read the issue, or subscribe to the periodical.

However, for the most part, circulation and promotion people are not able to influence or control the editorial content of their publication or program in any significant way.

When writing a direct-mail letter or ad describing the contents of their magazine, for example, circulation directors are generally restricted to describing articles the editor has or plans to publish; they can't list in the ad copy titles of articles they feel would get people to subscribe, then go to the editor and get those articles written.

Since interests of the circulation/promotion people rarely affect editorial content, they are not of concern to you as a public relations practitioner.

JI (Journalistic Integrity)

What do you think of when you hear the word journalist? Probably of big-time investigative reporters such as Woodward and Bernstein, as portrayed in the movie *All the President's Men*. If asked, you might say that, in your opinion, a reporter for your town's weekly "shopper" or a writer for an association or trade journal is not a "real" journalist.

The fact is, however, that most media people think of themselves as journalists to one degree or another (and, in fact, are). The editor of *Sludget Today* magazine realizes he is not a *New York Times* reporter, but takes his job no less seriously.

As a result, editors and program directors at most media, whether news-, feature-, or information-oriented, have journalistic ethics and values. They will not take actions that detract from or threaten their journalistic integrity or their image of themselves as journalists. For example, an editor at *Pulp and Paper* magazine will print a press release on your new Super Pulpmaker 5000 machine not to promote your company or generate sales leads for you but because she judges that it is news of value to her readers.

Avoid having a "slick" or "promotional" tone in your press materials, because such a style smacks of hype and is offensive to editors and writers. A common mistake businesspeople make is to take their ad, direct-mail letter, or brochure and simply retype the copy in press release format. This will turn off editors and gain your material quick rejection.

A better approach is to use the good, solid information (but not the sales talk) that is in your ad, direct-mail piece, or brochure, but rewrite it in a style similar to a newspaper article or feature article you'd find in any popular or trade magazine. Chapter 5 gives numerous examples of PR materials written in these styles.

Even if publishing your material does in fact promote you, your company, or your product—and even if you know it and the editor knows it—your material will be used (or not used) based on its merit and value to the readers, and not based on whether it helps you.

ESP (Editor Self-Protection)

Editors don't mind running questionable, unconventional, or controversial material *as long as they can attribute it to a quoted source.* If an editor writes, "Mr. Jones runs a questionable law practice," that editor is stating as fact in print something that may not be true.

On the other hand, if the editor writes, "'Mr. Jones runs a questionable law practice,' alleges Alma Smith, a disgruntled client," he is doing his job: that is, reporting what Alma Smith, a source for the story, said about the law practice.

For that reason, claims of superiority, of performance, and of excellence; out-of-the-ordinary statistics or figures; hard-to-believe statements or facts; or other items that might be questioned have a better chance of seeing print if you *put them in quotes* in your press materials *and attribute them to a source* (such as your company president or owner, for example). This technique was discussed in chapter 1.

THE TWO MOST COMMON
MISCONCEPTIONS BUSINESS-
PEOPLE HAVE ABOUT PR

The two most common misconceptions businesspeople have about PR are opposite opinions—you can believe one or the other, but not both at once.

The misconceptions:

Misconception 1. Media people loathe PR people, hate PR, prefer to investigate every story "from scratch" through good old-fashioned reporting, and avoid being influenced by PR at all costs.

Misconception 2. Media people are "in cahoots" with PR people, will do anything to please their advertisers or potential advertisers, are lazy and just want press releases they can copy and run word for word, and *want* to promote your product or service.

The truth is, the media world is like a bell curve. At one end, a small minority of media people fit the image of #1 above; at the other end, some fit the behavior pattern of misconception 2.

But in the middle of the bell curve is the vast majority of media people: the nine out of ten members of the working press who:

- Neither hate nor love PR people, but recognize that they are a permanent part of the "media machine" in this country and can sometimes be the source of interesting, usable material
- Do not avoid using, but at the same time don't actively seek out, PR materials—but simply consider PR as one of many sources of information and story ideas
- Are neither excessively lazy nor excessively workaholic, but are like the majority of Americans—they want to do

their jobs well but are pressured by deadlines and appreciate assistance that saves them time or effort
- Are not as dedicated to promoting your product or services as you are, but recognize that media coverage is beneficial to you, and don't mind giving you some of the coverage in exchange for a good story or material helpful to them and their readers

In short, contrary to what most businesspeople think, media people don't spend an inordinate amount of time worrying over the issue of PR versus purity in journalism. They are too busy putting the program together or getting the issue out. They are motivated primarily by ESI and RSI. Their decision whether to use a given story is based primarily on the quality of the material, not whether the story was gotten through reporting or provided by a PR source.

WHY EIGHT OUT OF TEN EDITORS *WANT* TO GET MATERIAL FROM YOU

Editors welcome PR materials if the materials are well written, relevant to their audience, noteworthy, and valuable.

You might think it a strange practice that a businessperson like you can write articles, send them to the press, and the press will use them or reprint them. "Aren't I doing the editor's job?" you may wonder. "Aren't their writers supposed to write the stuff?"

Most editors welcome PR materials, and here are the reasons why:

- *PR materials put expert sources at the editor's fingertips.* No editor or reporter can be an expert in every facet of a subject. Contributions from PR sources provide information and thinking from top executives, scientists, engineers, and other experts who, if they were not involved in promoting their company, would not make themselves accessible to the press.

- A writer working for a computer trade journal, for example, will, over time, become well versed in computer issues and gain a pretty fair knowledge of the technology. But she can't know every detail of every specialized area of software and hardware. So if she is writing an article on CASE (computer-aided software engineering), she will probably draw material from press kits provided by firms selling CASE tools, books, and seminars.

- *PR provides a free and infinite source of story ideas.* While it is part of an editor's job to come up with story ideas, this is the least worrisome aspect of being an editor. PR materials and query letters (letters suggesting article ideas) from freelance writers provide hundreds or thousands of story suggestions—at no charge to the publication.

  Most editors are inundated with article proposals, outlines, query letters, press releases, and press kits. All of these materials contain or propose specific topics the sender either wants to write about for the editor or wants the editor to write about the sender.

  As stated earlier, editors are not lazy, but they are human, and why knock your head against the wall dreaming up story ideas when you are getting them free by the hundreds? Although most PR materials and freelance submissions are never used, most *are* at least glanced at, and many are given serious consideration in editorial conferences where editors decide what stories to run.

- *PR materials save editors time and effort.* Assembling facts and figures for an article or on-air news story is time-consuming and labor-intensive. PR materials typically contain usable material surrounded by lots of puff and fluff. Editors are skilled at cutting this extraneous material and quickly extracting from a press release or kit only those facts they need for their story. They welcome PR mail, viewing it as free research material, and you benefit when they cite you as the source of the fact, quote, or statistic.

If the press release is written well enough and reads like a good article rather than an ad or promo piece, many editors may use all or most of it word for word. It does and can happen—which is why the *way* in which PR materials are written is just as important as the story content or angle.

- *Editors and program directors are feeling the effects of downsizing.* Like many companies, publishers and radio and TV stations in many states have had to let people go and operate with a reduced staff. This generally means each media person now has even more work to do, with tight deadlines always present. The editorial director at one publishing company told me, "We used to have 120 editors working on our various publications; now we have 60—and those 60 are doing the work of the 120."

  Lack of internal staff causes media people to rely more on outside help, including freelancers, syndicated columns, newswire services (AP and UPI), and PR sources. "Ready-to-use" material—releases, articles, even videos (for cable and broadcast stations) that can be used as is with little or no editing or fixing by the editorial or program staff—is more in demand than ever.

  If you can provide such material, you increase your chances of getting more and better media coverage than ever before.

- *PR contributions enable editors to provide comprehensive coverage of their field or industry.* Lack of time and staff prevent editors and program directors from going into the field as extensively as they'd like to dig up story ideas and scoops. Even if they had the time and staff, media outlets cannot possibly look everywhere or know what everyone is doing.

PR materials give editors a broad view of their area from a wide range of sources, and can sometimes help an editor or program director do a story he or she might otherwise have missed.

The bottom line is that PR materials are a welcome resource, not an intrusion, and editors and program directors use them daily. If other companies are sending PR materials to the media and getting coverage, why not you?

Chapters 5 and 6 give you a complete course in how to write PR materials that get used by editors and generate substantial media coverage. But before you can write an effective release or article, you need a hook—an angle or idea for a story. While this may sound like a difficult challenge, it is not, because there are really only seven basic story ideas that interest editors, and it is relatively easy to tailor your story to fit one of these key themes.

THE SEVEN KEY STORY THEMES THAT APPEAL TO ESI

The seven key story themes that have the greatest appeal to editors and program directors and will make your PR materials get noticed, read, and used are:

1. News
2. Interesting information
3. Useful advice

4. Controversy
5. Celebrity
6. Human interest
7. Timeliness

Let's take a brief look at each and see how a story can be structured around them.

Please note: In the following discussion I give as examples headlines of news and feature stories that illustrate the theme being discussed. However, because I took these from a random selection of magazines and newspapers, I do not know which, if any, were generated from PR materials or a publicist's efforts. If I were to guess, I'd say half of the articles originated from the publication's editorial staff and half from PR materials and sources.

Key Theme 1: News

News is the most basic story theme and the one with the greatest appeal to many media outlets, especially newspapers, newsletters, weekly magazines, and other periodicals that report recent events on a timely basis. News includes but is not limited to current events; anything that is new and noteworthy can be considered "news."

For example, the headline NEW STUDY SHOWS MAGNESIUM SAVES LIVES AFTER HEART ATTACK could be used on a press release distributed by a pharmaceutical company promoting a new line of magnesium tablets.

The headline INFORMATION SYSTEMS AND FORENSIC ACCOUNTING ARE TWO HOTTEST CAREER FIELDS IN SECURITY AND LOSS PREVENTION could be used on a press release distributed by an executive search firm specializing in data processing and financial recruitment.

Other examples of stories with a news-oriented theme:

BOSTON CITY SCHOOL SYSTEM APPROVES USE OF "VIDEO-TEXTBOOKS"; FIRST SCHOOL SYSTEM IN MA TO AUTHORIZE USE OF ELECTRONIC MEDIA IN THE CLASSROOM

RJR NABISCO COMMITS $5 MILLION/YEAR TO HELPING CHILDREN OF EMPLOYEES ATTEND COLLEGE AND JOB-TRAINING PROGRAMS

PRESIDENT URGES CHEMICAL COMPANIES TO DEVELOP SAFE ALTERNATIVES TO OZONE-DEPLETING CFC'S

A chemical company could use the last headline to introduce its new line of CFC substitutes.

Because the media's mission is to report what's new, the word NEW is extremely effective in press release and article headlines. Whenever you have anything new of any importance or note to announce, send out a press release letting editors know it is new. For example:

NEW ELECTRONIC DIGITAL THERMOMETER TAKES A CHILD'S TEMPERATURE IN 1.5 SECONDS BY TOUCHING EAR; DOES NOT REQUIRE RECTAL OR ORAL INSERTION

Once you get the editor's attention with the *new* theme, I would immediately start discussing *why* such a thermometer was introduced and is needed. (Taking temperature with a conventional thermometer is difficult for the parent and often traumatic for the child.)

Virtually any product announcement or other topic can be made more attractive to the media by placing the word NEW in the headline.

Key Theme 2: Interesting Information

It's become a cliché to remind people that we live in the Age of Information, but it's true. People seek, collect, and use in-

TIP

You can use the news theme—and the word new—in almost every release you distribute about a product, service, free offer, or just about any other topic.

The secret is in realizing that even a small change or modification allows you to call a thing "new." For example, the headline NEW TPS-43 RADAR DETECTS OBJECTS AS SMALL AS TWO FEET IN DIAMETER is more powerful than the same headline without the word new, because editors are interested in what's *new*.

But it's legitimate to use the word new even when what's new is in fact only a minor part of the whole. And, since you're probably improving and changing your product or service all the time, you can justifiably send out a news press release almost any time.

In our example, the TPS-43 radar is years old. But let's say engineering just made a minor modification to the shape of the antenna. Now you can send out a press release that says NEW VERSION OF TPS-43 RADAR USES IMPROVED ANTENNA DESIGN TO DETECT OBJECTS AS SMALL AS TWO FEET IN DIAMETER—and you would not be dishonest or deceptive in any way.

In the same way, let's say you have an accounting firm in business several years, and recently you bought a new software package for improving the way you handle client tax returns on your PCs. You send out a release that says ZIMMER AND ZIMMER OFFERS NEW "COMPUTER-BASED" TAX PREPARATION SERVICE; PC AUTOMATES PAPERWORK, SPEEDS COMPLETION AND FILING OF RETURNS.

You get the idea: Look for the one small aspect of what's new about what you are promoting, and then use the word NEW in your headline to make it a news story.

formation on all sorts of specialized subjects, from how to relieve colic in a baby to how to eliminate radon in your home.

One of the surest ways of getting your material into the media is to gather useful information, put it in the form of a press release, and send it to media outlets whose audience would be interested in such information.

Of course, you don't want to give away information just for the purpose of educating people; that would cost you money and not gain you any new business. Your goal is to become the leading authority in your field. One way to do that is to be seen as the source of expert information in your area, whether it's life insurance, tile manufacturing, quality control, or data communications networks.

Therefore, you use free publicity to disseminate information that establishes you as an authority, positions your product or service in the most favorable light, and motivates people to contact you to find out more about what you offer.

For instance, an association or group of psychiatrists could use the headline 10 PHYSICAL REASONS WHY YOU MAY BE DEPRESSED to promote their practices. The story could make the point that many depressions have biological causes, and therefore patients should seek help from a professional—a psychiatrist—who is a therapist as well as a medical doctor (a psychologist is just a therapist and is not an M.D.).

Other examples of recent stories based on the theme of interesting information:

MANY COMMONLY USED SPICES HELP FIGHT CANCER

AVERAGE UNEMPLOYED WHITE-COLLAR WORKER TAKES 7.3 MONTHS TO FIND A NEW JOB, OUTPLACEMENT FIRM SURVEY REVEALS

WEATHER CAN MAKE YOU SICK; CHANGES IN CLIMATE SHOWN TO AFFECT PEOPLE'S HEALTH

NEW TV NEWS SERVICE FOR DOCTORS MAY REVOLUTIONIZE
THE WAY DRUGS ARE MARKETED TO THE MEDICAL PROFES-
SION IN THE U.S.

A spice manufacturer could use the first headline to promote increased consumer usage of spices in cooking and eat-
ing. A placement firm could use the second headline to sell
consulting services or publications for job-seekers. A doctor
or a health newsletter could use the third to gain media attention. The fourth obviously promotes the TV service itself (a
TV service launched by Whittle and Philips Electronics as reported on the front page of the June 26, 1992, issue of the *Wall
Street Journal*).

Key Theme 3: Useful Advice

Even more effective than the theme of "interesting information" is the theme of *useful* information—do-it-yourself tips,
techniques, strategies, advice, and instructions. Some examples:

BEST VEGETABLES TO EAT TO WARD OFF CANCER—AND
HOW TO PREPARE THEM

HOW TO DETERMINE AND REALIZE YOUR TRUE CAREER
DESIRES

USE CAUTION WHEN TRAVELING DURING THE HOLIDAYS

ARE YOUR KIDS FIGHTING TOO MUCH?

TAKE YEARS OFF YOUR LOOKS

17 WAYS TO PINCH PENNIES—PAINLESSLY

HOW TO GET CHILDREN TO TAKE BAD-TASTING MEDICINE

TIP

A *survey* of your customers, clients, prospects, local community, or the general public is an effective way to produce interesting information suitable for publicity purposes. Doing a survey adds credibility and originality to the information you disseminate: It's credible because it's what people say, not just your opinion, and it's original because your survey—not someone else's data—is the source.

In the preceding examples, the statistic regarding how long unemployed executives take to find new jobs comes as a result of a survey performed regularly by Drake Beam Morin, a nationally known career management consulting firm. DBM receives wide publicity from this survey, because the press has come to rely on the firm as *the* source of this particular statistic. Reporters use the statistic in a variety of articles.

Do you sell a product or service to an audience hungry for information relating to its use, or to the need or problem it addresses? Build press releases around the dissemination of such information, with your firm as the expert source, and you will get lots of media coverage.

A pharmaceutical company, drugstore chain, or even a local pharmacy could use the last headline to promote itself in local media, such as weekly town shoppers. (Such papers are big users of how-to tips and advice as well as releases on any news concerning local businesses.)

One of the most effective PR strategies is to create a booklet, pamphlet, or special report (called a "bait piece") containing how-to information or helpful advice, then send out a press release offering it at no cost to anyone who calls or writes for it. As with the interesting information strategy, the useful information strategy requires that the information position you or your company as an expert in your field, be of sufficient interest to your potential clients so that they respond to the offer and contact you to get the booklet, and help position your product or service as the best solution to your prospects' needs, or at least get them interested in learning more about how your product or service relates to their needs.

Chapter 4 gives complete instructions for creating how-to informational booklets, reports, and pamphlets. Chapter 5 shows several examples of press releases built around the offers of such free booklets and reports.

Key Theme 4: Controversy

The press loves controversy. Controversy is best loved by the popular media, including daily newspapers, TV and radio talk shows, and supermarket tabloids. But even more low-key media outlets, such as business magazines, trade journals, and scientific publications, like a good fight if it's related to a topic of interest to the readers.

An effective PR strategy is to generate controversy by responding in the opposite to an opinion, stand, or belief stated by (a) an industry as a whole; (b) a major competitor; (c) an association or organization; (d) a governing body, such as Congress; (e) a powerful figure or authority, such as the baseball commissioner or the head of the Federal Reserve; (f) a guru, such as a well-known industry pundit, columnist, or speaker; or (g) anyone else who has expressed a strong view in the media.

The way it works is simple. Say Joe Guru, a columnist for

Banking Today magazine, says by the year 2000 every company in the United States will be doing business electronically through Electronic Data Interchange (EDI) and that we will have a "paperless" system of exchange (no checks).

As a consultant specializing in EDI implementation, you write a letter to the editor of *Banking Today* saying Joe Guru is totally wrong and EDI will *not* become the standard—*unless it's done right.* You then outline some of the problems companies have or mistakes they make that prevent EDI from being effective for them, and hint at how these problems might be solved.

The result? Your letter gets published, bringing you visibility. It gets read, because it's controversial. And, when readers see in the signature your name followed by the word consultant, they'll become interested in speaking with you about why they may be doing EDI wrong and how you can help them do it right—which is an ideal way to gain qualified prospects for your EDI consulting service.

Another example of using controversy to get publicity is in the field of investment letters. Many investment letter publishers sell their advice based on bold future predictions, and often subscribership remains brisk whether the prediction proves accurate or not. (If it's accurate, publishers claim they are gurus; if it's not, they give some technical explanation, sounding totally plausible, about why the prediction did not come true because of a new development or situation—and come out sounding smart and wise, anyway.)

So two competing newsletters might send out two different press releases. One guru says:

"DOW TO CLIMB TO 4,000 BY 1993"

while the other says:

"DOW TO DROP TO BELOW 2,000 BY 1993."

Even though neither really knows what will happen to the stock market, these predictions get widely quoted because they are controversial and make for interesting copy.

Another example: Let's say there is a debate in your industry about whether X will come to pass. X can be the adoption of a new standard, a new policy, new law, way of doing business, or some other major change.

The leading trade journal in your field comes out in full support of X. Your company would be better off if Y was made official instead of X. You can send out a release—or a letter to the editor—to all major media in your industry as well as general business publications having your president speak out in support of Y and against X. Even the magazine that is a big X supporter will probably print your rebuttal, because the press loves controversy and debate.

What is the biggest issue facing your industry right now? Do the media or your major competitors have a position on it? If taking the opposite position would be beneficial to your marketing effort, do it! You gain more attention by being a maverick than by being part of the herd.

Key Theme 5: Celebrity

The public is obsessed with celebrities and has an insatiable appetite for information, stories, and gossip about them. Indeed, magazines and TV shows, such as *Us* and *Lifestyles of the Rich and Famous*, are devoted almost exclusively to reporting on the activities of the jet set.

While at first you may think this has nothing to do with you—you're a businessperson, not a Hollywood mogul—the celebrity theme can and has been used successfully by businesses both large and small to gain visibility and increase their sales.

On a national level, many corporations have gained massive

media attention through the celebrity of their CEOs—Frank Purdue, CEO of Purdue Chickens and inventor of the oven-stuffer roaster, made famous through his TV commercials; Lee Iaccoca, CEO of Chrysler, who stars in TV commercials for his company and wrote a best-selling autobiography; and self-made billionaire William Gates, CEO of Microsoft, the world's largest software company, and the wealthiest person in the U.S.A.

On a local level, a business owner or president can gain a reputation as a local celebrity, or at least become very well known, by being active in civic groups, community projects, fraternal organizations, religious groups, or local industry, trade, or professional organizations.

Within an industry, executives can build notoriety for their companies and themselves by writing articles for trade journals, speaking at trade shows, or being on the board of important industry organizations.

If you or your boss isn't inclined to become a celebrity, you can always bring immediate attention to your firm by hiring a celebrity or semicelebrity to be your spokesperson or representative.

This may not be as expensive as you think. In his book *How to Make Maximum Money in Minimum Time*, marketing expert Gary Halbert says that many celebrities who are not superstars but still have some "marquee value" can be hired for $10,000 or so plus a bonus or percentage of the sale if the campaign is successful.

According to Halbert, spending this amount of money to have a celebrity as spokesperson for your product is often a good investment. It adds glamour and credibility to your promotion and has substantially increased sales for several of Halbert's direct-response clients.

Although superstars like Madonna and Michael Jackson cost millions of dollars and are affordable only by advertising giants such as Coke and Pepsi, numerous celebrities don't cost megabucks and do not restrict themselves to representing major corporations or national brands. Many athletes, singers, actors, and entertainers who are no longer at the peak of their earning power can still generate "celebrity excitement" and can be used profitably by smaller firms. You see them making personal appearances in malls, hosting local events, or starring in TV infomercials. Why not feature them in your PR too? Celebrities make news, and news gets printed.

For more information on how to get a celebrity to endorse your product or appear in your next promotion, read Halbert's book *How to Make Maximum Money in Minimum Time*. Call 305 743-5291 to order.

Key Theme 6: Human Interest

"Human interest" means noncelebrity-oriented "people stories." *People* magazine runs a lot of these articles. Popular human interest subjects include people who overcome adversity or illness; unusual pets; uncommon acts of bravery or kindness; rags-to-riches stories, business success, and entrepreneurship; outstanding achievements of children, young adults, or the elderly; inventors, artists, and others who produce odd or unusual creations; unusual hobbies, careers, or professions; and people who have been through extraordinary experiences.

Of the seven categories, human interest is probably the one you are least likely to use to promote your business . . . yet there *are* some PR opportunities for you here.

A few suggestions:

- *Profile interesting people.* An employee with an unusual background or hobby can be the subject of a PR story. The media is more interested in a local businessperson who moonlights as a wine taster or raises king cobras than the usual press release announcing that Joe Blow has been promoted from assistant vice president of the bank to associate vice president.

- *Be unusual.* A business that does things in an unusual way can get big media coverage. Ben & Jerry's Ice Cream, for example, was featured in a recent national TV program that showed how, unlike other ice cream makers who waste left-over ingredients, Ben and Jerry use their excess ingredients to feed farm animals.
- *Do something extraordinary.* A good example, mentioned earlier, is RJR Nabisco's committing $5 million to paying for the college tuition or other vocational training of employees' children. Any time you do a good deed, publicize it—and don't be ashamed about doing so or listen to people who tell you it's crass to take credit for your good deeds. (Getting credit doesn't make the deed less beneficial to the recipient.)

Here's a good example of a PR opportunity based on a human interest angle.

An article in the *Wall Street Journal* (June 26, 1992, p. B1) profiled a young Russian writer who recently completed an unusual work of fiction: a manuscript consisting of just one word—Ford—repeated 400,000 times.

When asked why he selected the word Ford, the writer, who speaks English, said, "Well, I like Ford cars," adding "Maybe Ford will give me some money or something."

You can see that the oddball nature of this story makes it perfect for the media. So what's the PR opportunity?

If I were a high-level executive at Ford, I would take advantage of the media appeal of this story and blast it out for wide, continuing media coverage for as long as I could.

I would start by giving the writer a brand-new Ford and sending a release announcing the gift to all major media; the car would be presented to the writer in Russia at a press conference, with plenty of photo opportunities. I might also consider publishing the writer's *Ford* book and using it as a promotional giveaway or novelty. (Well . . . maybe not.)

Key Theme 7: Timeliness

The media is focused on the present; they report what is happening today. If you can tie your promotion to current events, conditions, and happenings, you increase your chances of getting your story picked up by the media.

For example, a manufacturer of high-efficiency shower nozzles, no-drip faucets, and other water-saving devices will get the most exposure distributing a press release entitled HOUSE-HOLD WATER CONSERVATION TIPS during a water shortage or drought than when the reservoirs are full and water is plentiful.

Timing can be critical. At a party, my wife and I met a couple who self-published a hardcover book predicting massive bank failures; they printed 10,000 copies and sold only 200; in the early 1980s, no editor was interested in such a doom-and-gloom book. Had the book come out at the start or height of the S&L scandals and the numerous bank collapses, the media would have given it much more attention—because it would have been timely.

Most businesses can increase PR results through careful timing and by creating PR campaigns that take advantage of current conditions, events, and affairs.

For instance, an accounting firm could do a press release on last-minute year-end tax-saving strategies in late autumn and early winter, so that the media can get the story out before the end of the calendar year—the deadline by which consumers must take action to benefit from the strategies.

Another release, on income tax preparation tips, would go out in January, February, or March, when most people are doing their taxes.

A third release, on how to improve finances in a recession, could be used whenever the economy gets sluggish.

HOW TO DETERMINE WHICH OF THE SEVEN KEY THEMES TO USE IN YOUR PR MATERIALS

Are any of these seven themes already present or inherent in what you want to publicize? The checklist in Figure 2.1 can help you assess whether your story contains news, interesting information, useful advice, controversy, celebrity, human interest, or timeliness.

Figure 2.1.
Checklist for Identifying Key Theme of Story for PR Campaign

INSTRUCTIONS: Put a check mark in the box next to every question to which you give a "yes" answer. Key themes under which you have checked one or more boxes are the ones you can apply most easily to your PR campaign.

News

- ☐ Is what you want to promote new?
- ☐ Is it important?
- ☐ Is it noteworthy?
- ☐ If it is not entirely new, is there a segment or one aspect of it that is new or improved?
- ☐ Has the product or its most recent improvement or upgrade not been announced or widely publicized? If so, it can be introduced now as "new" because it *is*

new (as far as the general public and the media are concerned).

Interesting Information

☐ Does what you want to promote contain interesting information?

☐ Do you have unique knowledge you can share with the public?

☐ Have you collected unique statistics that you can make available?

☐ Have you compiled interesting information that people would want to know about?

☐ Have you discovered anything unusual or out of the ordinary about your subject that can be the basis for a story?

Useful Advice

☐ Are you an expert in your field?

☐ Do you have information and advice you can share to help your prospects solve their problems or improve their lives?

☐ Do you have information and tips you can share on mastering a particular skill or accomplishing a specific task?

☐ Do the prospects seek information (which you can provide) on how to evaluate their need, problem, or requirement?

☐ Do your prospects seek information (which you can provide) on how to evaluate, specify, buy, install, use, and maintain your generic type of product or service?

Controversy

- ☐ Do you or your company have a stand or opinion on an important topic or issue?
- ☐ Is the issue controversial?
- ☐ Is your stand or opinion controversial?
- ☐ Do you strongly agree or disagree with the stated opinions of gurus, pundits, authorities, and others who have spoken out on or written about this topic?
- ☐ Would openly expressing your opinion or stand be beneficial (rather than harmful) to your marketing efforts?

Celebrity

- ☐ Are there one or more celebrities or semicelebrities you can identify whom you feel would be appropriate spokespeople for your company and a good "fit" with your corporate policies and philosophies?
- ☐ Are you ready and able to hire such a celebrity if the up-front fee is affordable?
- ☐ Is there someone in your organization who is (or can be made to be) a minor celebrity or "known personality" in your industry, community, or field?

Human Interest

- ☐ Are there any good human interest stories within your company you can capitalize on for PR purposes?
- ☐ Do you have any employees with unusual interests, hobbies, or backgrounds?
- ☐ Is there anything unusual, odd, or otherwise of special interest to the media in the way you do business?

☐ Is there any action you can take (for example, charitable contribution, participation in community programs) that can be used as the basis of a human interest story featuring your firm?

Timeliness

☐ Are there seasonal trends to which you can tie seasonal PR efforts?
☐ Are there special events that can be publicized?
☐ Are there anniversaries, milestones, and the like (such as your hundred-thousandth customer, your tenth anniversary) that you can publicize?
☐ Is there any tie-in between your activities and current conditions and events?

If elements of one or more of these seven key themes already exist in what you want to promote, you can stress them and build a release around them.

HOW TO *CREATE* NEWS, INFORMATION, ADVICE, CONTROVERSY, CELEBRITY, HUMAN INTEREST, OR TIMELINESS IF IT DOESN'T ALREADY EXIST AND THEN USE IT AS A THEME IN YOUR PR MATERIALS

Let's say you examine what you are promoting, and you don't see any angle you can use to publicize it. The seven key themes don't seem present; the story just seems boring or dull—there's nothing there, no media appeal. What to do?

Do not try to get media coverage when there is nothing to cover. If there is no "meat" to the story, either drop the story and look for another topic, or try to work with what you have by adding elements of interest to it. That is, if there's no news to report, your best chance of getting media coverage is to *create* something newsworthy, then publicize it.

Example: Let's say you are a widget manufacturer and you find nothing promotable or newsworthy about your widgets or your company. Here's how you can *create* interest using the seven key themes:

1. *News.* The widget is not new, but chances are there's *something* different about this year's model. Even if it's something as minor as adding some grease to the screws, that's enough "new" to form the basis of a release promoting your product as a "new" and improved version—for example, NEW "PRE-LUBRICATED" MODEL OF WIDGET X ELIMINATES NEED FOR LUBRICATION; MAKES INSTALLATION QUICKER AND EASIER. If there is truly nothing new this year, just take the last improvement you *did* make that was never announced, and use that as the basis for a "NEW MODEL" press release.

2. *Interesting Information.* What do you know about widget making, widget selection, or widget use that your customers do not? Feature this in a release. Editors at technical journals are hungry for new facts about technology of interest to their readers and will print it. For example, if you recently did a customer survey to gather information about buying habits, you might issue a release with a headline like this:

AVERAGE MACHINE SHOP GOES THROUGH 1,400 WID-GETS PER MONTH
NEW STUDY LOOKS AT USAGE AND BUYING HABITS OF WIDGET USERS

Editors at machine shop magazines will probably run your release as a news story, since machine shop people are naturally curious as to how their colleagues buy and use widgets.

3. *Useful information.* Limitless possibilities here. For example:

> HOW TO BUY THE RIGHT WIDGET FOR YOUR APPLICATION
>
> 7 WAYS TO IMPROVE WIDGET PERFORMANCE IN YOUR PLANT
>
> DESIGN CONSIDERATIONS FOR OEM'S USING WIDGETS IN LARGE SYSTEMS
>
> 10 TIPS FOR TROUBLESHOOTING WIDGET-RELATED EQUIPMENT PROBLEMS

Your prospects want information on how to evaluate, specify, buy, install, use, operate, repair, and maintain widgets. PR is the ideal tool for disseminating that information in a way that gains you maximum visibility and inquiries at minimum marketing cost. Chapter 4 covers this strategy in detail.

4. *Controversy.* This is a bit more difficult to use with our widget example, but not overly so. In every industry there are debates over how things should be done or what technology is best.

In a certain application, for example, engineers may be divided as to whether a widget or a transducer is the best device to use. You can jump into the controversy—and get considerable coverage—by issuing a press release that states categorically that widgets are better than transducers for the application . . . and authoritatively tells why. Be sure your release backs up your opinion with facts, figures, graphs, charts, lab tests, field tests, circuit diagrams, and other proof.

5. *Celebrity.* Take the senior engineer on your staff who has the best reputation in the field, or holds the most widget patents, and set him up as the authority on your topic—in effect, making him a minicelebrity within the wonderful world of widgets. This can be done through press releases, your company newsletter, articles, presentations of papers, entering and winning awards, getting him a regular column in the leading industry journal, having him honored by his technical society, and so on.

6. *Human interest.* Is it difficult for kids in your town to get a summer job? Start a "Worldwide Widget Summer Job Program" that offers good-paying summer jobs for local high school students. Are good engineers hard to find? Establish a college scholarship for bright science students who study engineering in college, and hire them every summer as interns. It's easy to take some action, even a small one, that can get you press coverage based on a human interest angle you create.

7. *Timeliness.* Tie in your widget technology to current themes in the news. For example: Global warming, caused by carbon dioxide emissions in the atmosphere, is a hot issue right now (no pun intended). Put out a press release explaining how improvements in your widget technology have virtually eliminated emissions from your widgets, while your competitors' widgets produce a significant quantity of carbon dioxide.

CHAPTER 3

HOW TO TARGET YOUR AUDIENCE

TARGETING YOUR PR EFFORTS

As discussed in chapter 1, one of the two characteristics that
distinguishes Targeted Public Relations from conventional
public relations is that TPR concentrates on reaching a small,
narrow segment of the market—the people who are potential
buyers of your product or service.

You must follow two simple steps to implement the "targeting" segment of your Targeted Public Relations campaign:

1. Define and select your target markets.
2. Identify and locate appropriate publicity outlets that
   reach your target markets.

Let's look at this process in detail.

DEFINING AND SELECTING YOUR TARGET MARKETS

"Target marketing" means instead of attempting to convince everyone to buy your product, you focus on one or more *segments* of the marketplace. These "target markets" represent real, reachable prospects for what you are selling.

What is a market "segment"? Example: Instead of just thinking of their market as "businesses," a photocopier manufacturer might target its marketing efforts at several distinct submarkets within the business marketplace: home offices, small businesses, large corporations, engineering firms and other businesses that need to duplicate technical drawings, ad agencies and other firms that need color copying capability, and so on.

In the same way, a company manufacturing air pollution control equipment might sell to many different vertical markets: chemical plants, pulp and paper plants, food processing, iron and steel mills, utilities.

Targeted marketing offers two distinct advantages:

First, it is usually more effective than general or "mass" marketing. In mass marketing, your message must necessarily be generic so that it appeals to a diverse audience. This means it does not speak directly to the needs of individuals or to groups of individuals with shared backgrounds, interests, problems, or concerns.

Targeted marketing, on the other hand, allows you to tailor your message directly to the needs, concerns, and interests of your prospects, because you are communicating with one distinct market segment of like individuals.

Example: My wife and I wrote a book, *Information Hotline* (now out of print) that was a directory of toll-free consumer hotlines and help lines, along with information on what each hotline service provided. The publisher did a conventional

mass mailing of a generic press release saying something like
NEW BOOK, "INFORMATION HOTLINE," GIVES READERS ACCESS
TO HELP VIA TELEPHONE. This release generated virtually no
response.

In a follow-up, my wife and I created a number of releases
promoting the book to several distinct target markets, based
on the fact that the hotlines in the book were organized in
categories appealing to different audiences.

For example, to gardening magazines, we sent a press release with the headline NEW BOOK OFFERS FREE ADVICE TO
GARDENERS VIA TOLL-FREE GARDENING HOTLINES. For those
concerned with fitness and health, we wrote a release with the
headline HEALTH AND FITNESS TELEPHONE HOTLINES PRO-
VIDE FREE INFORMATION AND ADVICE ON EXERCISE, NUTRI-
TION, AND COPING WITH ILLNESS. The release listed half a
dozen or so of the many health hotlines collected in the book
under the heading "Health and Fitness" and was mailed to
fitness, exercise, and popular health magazines.

We did a series of such releases, each targeted to a different group of consumers, each going only to the magazines
read by those groups. This generated quite a bit of publicity—
much more than the general, "generic" press release had
done.

The second advantage of targeting is that it reduces marketing costs. Sending a general press release on *Information
Hotline* to the hundreds of feature editors and writers who
might find such a book interesting enough to write about could
cost hundreds or even thousands of dollars in printing and postage costs, depending on the quantity mailed.

But sending our "Gardening Hotline" press release to the
top fifty or so publications and columnists writing about gardening cost us less than $50 in photocopying and postage.
Other versions, aimed at different vertical markets, cost
about the same. Reason: Since target marketing narrows the
market, it reduces the size of the audience and the number of

available media outlets that reach this specific group. Therefore, you mail press releases to fewer publicity outlets. So in addition to increasing PR effectiveness, targeting reduces costs.

Even Madison Avenue is getting into the act. Once the giant package goods manufacturers treated all markets pretty much the same. Now they're targeting specific markets too. For example, most of the major fast-food chains and soft-drink producers have separate campaigns targeted toward blacks, other campaigns toward Hispanic consumers. Why? Because *targeting works.*

NINE WAYS TO TARGET YOUR MARKETING AND PR EFFORTS

You can target your market in any of several ways (or a combination of ways). The nine major ways include: industry, company size, location, job function or title, product application, distribution channels, affinity groups, specific users, and buying habits. Once you select your target market, you must then seek out, identify, and collect information on the publicity outlets reaching your various market segments. This is also discussed in the following text. (Note: For additional information on the directories or publicity lists mentioned here, see the appendix at the end of the book.)

Industry

You can target by industry, specifying industry segments by name or by SIC (Standard Industrial Code). The Standard Industrial Classification system uses a series of eight-digit codes to organize U.S. businesses into 15,000 categories and subcategories. The definitive reference work to SIC is Dun & Bradstreet's *SIC 2 + 2 Standard Industrial Classification Manual,*

available from the Direct Marketing Association, DMA Book
Distribution Center, 1650 Bluegrass Lakes Parkway, Alphar-
etta, GA 30201, 404 664-7284.

Example of targeting by industry: A client of mine sells
plastic diaphragm pumps. I was asked to write two different
press releases describing the same product.

Why two different releases? Because the users in different
markets were interested in different performance features.
Buyers in the chemical industry were interested primarily in
corrosion resistance; buyers in the pharmaceutical industry
were more concerned with purity and cleanliness. Press releases sent to the editors at top trade journals covering these
markets stressed these different themes. The advantage of
doing this? Editors respond better, because the press materials they receive talk about what is of interest to their
readers.

Many of the available directories of publicity outlets are
organized by industry segment, cross-referenced by industry
segment, or at least allow you to specify industry-specific publications when ordering mailing lists. The volume of *Bacon's
Publicity Checker* covering business magazines is especially
helpful when you are looking for the publications covering a
particular industry segment. For details contact: Bacon's PR
Service, listed in the appendix.

Size of Company

Your market can be segmented according to size of company.
I see American business divided into three basic markets:
small business, middle-size companies, and large corporations. How you define "small," "medium," and "large" for your
marketing and PR purposes is really up to you. But here's
how I think of it:

Small companies are generally privately owned, usually
family-run businesses, with anywhere from one or two em-

ployees up to thirty, forty, maybe fifty employees. For a manufacturer, this means sales under $10 million; for a service firm, sales under $2 million.

The small company is usually run by an owner who keeps a tight rein over all aspects of the business. Entrepreneurs are skeptical, pressed for time, not terribly interested in technical details, bottom-line oriented, and cost conscious.

Home-based businesses are a distinct submarket within the small business market. Many computer, fax, copier, telephone, furniture, and office supply companies are aggressively targeting this market segment because of the rising popularity of working at home. The disadvantage in targeting this market, however, is that home-based businesspeople are usually frugal, on a limited budget, and rarely offer opportunities for repeat business or volume sales. They tend to buy only one of everything, and that only after much deliberation. And they also tend to require a lot of after-sale support and service.

The second market segment is medium-size companies—from several dozen to several hundred or more employees, with sales usually above $10 million if a manufacturer (or above $2 to $3 million if a service provider) but less than $100 million. Your prospect here is probably not the owner, but he or she may very well report *to* the owner. Some prospects have a lot of autonomy and authority; others have to check with the boss to spend $50 on office supplies. This market segment is difficult to put neatly into a single category, because it is so big: There's a lot of difference, for example, between a firm with $10 million in sales versus a firm with $150 million in sales.

Large corporations make up the third segment of the market. Typically, these include the Fortune 500 firms and those of similar size: big companies with thousands of employees and annual sales in the hundreds of millions of dollars.

Typically, managers in these firms are part of a chain of

authority and must consult with others in their company to make a purchase decision of any consequence. Prospects at big corporations frequently are as concerned with making an "acceptable" buying decision (one that pleases the immediate supervisor or top management committee) as they are with bottom-line results. Many hesitate to take risks.

What publicity outlets reach businesspeople? These would include:

- General business magazines
- Local and regional business magazines
- Chamber of commerce magazines and newsletters
- Industry-specific trade journals
- Industry-specific newsletters
- Business sections of major daily newspapers

There is a lot of overlap in readership among these publications, and so you can't strictly target publicity outlets by size of business in your PR mailings. For example, *Business Week* is written for corporate executives, but I'm sure many small business owners read it too.

The best you can do when targeting PR by size of company is to give a little extra attention and focus to those publicity outlets known to concentrate on your market segment. For example, I'd probably devote a separate effort to getting my material into *Inc.* if targeting small to medium-size businesses; for reaching top executives in large corporations, I might concentrate on *Across the Board, Forbes*, and *Fortune*.

You can get a good feel for the audience of any business publication simply by flipping through a recent issue. Or you can read the descriptive listings of these publications in *Writer's Market*, available at your local library or from F&W Publications, 1507 Dana Avenue, Cincinnati, OH 45207, 513 531-2222.

Although *Writer's Market* is published primarily for freelance writers as a guide to where they can sell their work, businesspeople seeking publicity will also find it useful: The listings are more detailed than in the standard publicity outlet directories, especially concerning the readership of each publication and the types of articles sought by their editors.

Location

Some marketers target PR geographically; others do not. Most of my manufacturing clients, for example, sell to customers across the country, and geography does not affect their marketing efforts. Distributors, on the other hand, might market only in their immediate and surrounding states, because they can offer delivery that is both fast and economical only to prospects who are nearby.

Many companies selling professional, consulting, and technical services to businesses are often similarly restricted to serving markets within the immediate geographic area of their headquarters or branch offices.

Companies that sell to businesses from retail outlets—value-added resellers of computer systems, for example—also serve a market within driving distance of the shop or store, as do firms that offer on-site repair services.

Even some companies that sell products may do target marketing based on location. One of my clients, a metals firm, finds that marketing efforts do better in some states than others, and he deletes the poorer states when renting mailing lists.

In today's global marketplace, many U.S. firms are looking to expand into overseas markets. Most certainly, a separate international campaign will be developed; larger, more sophisticated marketers may even have separate campaigns aimed at different regions (Europe versus Asia) or even countries.

To target by location, you can select from *Bacon's Publicity Checker* and many of the other media directories listed in the appendix those newspapers, business magazines, and consumer magazines with circulations limited to a specific town, region, or state.

In addition, a few directories list all major media in a specific city or area. These include:

METRO CALIFORNIA MEDIA
Public Relations Plus, Inc.
P.O. Drawer 1197
New Milford, CT 06776
800 999-8448 or 203 354-9361
Lists publicity outlets covering most of California.

NEW YORK PUBLICITY OUTLETS
Public Relations Plus, Inc.
P.O. Drawer 1197
New Milford, CT 06776
800 999-8448 or 203 354-9361
Lists more than 2,600 publicity outlets within a 50-mile radius of midtown Manhattan.

Job Function or Title of Prospect Within the Company

Another means of targeting prospects is by job title. By concentrating your marketing efforts on those people who are responsible for buying, recommending, or specifying your type of product or service, you eliminate the waste of marketing to people not involved with your product or its purchase.

Although PR mailing lists are not categorized by job title, certain magazines are aimed at people with specific job titles. *CEO*, for example, is written for chief executive officers; *Purchasing*, for purchasing agents. Consult the publicity directories listed in the appendix to research publications that are job title–specific.

Application or Use of Your Product

You can target your marketing efforts based on how the prospect uses your product. A good example are the pocket planners, daily calendars, time management systems, and other pocket schedulers and diaries sold to businesses.

Some manufacturers sell them to be used personally by the buyer. Their catalogs and mailings go into elaborate detail about how the time management systems work, how they save you time, make your life more efficient, and so on.

Other manufacturers market these items as gifts to be bought by businesses and given to customers, prospects, and colleagues. When selling these same items as a gift, rather than for personal use, copy is much shorter and doesn't detail how the systems work. Instead, it stresses the high value, elegant look, leather cover, personal imprint, and other aspects that make the books and diaries an appealing gift item.

Press releases should be slanted similarly depending on how you want your product to be positioned in the marketplace. Example: One client sells a software package used by systems analysts to develop applications, but saw that they needed software to help them generate reports in different formats. Since the client's product could handle this function well, a separate marketing and PR campaign positioned the product as a first-rate "report generator."

Channels of Distribution

You can target different promotions aimed at getting response from different people in the distribution channel—end users or customers, distributors, agents, resellers, wholesalers, agents, reps, OEMs (original equipment manufacturers), VARs (value-added resellers), stores, catalogs.

Promotions aimed at end users or customers naturally stress the benefits of using the product, while promotions aimed at the distribution channel tend to stress how much money or profit the distributor can make by carrying the item in his or her line and selling it aggressively.

Marketers sometimes use the term push to describe marketing to the distribution channel and pull to describe marketing to the end user or customer. This is because promotion to dealers is aimed at pushing the product on them, and getting them to push it onto their customers, while marketing to customers creates demand that pulls the product through the distribution chain from manufacturer to distributor to end user.

PR aimed at pushing the product through the distribution channel by promoting it to the trade should be sent to trade publications, while PR aimed at pulling the product through the distribution channel should be sent to magazines read by consumers and other end users.

For example, to promote a book such as this one to the trade, press releases will be sent to *Publishers Weekly*, *Library Journal*, and other magazines read by those in the book trade. To promote this book to potential buyers such as business owners, managers, executives, and marketing professionals, press releases will be sent to such publications as *PR Journal*, *Advertising Age*, *Business Marketing*, *Inc.*, and *Business Week*.

Is it better to concentrate your PR efforts toward end users or the distribution channel? It depends on the market. If customers tend to buy the product directly from the manufacturer and distribution channels account for only a small percentage of sales, then naturally you concentrate your PR efforts on the end user.

In other markets, distribution channels are pretty important. Take books, for example. If bookstores don't buy a particular book from a particular publisher and put it on the shelves, it has very little chance of selling. And with 50,000 new books published each year, most get little or no shelf space in bookstores. So selling the distribution channel is essential.

A similar situation exists in supermarkets. With too many products competing for limited shelf space, many packaged goods manufacturers actually *pay* the supermarket a fee to stock and display their products.

It's the same with many PC software packages. There are thousands of software packages on the market, yet most computer stores have room on the shelves for only a few dozen titles. If they don't carry yours, you either have low sales or must direct sales through other channels, such as catalogs, space ads, or direct mail.

How do you overcome this resistance? At first you might think heavy marketing to the distribution chain is the answer. But let's say you do this, and the bookstores carry your book. Readers might see it and snap it up. But perhaps they've never heard of it, so they walk right by it. With no demand from the end user, the title will be pulled quickly.

Often, creating a heavy customer demand is effective in getting the distribution channel to buy your product: After all, if your book gets rave reviews and dozens of people ask for it every hour, the bookstore will naturally want to carry it and order many copies from you.

For products where the distribution channel is important, then, you will probably target both the customer and the distribution chain. In most cases, the bulk of your effort will go toward end-user marketing; a much smaller portion toward dealer and distributor promotion. Exceptions? Of course.

If you study the publicity outlets as described in the media directories listed in the appendix, you will see that many industries have different magazines aimed at various segments in the distribution channel. In the computer field, *VAR* magazine is aimed at value-added resellers who customize, repackage, and resell software for specific applications, while *Dr. Dobbs' Journal* is written for people who design and write software.

Affinity Groups

An "affinity group" is a group of prospects with similar interests. These might include classical music "buffs" . . . computer "hackers" . . . bodybuilders and "health nuts" . . . and
other people who vigorously and enthusiastically pursue specialized hobbies, interests, or activities.

When you market a product that appeals to their common
interest, you get much higher results than with mass-
marketing of the same product to the general population—
because the people in the affinity group have a demonstrated
interest in your product category or in the benefits your product provides.

A good example might be computer enthusiasts who use
Prodigy, Dialog, CompuServe, electronic bulletin boards, and
other on-line computer services. If you did a promotion for a
bulletin board or other on-line electronic information or communications service, and targeted the general population of
computer users, you might be unsuccessful—not because your
service or promotion are bad, but because the average computer user isn't "into" on-line communication, doesn't actively
use a modem, and is intimidated by the whole thing. On the
other hand, if you could target your promotion to existing
users of such services, selling them an additional service—
yours—would be much easier, because you'd have to sell the
service only, not the whole concept of on-line communication
or buying a modem.

This is a good example of marketing made more efficient
through targeting. It's always easier to "preach to the converted"—it makes more sense to advertise your steaks to beef
lovers rather than trying to convince vegetarians that meat is
good for them. Targeting to an affinity group assures that
your audience is already converted before you start preaching
to them.

PR lends itself very well to affinity-group marketing, because in today's publishing industry, the general-interest magazine has given way to the special-interest magazine. Most successful magazines today cover a niche: They report on a specific topic for an audience composed of people with a strong interest in the topic. Examples include bodybuilding magazines, karate magazines, gun magazines, pet magazines, computer hobbyist magazines, car magazines, gourmet magazines, and home magazines. By selecting these publications from the media directories listed in the appendix, you can easily build a list of publicity outlets that reach your affinity-group audience.

Users of Specific Devices, Products, Machines, Systems, or Technologies

Targeting members of this category is a simple, sensible strategy. Its premise: If you're selling fax paper, you'll do a lot better selling to people who own fax machines than to those who don't.

A good example is in the computer field: If you have software that runs only on a Macintosh, you can go to a source of publicity outlets such as *Bacon's Publicity Checker* or *MediaMap* and select publications written specifically for Macintosh users. This increases the odds for success and eliminates waste; the editor of a magazine for IBM PC users isn't going to run a story on your Macintosh software (no matter how great the program) because readers *can't run the software*—they don't have the right machine.

Buying Habits

Although this is not a major method of targeting the market, there is some evidence that you can increase marketing results by tailoring your marketing efforts to fit the buying habits or patterns of the target prospects.

In consumer direct marketing, for example, results show that mailings using a *sweepstakes* do best when mailed to lists of people who have previously responded to sweepstakes mailings. Apparently, these people enjoy sweepstakes and will go through the trouble of entering, more so than the general population that contains a number of people who do not have patience for sweepstakes and do not respond to mailings.

So, if your company is running a big contest or sweepstakes as a promotion, you want to make sure that, in addition to announcing the promotion to all the regular media, you hit publications such as *Contest News* and any others highlighting sweepstakes and contests.

Or, if most of the orders for your product or service are placed using credit cards, you might contact the person at American Express responsible for producing the newsletter mailed with its monthly bill, and see whether you can get a mention in one of its service articles or resource lists.

THE TARGETING DECISION

Deciding how to divide your total marketing effort and expenditure among various target markets—what the markets should be, how many different target markets to address, how much time and effort to spend on each, which markets to ignore—is one of the most important and difficult decision any marketing manager has to make.

While it doesn't cost a lot of money to mail a press release, it does take time to plan and write one. The more target markets you have, the more material you're going to have to create, and the more time it will take you to create and mail it.

Should you target? How broad or narrow should your focus be? Which markets are primary? secondary? Keep in mind that your PR will not be the only aspect of your marketing that is targeted; targeted marketing means direct mail, print advertising, and other media will be targeted as well.

Here are some questions and answers you might find useful in working through this difficult issue in your own marketing plan.

Does Your Product or Service Lend Itself to Targeting?

In my experience, most products and services lend themselves to a targeted approach, but some don't.

An example of a service that benefits from targeting? Transportation—shipping, warehousing, freight forwarding, and so forth. One client of mine, a marketing genius, has dramatically increased the sales of his air freight forwarding business by targeting specific marketing segments and establishing himself as *the* transportation expert in those niches. For example, after discovering that medical clients have specialized needs that are inadequately handled by general shipping and courier services, he recently formed a subsidiary that handles nothing but medical shipments.

An example of a product that did *not* lend itself to target marketing? A company in my area of northern New Jersey sells a software utility for improving the performance of mainframe computers. It does the same thing on every computer, it's a function every data processing manager in every company would want, and the desire for this function doesn't vary based on size of company, type of computer, or industry. Therefore, niche marketing does not make sense, and it is advertised in general-interest computer magazines.

Take a look at your product or service. Does it lend itself to targeting by size of prospect company, industry, SIC code, or any of the other characteristics discussed in this chapter? If so, great. If not, perhaps target marketing is not for you.

Do Clear, Distinct Targets Emerge?

As your business progresses, certain markets may emerge as "naturals"—ones that are attractive, lucrative, have a strong need for your product, can benefit from your service, and are a good "fit" for your company. These become the primary markets you target.

On the other hand, perhaps no distinct vertical market opportunities emerge, or no single market is clearly the right one to pursue. In this case, you must think through whether specific markets can be targeted logically, based on a combination of common sense and experience supplemented by market research.

One excellent resource for market research when targeting vertical market segments or industries is *FINDEX*, which lists commercially available market research, reports, and surveys, organized by industry. You just look up your target market, read the descriptions of the reports, and call the report publisher to get more details or order the material. For more information on FINDEX, contact Cambridge Information Group, 7200 Wisconsin Avenue, Bethesda, MD 20814, 301 961-6750.

Are There Distinct Media Targeted to These Markets?

If there are no specialized newsletters, magazines, radio shows, or cable TV programs covering a vertical market or industry segment, you probably will have to give up the idea of targeting it as a distinct market. After all, if there is no radio show they listen to, no magazines they read, or no associations they belong to, how will you reach them? You can't. For Targeted Public Relations to be successful, media reaching those target markets must exist.

Do You Offer Something of Interest to This Market and the Media Covering It?

Just because a particular vertical market looks attractive to you doesn't mean you look attractive to the marketplace. If you are going to succeed with target marketing, you must offer something these prospects want—something they can't get from other vendors. Your product or service must address a need that is currently going unfulfilled, or else perform better than other products or services they are using now or can buy elsewhere.

Does some attribute or feature of your product or service make it especially well suited for a particular niche market? Then you have a good chance of succeeding in that market.

Having something of interest to offer the market applies to the media as well as to the public. You must have a story to tell that uses one of the seven basic hooks (listed in chapter 2); otherwise, editors will not give you the publicity you seek.

If there's no special reason why your product or service is suited to this market, either you have to change the product or service, or you at least have to create the *perception* that it was especially designed with that market's needs in mind. What works best is a combination of the two techniques: tailoring the product or service to the needs of the market, coupled with a promotional campaign that establishes your firm as a specialist in serving these unique needs.

Again, the same applies to the PR needed to reach this market: If you have no story of interest to offer the editors and program directors, either you have to find one, or you must create one, using the strategies outlined in chapters 2, 4, 5, and elsewhere in this book.

Do You Have Credentials or Credibility in These Markets?

I know of several software vendors who had great products running on specific hardware platforms who thought they could naturally expand their sales by migrating these proven winners to other platforms. But they found it wasn't as easy as they thought it would be. Why? Because they had no *reputation* or *credibility* in these new markets. They would say, "Our software is proven in 30,000 IBM installations!" The prospects would reply, "Yes, but we're a DEC shop. Have you got anything running on a VAX?" Not having these reference installations made expanding into the DEC marketplace slow going.

Do you have credentials or credibility in the marketplace you want to target? Even a small amount of prior experience, or a limited presence, can be made to seem impressive and help make prospects comfortable with you as a vendor.

But if you haven't served this market before and prospects don't know you, extending into the market will be much tougher for you. The best technique for gaining quick visibility in new markets is a combination of an aggressive but low-cost public relations campaign combined with networking, participation in major trade associations and professional societies, and trade show exhibits at the industry's major events.

Another good strategy for gaining credibility fast is a name change. This is usually done by establishing a division or subsidiary with a name indicating experience and specialization in a particular market. For instance, would a hospital looking for a collection agency be more likely to hire Retrieval-Masters Creditors Bureau (RMCB) or American Medical Collection Agency (AMCA)? The latter, obviously. That's why RMCB's owner *formed* AMCA as a separate company when he decided to pursue the medical collections field aggressively.

What's Your Budget?

Your budget is another factor determining whether you will do mass marketing or niche marketing. Actually, only the largest Fortune 500 corporations and other giants can afford mass advertising. Small and medium-size companies, whose marketing budgets are much smaller, do well by avoiding mass marketing and instead concentrating on niche markets that the larger companies ignore.

A finite budget must be divided in some fashion among a finite number of target markets. If you determine that a target marketing campaign costs you $10,000 a year, and your marketing budget is $50,000, then you can afford to target five niche markets, maximum. You might, however, choose to spend $20,000 on your primary target market and $10,000 each on three secondary markets. It's entirely up to you, but that's the kind of decision you'll have to make.

What Are Your Resources?

Budget is one constraint on marketing activities; another is resources—usually staff and time. Do you have the time or staff to manage five ongoing campaigns? Your own resources determine how "thin" you can spread yourself. With a large staff, assistant PR managers can each take charge of a different vertical market. If staff is limited, you may decide it's better to concentrate your energies on a smaller number of niche markets.

Does It Work?

Target marketing usually works, but the question is "Does it work for you?" Set objectives, measure results, and then decide. Often you find that a market segment you thought would be profitable is not, and so you should switch to a different segment.

For instance, you're not making money installing turnkey computer systems for individual doctors' offices but realize the same software could work for group practices, which buy more terminals and larger systems for a higher price tag. So you switch your focus and become successful.

Target marketing almost always works, to some degree. The question is: Is the incremental improvement in marketing results it generates worth the extra time, effort, and expense of maintaining an ongoing marketing campaign aimed at that specific audience?

If yes, keep going, make your money, and look to duplicate your success in similar or different markets. If not, regroup. See if the same campaign can work on a slightly different market segment, or consider switching to a different market altogether.

CHAPTER 4

FREE INFORMATION: THE ULTIMATE PR OFFER

GETTING PEOPLE TO RESPOND TO YOUR PR EFFORTS

As noted in chapter 1, the two fundamental differences between Targeted Public Relations and conventional public relations are that Targeted PR is aimed at a specific audience or market segment versus a mass market and Targeted PR seeks to generate not just visibility but also a direct response—an inquiry or order received as a direct result of the placement of your PR story.

In chapter 3 we discussed the targeting aspect of Targeted Public Relations and how to aim PR efforts at specific market segments. This chapter shows how to double, triple, or even quadruple the direct response to your publicity placements using the offer of free information. Chapters 5 through 10 discuss applications of the free information offer in such PR tools as press releases, feature articles, speeches, presentations, seminars, newsletters, and radio and TV appearances.

THE IMPORTANCE OF THE OFFER

YOU MAY HAVE ALREADY WON $10 MILLION

THE GREATEST SPORTS BLOOPERS VIDEO—YOURS FREE
WITH YOUR PAID SUBSCRIPTION TO *SPORTS ILLUSTRATED*

AFFIX THE TOKEN TO THE REPLY CARD FOR YOUR *FREE*
SAMPLE ISSUE

BUY ONE—GET ONE FREE

FREE TOTE BAG WHEN YOU BECOME A MEMBER

Traditional marketers who are heavy users of direct mail
realize the importance of finding the proper offer and phrasing
it so as to wake up bored consumers, get them to take notice,
and persuade them to respond to ads and mailings.

PR practitioners have traditionally ignored offers, not con-
sidering them important. The typical press release, for example, requests no action and does nothing to motivate the
reader to respond. It simply makes an announcement that the
firm mailing the release hopes it will be reprinted in the newspaper.

Not having an offer in your PR is a mistake. The offer is
almost as critical to public relations success as it is to traditional direct-mail marketing.

To get maximum response and results from *your* public relations programs, you must be aware of the following:

- The offer is of utmost importance to the success of a PR
  campaign.
- The strategic planning, selection, and experimentation
  with various offers can make or break a PR campaign,
  regardless of how well written the piece or how timely
  the story. As a rule, the more valuable and attractive the
  offer seems to the reader, the better your response.

- The presentation of the offer—the copy used to describe it, the emphasis it receives—is also of critical importance. As a rule, the more you emphasize and stress the offer in your release, the higher your response rate (assuming the editor prints your offer in the piece written about you).
- The clearer and more understandable your offer, the better your response. The lack of a clear, distinct offer can significantly depress response.
- The offer must appear to be objective, neutral, and of general service or benefit to the publication reader or radio show listener—not pure hype or promotion for a product or service you are selling.

WHAT EXACTLY IS AN OFFER?

I define the "offer" as:

What your prospects *get* when they respond to your article or broadcast appearance—combined with what *they* have to do to get it.

Note that the offer has two components:

1. What the prospect gets.
2. What the prospect has to do to get it.

The simplest, most popular offer in marketing is probably the offer of a brochure describing a product or service. In a press release announcing a new product, for example, this offer is found in the last paragraph and typically reads: "For a free brochure on the Widget 2000, write Johnson Engineering, 100 Maple Avenue, Anytown, USA, or call

XXX XXX-XXXX." What prospects get is a brochure describing your product. What they have to do to get it is to call or write you.

This offer can and does work for many, many products and services . . . usually those sold to business and industry, not consumers. Reason: Editors of trade journals will gladly mention the availability of your brochure in the short write-ups they print in their "new product" or "new literature" sections, and will give an address and phone number that readers can use to request your literature. Many publications will also run a reader service number with your new product or new literature blurb; the reader can request a copy of the literature by circling the corresponding number on a postcard bound into the magazine and mailing it back to the publication, which turns the inquiries over to you for fulfillment.

Editors of consumer magazines and newspapers, however, will probably *not* include mention of your brochure or a contact address where the reader can get product information, because they do not want to appear to be promoting and endorsing your company, service, or merchandise.

Despite the effectiveness of the free brochure offer, in most cases you can come up with a much more attractive offer—one that will get many more people to be interested in your proposition and respond to your articles, and will also be usable by editors at consumer as well as trade publications.

A "SOFT OFFER" OFTEN WORKS BEST

My definition of a "soft offer" is as follows:

> An offer in which the prospect requests some type of printed material that is mailed or shipped to him or her, and makes this request by writing or phoning or some other mechanism that does not require face-to-face or

other personal communication between the prospect and the seller.

The important thing to note about the soft offer is that it's the most painless, risk-free way for prospects to raise their hand, get in touch with you, and say "I may be interested—tell me more" . . . without having to subject themselves to sales pressure of any kind.

The soft offer appeals to those prospects who do not have an immediate need and are "just looking" . . . or to those who have an immediate need but want to gather preliminary information without speaking to your agents or sales reps. The soft offer generates a high level of response because there is no sales pressure or risk of being "pitched" by high-pressure sales types. It promises details on the offer that prospects can review at their leisure.

Many marketers mistakenly believe that all people who respond to soft offers are just collecting free information and are therefore not serious, *real* prospects. For this reason, they avoid soft offers. They say, "If prospects don't pick up the phone and call me, they're not really interested, and I don't want to waste time and money sending them an expensive catalog or booklet they're just going to file or throw away."

While there's some validity to this point of view, usually it's not true. Soft leads can be extremely profitable, and often these leads convert to a large number of sales.

Even if response to a PR item generates a large quantity of leads of only so-so quality, and the conversion rate of leads to sales is mediocre, the promotion can be immensely profitable because of its low cost.

Importantly, the offer in your press release must be "neutral," not promotional—that is, it must offer printed information, a free evaluation, a free product sample, or other items or services of value to the reader—because editors do not want to appear to be giving a "free ad" to your firm.

For example, if you end your press release by saying "Call XXX XXX-XXXX to schedule an appointment with a career counselor at Careers Are Us; cost is $50," most editors won't put this call to action in their article about you, because it seems promotional and self-serving.

However, let us change the closing paragraph of the press release to read, "For a free Self-Scoring Assessment Test you can take at home in 5 minutes to determine what careers fit best with your skills, likes, and personality, write to Career Consultants at 100 Maple Avenue, Anytown, USA, or call XXX XXX-XXXX." Many editors will run such an offer as the last paragraph of their article about you.

Why? Because publications exist to serve their readers, and giving the readers a free self-assessment career checklist helps the editor to serve the readers—at no cost to the magazine, since you are the one supplying the free material. Such a blurb can generate hundreds of requests from career changers and job seekers, many of whom, once they respond, can be convinced by mail, telephone, or in-person selling to sign up for your expensive career counseling service.

ENHANCING THE SOFT OFFER

The typical industrial marketer uses a fairly standardized soft offer that is either "more information" or "free brochure." While this is adequate in many cases and can work, there is vast room for improvement.

The key is to maximize requests for the free information you offer by making the package you are offering seem important, interesting, useful, valuable, desirable, and highly specific and relevant to the prospect's interests and needs. For example, a booklet of useful how-to information has more appeal than a sales brochure hyping the company's service.

There are a number of ways to do this. The most popular,

and probably still the most effective, is the offer of a free booklet or special report.

"Free Booklet" and Other Free Information Offers

The term bait piece refers to free information advertisers offer in their mailing pieces or ads to generate a high number of inquiries. The term bait is used because the free booklet is offered not to give away free information or educate the reader (as the reader is led to believe) but to "hook" him or her by generating a response or inquiry that can be followed up by telephone and field sales personnel.

Here is a secret many PR practitioners do not know and will find difficult to believe:

The "free booklet" (or "free report" or other free information offer) will *dramatically* increase response to your PR placements compared to what the response for essentially the same article or blurb would be without the free information offer.

Why are free booklet offers effective? For several reasons.

First, today's consumer and business prospects, despite being overloaded with reading material, are information seekers, always on the lookout for advice, ideas, and information to help them do their jobs better, improve their health, make more money, get more out of life, gain financial security, and so on.

Many publishers charge handsomely for such information sold as seminars, audiocassettes, books, newsletters, and manuals. So when people see that they can get similar information from you as a free booklet or special report, they respond. After all, if it's free, they have nothing to lose.

Second, most people are so busy they flip through their

magazines and newspapers at a frantic rate. The free booklet offer, perhaps appearing in a concise article highlighted in a box or sidebar, has attention-grabbing power. It forces readers to slow down, stop, and read more carefully. Readers think, "Oh, this is one of those articles offering something free. Let me take a look for a second and see what I can get." So they call or clip the coupon and request the booklet, recipe, calorie counter, or whatever it is you are offering.

Third, people like getting things for free. In the marketing seminars I give nationwide, someone in the audience always says, "Aren't free offers much less effective in today's market? For instance, how excited can an executive get about a free booklet or report?"

The fact is, whether they get *excited* is irrelevant; they do get *interested,* and the specific offer of free information dramatically increases PR response rates.

Fourth, being perceived as *the* authoritative source of accurate, up-to-date information in your field enhances your competitive position in the marketplace. "If you are not recognized as the primary source of information and applications knowledge about your product realm, you are in danger of being left out of the next major loop of marketing: knowledge-based marketing," writes marketing consultant Don Libey in *The Libey Letter* (February 4, 1991). "When the products are homogenized, only the knowledge and information, above and beyond the expected, will differentiate you from the competition."

The Importance of the Free Booklet Offer

The free booklet offer is so effective, and so important, that I think it's a mistake for most marketers using PR to generate leads not to use such an offer as part of the press release.

The reason is simple: Unless prospects have an immediate, urgent need to pick up the phone and call you, seeing an article about you is largely a matter of indifference to them. While it's a big deal to you, they'll forget about it five minutes after they read it—if they see it at all. Prospects feel no need to respond, and don't.

People doing *conventional* PR campaigns get very excited every time one of their press releases is picked up and an article is written that mentions or features them. "Look at all the visibility we are getting!" they exclaim. "This will really create a positive image for us."

They forget or don't realize a basic fact of life: What seems important or a big deal to you and the people in your company won't be noticed or given any attention by 99.99 percent of the rest of the world. Or if they do give it some attention, it will fade from memory in a day or so.

But if you get readers to *take some sort of action* during the two minutes they spend reading the article about you, you'll have captured the name, address, and phone number of those prospects *as a result of their short-term interest.* So even though they soon forget about you, *you* don't forget about them.

Instead, you follow up with a barrage of letters, brochures, phone calls, and contacts until you convince them to buy what you are selling. But without a response mechanism built into your PR placement, such as a free booklet offer, prospects will never contact you, and so you will never know who read the article and was interested in you.

The free booklet offer solves that problem. It says to prospects, "Even if you have no immediate need, don't have time to read our mailing, and don't want to think about this topic right now, at least call or write us. You'll receive something of value in return." The offer converts inaction to a response.

How to Create Successful Free Booklet Offers

What are the steps to creating and using successful free booklet offers?

First, pick a topic for your free booklet or report. The topic should be something that interests readers while at the same time helps sell them on your system, product, service, or idea.

For instance, to promote a line of business software, IBM published a free booklet (actually, it was a full-length paperback book) telling small businesses what to look for when evaluating software packages. The book helped readers by showing them what features to look for when "shopping" for software. At the same time, it helped IBM promote its software, because the comparison checklists highlighted many of the features found in the IBM products.

The free book "creates a specification" readers use to evaluate potential software. The information is believable because it is packaged in the form of a book rather than a promotional brochure. Readers then go to IBM for a software demonstration; IBM has become a credible source in their minds because, after all, they "wrote the book." When prospects check out IBM's software, they find (surprise!) that it fulfills the specifications outlined in the book—therefore, it must be good—and a sale is made.

The topic you select can persuade readers to favor your product or service, but the "sell" must be soft and subtle. Typically, your free report or booklet explains a certain way to do a thing or how to select a product to do it. While this discussion must appear unbiased and editorially neutral, you will slant it so readers come away favoring *your* approach.

The booklet you write contributes to the selling process in two ways: first, by predisposing readers to accept your methods as standard and desirable; and second, by positioning you and your firm as experts in the topic (the folks who "wrote the book").

The topic must also be interesting and relevant to readers. A small-business owner would not be interested in "How IBM Designs and Codes Its Software Systems" but would be interested in "How to Choose the Right Software for Your Business." The booklet must appeal to readers' self-interest while promoting your own—that's the balance you must achieve.

Your Free Booklet Should Have a Catchy Title

After topic selecting, you need a catchy title. A title with the words "how to" in it—"How to Reduce Costs and Increase Productivity by Implementing EDI (Electronic Data Interchange)"—can be effective; people want to know how-to-do things. Number titles—"7 Ways," "6 Steps," "14 Winning Methods"—also make your booklet more attractive to readers, because they arouse curiosity: People want to know what the seven ways, six steps, or fourteen methods are.

Here are some typical titles from successful free booklets offered in promotions by the companies listed in parentheses:

"15 Ways to Improve Your Collection Efforts"	(RMCB)
"14 Winning Methods to Sell Any Product or Service in a Down Economy"	(CTC)
"10 Steps to Better Technical Writing"	(CTC)
"Should I Personalize? A Direct Marketer's Guide to Personalized Direct Mail"	(Fala Direct Marketing)
"Choosing Business Software"	(IBM)
"Aldus Guide to Desktop Design"	(Aldus)
"Family-owned Businesses: The 3 Most Common Pitfalls . . . and How to Avoid Them"	(Consulting Dynamics)
"A Special Report: Productivity Breakthrough Projects"	(JMW Consultants)

"33 Ways to Make Better Displays: What Every Marketing Executive Should Know About Point-of-Purchase Display Marketing"	(Display Masters)
"Steel Log: Glossary of Metal Terms"	(Specialty Steel)
"7 Questions to Ask *Before* You Invest in DP Training . . . and One Good Answer to Each"	(Chubb Institute)

The title of your bait piece is all important because it determines, in large part, whether you can get prospects interested enough to send for it. So choose the title with care.

For instance: If you are selling desktop publishing systems and your target market is advertising agencies, how about a booklet titled "What Every Ad Agency Executive Should Know About Choosing and Using a Desktop Publishing System to Reduce Production Costs and Increase Client Satisfaction"? If you owned an ad agency and were losing clients because you didn't offer desktop publishing capability, would you send for this free report? I should think so!

When choosing a topic and title, it's better to make it narrow and more targeted than broad and general. By narrowing the focus, you can cover one specific topic of great interest to your prospects with sufficient detail to gain their attention and whet their appetite for further contact with you.

Fala's booklet, "A Direct Marketer's Guide to Personalized Direct Mail," is effective because it zeros in on one specific topic of interest to direct marketers—use of personalization in direct mail—rather than the broader, less meaningful topic of "direct mail." It positions Fala as the expert specifically in *personalized* direct mail production.

Booklet, Tip Sheet, Report, or Manual?

After selecting the topic and title, think about format. Do you want to publish a booklet, report, fact sheet, or poster? Or how about a book or manual? Or do you plan on putting your information on audiotape, videotape, or computer disk?

A fact sheet or tip sheet is the most basic format. In a fact sheet, your information is typewritten or typeset and printed on one or both sides of a single sheet of 8½-by-11-inch paper. Such sheets can be produced quickly and inexpensively.

For example, you can offset print or photocopy 500 single-sided tip sheets for $30 to $50. To enhance their perceived value, print on yellow, gold, or other brightly colored stock rather than white. You can make the mechanical at no cost using a typewriter or desktop publishing system. Or you can offer reprints of articles you've written, calling them "tip sheets."

Tip sheets can be effective, but some marketers think they look cheap. One solution is to print your tip sheet as a poster, using a larger size and better stock of paper "suitable for framing." The Communication Workshop, a New York City consulting firm, has had great success promoting its writing seminars with a series of one-page posters on grammar, sexist language, and similar writing topics.

Many marketers offer free information in the form of a booklet or special report. A booklet implies a smaller-size publication, either folded or saddle-stitched (staples through the spine). The information is more detailed than a tip sheet but less detailed than a book or scholarly article. The booklet page size can be either 4 by 9 inches to fit a standard #10 business envelope, or 5½ by 8½ inches to fit a 6-by-9-inch envelope.

A "special report" is similar to a booklet except it has full size (8½-by-11-inch pages) and is mailed in a 9-by-12-inch envelope. The report can be typewritten, desktop published, or typewritten with a desktop-published cover.

Such reports are often run off on a photocopier, collated, and put in a clear plastic or other attractive cover. If you want to tailor versions of the report to different audiences, you can keep the body of it the same, then just change the introduction and the front cover for each audience.

Even though you intend to give away your booklet or report for free, put a price on the front cover in the upper right-hand corner. This serves a couple of functions: First, it adds to the perceived value of the booklet or report—people are more interested in getting a $7 item for free than they are in getting a free item for free.

Second, it allows you to charge for the item when you get inquiries from those who are not potential customers—students, brochure collectors, and so on. Third, it allows you to request payment gracefully from the occasional person who calls you up and wants multiple copies for a seminar, presentation, class, or to distribute in some other fashion. This does happen every once in a while, and it can be costly.

What should this pricing be? Say $1 or $2 for a tip sheet, $3 to $10 for a booklet, $7 to $15 for a special report, $5 to $15 for a book, $15 to $25 for a manual. These prices seem credible and fair; if you make the price too high, prospects realize it's a scam to make the offer seem better than it is.

If your report is long (fifty pages or more), you can increase its perceived value still further by putting the pages in a three-ring binder and calling it a "manual." You can duplicate your manual in small quantities using your office copier.

If you are going to produce the manual in volume, don't imprint the cover directly on the binder. Instead, leave the binder cover blank and use a title page. Or print the cover on a separate glossy sheet and buy notebooks with a front cover "trap-in"—a clear plastic sleeve that allows you to easily insert and remove the cover. This way, if the report changes or becomes dated, you are not stuck with hundreds of unusable (and expensive) custom-imprinted binders.

Using a Book as the Free Bait Piece

If the free-information bait piece is lengthy and a proven success, you may want to go to the next step and produce it as a self-published book. As mentioned, IBM did this. CoreStates Financial Corporation similarly promotes its expertise and technology in EDI (Electronic Data Interchange) by giving away a self-published book on the subject.

The advantages of offering a book versus a booklet, tip sheet, or report are twofold. First, the book has a higher perceived value, so more people will send for it. And second, a book has a longer shelf life—a self-published promotional book is like a brochure that prospects will keep for a long time.

Producing a book requires more of an investment in effort, typesetting, and printing than a booklet, report, or manual. Because of printing economics, you will have to order a minimum of 500 copies of your book, and will probably get the best price/volume "deal" when you order 2,000 or 3,000.

Be sure to get quotes only from printers who specialize in short-run (less than 5,000 copies) printing of books. General printers charge two to three times as much because they are not set up to print books. For a directory of book printers, contact Ad-Lib Publications, 51½ West Adams Street, Fairfield, IA 52556, 515 472-6617.

A book has an extremely high perceived value and is also perceived as being an unbiased, "legitimate" source of information. Because you want to keep the cost reasonable, you should plan to publish a small book rather than a big one.

A small paperback book can contain as few as 60 to 80 pages with as little as 15,000 words of text (the equivalent of 60 double-spaced typewritten pages). Again, don't forget to put a cover price on the book—about $10 to $15 for a small paperback seems right.

WRITING YOUR BAIT PIECE

You have selected the topic, title, and format. Now it is time to determine the contents, make an outline, and write the copy.

The most important thing to keep in mind when writing "informational premiums" such as free booklets or reports is that the contents must deliver on the promise of the headline, convey useful information helpful to the reader, and be accurate.

The contents do not have to be revolutionary or give the reader all new information. Many people read to affirm current beliefs or reinforce existing knowledge. So even if your booklet mostly repeats what they already know, they'll be happy with it, and, more important, they'll think you're a wise, knowledgeable expert on the topic.

However, if you can give readers one or two genuinely new ideas or things they may not have thought of before, so much the better. It will make your booklet or report even more valuable to them.

Do not put any selling or advertising message into the body of the booklet. The contents should be pure information. You have promised readers knowledge; you impress them by conveying that knowledge. If you turn the booklet into a sales pitch, the people who sent for it expecting helpful advice will be angry, disappointed, turned off, and not inclined to do business with you.

How much information should be included? It depends on the length and format. A full-length book, for example, must obviously contain more detail than a one-page tip sheet.

As a rule, make your booklet or report helpful and fascinating, but don't overdo the detail. You want to tell prospects enough to get them interested in hiring you to solve their problem; you don't want to tell so much in your report that they no longer need your firm or your product.

If the body is pure information, can you do any selling in the booklet? Yes, but keep it low-key. On the front cover, under the title, put your firm as the author, giving the address and phone number.

Repeat this information on the back cover, adding a more complete description of your company, your product or service, how you can help readers, and the next step they should take to learn more about your product or service. This should read like the "about the author" bios you find on nonfiction how-to books written by business experts—giving enough information to whet readers' appetites without being too blatantly sales-oriented.

In reality, however, the back-page company bio is a sort of advertisement for your product, service, or company, and therefore the most important part of the bait piece. Be sure it tells your story completely yet concisely, giving enough information to get prospects interested in your product or service while not seeming to push for the order too hard.

MAGNETIC AND ELECTRONIC MEDIA

One way to create additional interest and make your bait piece stand out even more is to produce your information in the form of an audiocassette, videotape, or computer-based presentation.

One advantage of these formats is that they are not widely used and are therefore a bit unusual and likely to get greater notice. Also, audiotapes, videotapes, and floppy disks tend to stand out in an in-basket crowded with paper. Plus, they have higher perceived value than printed material and so won't get thrown away by secretaries who screen mail.

Experience has shown that business prospects will take the time to either listen to or view the tape or disk, or at least make sure it gets passed on to the right prospect within the organization. Printed pieces are not treated with the same respect.

Finally, even if prospects don't immediately listen to or view the tape or disk, they will probably keep it in a desk drawer rather than throw it away. So every time they open the drawer, they see the tape or disk imprinted with your company name and phone number.

Audiocassettes are the easiest and least costly audiovisual medium to use as information bait pieces. Some marketers using audiocassettes think that briefer is better, and limit the message to ten or twenty minutes. But if the tape contains pure, useful information, it can be much longer. I have been successful promoting both my seminars and my consulting and copywriting services using cassettes on marketing and sales topics that are ninety minutes long.

Audiocassettes don't require the high level of production that videocassettes do. You can record a live presentation or speech at work, a meeting, or an industry event, edit it in a studio, and offer it as an attractive bait piece on audiocassette.

What will all this cost? Hiring someone with professional-quality recording equipment to record a presentation costs $100 to $200 a day plus travel expenses. Studio time goes for $35 to $75 per hour and should take less than half a day. Duplicating my presentations onto C-90 (90-minute-long) audiocassettes, including a laser-printed cassette label and soft plastic box, costs less than $1.50 per cassette in quantities of less than fifty.

Videos are another story. You can expect to pay a professional at least $1,000 or $2,000 to record you live or in a studio. If you want a full-blown production with sets, special effects, and live location shooting, a ten-minute video can cost $5,000 to $15,000 or more, just for production. Cost to duplicate 1,000 copies of a ten-minute video is about $2.50 per cassette with a cardboard box and typed label; plastic boxes and four-color packaging can run much higher.

A relatively new promotional medium is the floppy disk. Sales and informational presentations can be put on floppy disks that prospects can run on their own personal computers. Some direct marketers are reporting success with this medium, though I have no personal experience with it (other than conventional demo disks for software, which is a different thing).

Here are some companies that can help you create information premiums using electronic/magnetic media:

For audiocassette duplication:

Dove Enterprises
907 Portage Trail
Cuyahoga Falls, OH 44221
800 223-DOVE (3683)

For videotape duplication:

Mighty Mountain
RD #1 Box 8100
Lyndonville, VT 05851
802 626-8100

For presentations on floppy disk:

CompuDoc Inc.
1090 King George Post Road
Suite 808
Edison, NJ 08837
908 417-1799

SOURCES OF READY-MADE FREE
BOOKLETS AND SPECIAL REPORTS YOU
CAN OFFER AS BAIT PIECES

One reason why more marketers don't use the bait-piece offer despite its proven effectiveness is as follows: "It sounds good, but we have a limited budget and staff. I don't really have the time to write and design—or commission someone to write, design, and print—a really good booklet or special report."

There are several solutions to this problem. One is to have your PR firm or department write and place a feature story on your preferred topic in an industry trade journal, then simply reprint the article as a tip sheet or booklet. This eliminates the need for you to write, typeset, and design an original piece.

Be sure the PR agency or department retains reprint rights or gets reprint permission from the magazine in which the piece is first published as an article. When you offer the reprint, call it a tip sheet or special report, not an article reprint, as the former imply higher perceived value. Somewhere in small type on the reprint you can cite the publication and date of the article's original appearance.

You might ask, "But will one magazine run a blurb offering a bait piece that is essentially a reprint of an article that appeared in another magazine?" The answer is yes, as long as your press release calls it a tip sheet, not a reprint, and as long as it was not published by one of its direct competitors.

Another way to offer free reports as bait pieces without paying to create them yourself is to reprint existing materials that deal with your topic, would be interesting to your prospects, and are in line with the service or product you sell.

If you're a member of a professional society or trade association, your group may offer informative publications that members can distribute or reprint without charge or for a reasonable sum. When reprinting, add your own front and back covers with your company name, description, and contact information.

Many medical societies and associations as well as some pharmaceutical companies, for example, offer informative booklets on various aspects of health care that member physicians can reprint. Most doctors simply leave copies for patients on a table in the waiting room. But one orthodontist in my area reprinted such a booklet with his office address and phone number, added a personal cover letter, and mailed it, with good results, to potential patients in town.

If you're an agent, representative, distributor, or dealer, your manufacturer or wholesaler may provide you with booklets and other literature you can reprint or add your label to. You can offer these to prospects as bait pieces with no creative or other development costs on your part.

Another well-kept secret: The U.S. government is one of the biggest producers of informational booklets and special reports, and a large number of these *are not copyrighted.* Therefore, you can reprint them and use them for promotional or any other purposes. (The government asks but does not require you to acknowledge it as the original source of the material.) One local radon testing firm, for example, offers a report on "radon in the home" that is simply a reprint of a government publication with the firm's name and phone number imprinted on the top.

For catalogs of the various government publications available for free or at reasonable cost contact:

Consumer Resource Center
Pueblo, CO 81009
719 948-3334

Superintendent of Documents
Government Printing Office
Washington, DC 20402
202 783-3238

Using existing publications as bait pieces works if you have a product or service for which a "generic" bait piece would be an effective promotional device. For instance, if you're generating leads for an executive fitness program, you could probably increase response by offering a free package of booklets on health, diet, and exercise that are reprints of some of the copyright-free publications offered by the U.S. government.

On the other hand, if you are selling a highly specialized technical product, probably no existing report would be useful. You will have to create your own.

While in many cases you can "make do" using existing publications as bait pieces, I usually recommend to clients that they create their own customized information premiums, because an original publication can be made more interesting to the audience and more relevant to the client's product or service.

FOUR REASONS WHY MORE MARKETERS DON'T USE FREE BOOKLET OFFERS

Offering a free booklet, report, or other information piece in your press releases can dramatically boost response. In fact, it is one of the few "sure-fire" rules of PR that works almost every time. In virtually every campaign where I have been able to persuade clients to offer a free booklet or report in their press release, that release has generated substantially more inquiries and leads than any they had previously mailed. Few other strategies are so basic, simple, and easy to use while consistently delivering such excellent results.

Despite this, many clients avoid offering a free booklet, based largely on the following erroneous beliefs. If you are not using the bait-piece strategy because of one of these fears, this list may be helpful in overcoming your particular objection.

1. *It's a cliché.* "Offering a free booklet isn't original." "It's a cliché." "Can't you think of something more creative?"

   The number-one reason marketers avoid free booklet offers is that they think it's old hat and are looking for something original.

   My answer is simple: So what if it's old hat? So what if it's a "formula"? The fact is, it *works*—consistently and repeatedly, for hundreds of companies in all industries. The fact that free booklet offers are not original is true but unimportant. What's important is that such an offer will generate more leads per ad or mailing, producing more inquiries, more sales, while lowering marketing costs.

   If you don't believe me, pick up any issue of *Glamour, USA Today, Cosmopolitan,* or *Family Circle* at the newsstand. Chances are, you'll find at least two or three little articles or blurbs offering free booklets put out by manufacturers or service firms to promote their products or services—proof that editors like and do use such releases.

2. *It's overused.* Another common objection is "I like the idea, but free booklet offers are so overused in our industry. Take a look at our trade magazines and you see lots of new-product blurbs and feature articles offering free brochures. So how could our making such an offer compete with all this clutter?"

   This argument makes sense but is refuted by experience. While some marketing techniques *do* lose effectiveness if overused, the free booklet offer is not one of them. In fact, the opposite is often true: Prospects in a particular industry become accustomed to seeing free booklet offers and eagerly seek them out in trade publications. If your PR program lacks such a bait-piece offer, prospects are less likely to contact you in response to an article or item they read about you.

3. *Our competitors already offer a free booklet.* The natural tendency is to think "Our competitor has already published a booklet on the topic we were thinking of, so they've beaten us to it, and there's no sense going ahead with ours."

The *right* strategy, however, is to go ahead with your own booklet and either choose a topic that's different but still helps promote your product, or choose the *same* topic and produce a report or booklet that's *better.*

How do you make your booklet better? Give tips and strategies the competition does not. Include a helpful glossary, charts, conversion tables, a bibliography, checklists, names and addresses of resources, graphs, and other useful references. Use pictures and illustrations to make your point clear. Reveal inside information and details the competition keeps secret.

Even if the topic is similar, select a title that's clearly different from the competition's. Having the same or a similar-sounding title confuses prospects and isn't good for either you or your competitor.

4. *My prospects already have too much to read.* The fourth argument against free information offers is either "My prospects already have too much to read, so the last thing they want is another booklet or report" or "My prospects are not readers."

While many prospects do already have too much to read, they will still seek out and send for yet another booklet or report *if they perceive that it contains information that is relevant, helpful, and tailored to their needs.* Prospects may have six inches of paperwork stacked in their in-baskets, yet if their most pressing problem is cutting energy costs in the plant, they *will* respond to a notice or short article offering a free report entitled "Six Proven Ways to Cut Energy Costs in Your Plant This Year."

Ideally, you want your prospect not only to send for but also to read your booklet or report. However, even if a prospect sends for but does *not* read your free information, the bait-piece offer has still done its job: namely, to generate an inquiry from a prospect who would otherwise not have contacted you.

Therefore, the fact that prospects are too busy or not inclined to read the material you send is not a good reason not to offer such information; the key is that it overcomes inertia and gets them to respond. Once you receive the inquiry, you can start the selling process to convert the lead to a sale. But with no response, you get nowhere. And free booklet offers *increase response.*

SHOULD YOU CHARGE FOR YOUR BOOKLET OR REPORT?

In most cases, no. If you're offering a booklet or report to generate leads rather than to make money on the sale of the booklet, then the booklet or report should be free. Unless your primary business is that of selling books or reports by mail, and you are offering this booklet or report to build your mailing list, you should not charge for it. Doing so will dramatically decrease your response rate and slow down the flow of leads—which defeats the reason for offering the bait piece in the first place.

One argument for charging is that people who pay for the booklet or report are better qualified as prospects. This isn't true (unless, again, your main business is the selling of books or reports by mail). Does asking them to pay $5 for your booklet make prospects more qualified to buy your widget? I don't think so. In fact, it only serves to prevent a lot of qualified prospects who would have requested your widget booklet if it were free from doing so.

The basic offer options for bait pieces are as follows:

- Free booklet or report when you call or write
- Free booklet or report available only to qualified prospects
- Free booklet or report with self-addressed stamped envelope
- Free booklet or report with self-addressed stamped envelope and $1 or $2 to cover handling
- Booklet or report for a price of $5 (or whatever you want to charge)
- Booklet or report free to qualified prospects; $5 (or whatever you want to charge) to the general public and others who are not qualified prospects

If the cost of printing and distributing booklets is a real hardship for you, you can recover that cost by requesting the reader to supply a self-addressed stamped envelope and $1 or $2 to cover printing and handling. But I don't recommend this. For most marketing programs designed to generate leads, the free booklet offer should be just that—entirely free.

CHAPTER 5

Using Press Releases to Generate Visibility and Immediate Response

WHY CONVENTIONAL PRESS RELEASES DON'T WORK

The "conventional" press release is a one- or two-page typed document of news or information about a company and its activities.

Here's a typical example:

FROM: XYZ Company, Anytown USA
CONTACT: Paul Paterson at XXX XXX-XXXX

For immediate release

JOE JONES NAMED EXECUTIVE VICE PRESIDENT AT XYZ COMPANY

ANYTOWN, USA—Joe Jones has been promoted to executive vice president at XYZ Company. In his new position, he will be responsible for managing U.S. operations as well as long-range strategic planning for all business units.

Before being promoted to executive vice president, Mr. Jones had served for 5 years as a senior program manager for the ABC Division of XYZ Company.

Prior to joining XYZ, he had been a program manager for Another Bigco in Sometown, USA, and had also worked as a staff analyst at SmallCo in Another-town, USA.

Mr. Jones holds a B.S. in systems engineering from Nice College and an M.B.A. in finance from NightSchool U. He is a member of Tau Beta Beta Rho and the Society for Systems Engineering.

Mr. Jones currently resides in Anytown with his wife, Janet, and his three children, John, Jamie, and Jack.

Most publications receiving this release will ignore it. One or two industry publications will run a one-line mention of Joe's promotion, as will his alumni magazine. If he lives in a small town, the weekly newspaper may run a short feature article with his picture and the text of the release. The result is minimal coverage; minimal visibility gained; zero leads, inquiries, or new business; and in short, no return on the time and money invested in preparing or distributing the release.

Perhaps 90 percent of the press releases distributed are similar in nature to this fictional example, generating a similar lack of interest, media coverage, and marketing results.

There are a number of reasons why press releases of this type, despite their popularity, are so ineffective.

First, the topic is a nonevent. Hundreds of people get hired or promoted every day. So there is nothing to differentiate the announcement from the other dozen or hundred or more the editor receives that week.

Second, the topic is not meaningful. The promotion is important to Joe Jones and his family—but that's about it. There is nothing to interest an editor or a reader: zero RSI, zero ESI.

Third, the announcement does not help promote Joe's firm or sell the firm's products, other than by mentioning the company name.

Fourth, there is no reason or incentive for the reader to pay attention—no benefit or usefulness in the information presented.

Fifth, there is no call to action, no response for a reader to take if he or she wants to do business with Joe or his firm.

Despite this lack of effectiveness, the "Joe Jones got promoted" press release is the most commonly used and most popular; nine out of ten releases are structured just like it. (Other themes include expanded facilities, new hires, awards won, other honors, corporate reorganization, openings of new facilities, company anniversaries, and so on.)

Such releases are popular with publicists for two reasons.

The first is that they're easy to do and can be prepared quickly without much effort, research, or creative thought.

The second has to do with the way PR firms and professionals are compensated by their clients.

Many PR firms work on retainer: In exchange for a fixed monthly fee, they produce a set number of releases and articles. To fulfill their contractual obligation, the PR firm looks around the company, asks "What's new?" and writes and distributes releases on these topics.

If there's a lot going on that month, the releases have substance and will work. If there's nothing noteworthy, the PR firm still has to produce X number of press releases. So it may be forced to "scrape the bottom of the barrel" and write bland releases on "nonevents" such as Joe Jones's promotion or Sam Smith's being elected treasurer of the local fraternal club.

A BETTER ALTERNATIVE

In Targeted Public Relations, we use the Direct Response Press Release (DRPR), which is much more effective than the conventional press release.

There are three differences between the DRPR and the conventional press release:

1. The Direct Response Press Release has "real" content—meat.
2. The Direct Response Press Release has ESI and RSI.
3. The Direct Response Press Release has an offer.

What does this mean?

First, the Direct Response Press Release is always built around a genuine story, a real event, important information, or other "meat."

How is this done? Using the checklist in chapter 2 (Fig. 2.1), you analyze a proposed subject or topic to see if it contains within it any of the seven key themes most likely to have strong media appeal.

If the topic contains this media appeal, we write a press release around it, so that it gets noticed and used. If the topic is found not to contain inherent media appeal, we *don't* go ahead and put out a press release on it anyway, as some people would. Instead, we either drop the topic and find another . . . or we *create* media appeal, as outlined in the last section of chapter 2.

Second, a DRPR has strong ESI and RSI. This means we do not put in the press release what interests us; rather, we build the story around something that would interest our prospects—the readers of the publication and listeners of the program.

Too many people write press releases from the manufacturer's point of view. They put out story after story about things that are of interest only to the company and its managers.

This is done either in the mistaken belief that others care about you and your company as much as you do (which isn't true) or to stroke someone's ego: Often an executive will order the PR department or agency to put out a release on a person or his or her accomplishments as a way to recognize and honor that person. It may flatter the subject of the release, but editors don't care . . . and neither do your prospects.

As with any effective marketing effort, good public relations focuses on the prospect, not the product. As far as PR goes, think about not what is important to you; concentrate on what is important to your prospects. What are their problems, their needs, their most pressing concerns? What information, advice, products, services, tips, or guidance do they require to improve their lives, do their jobs better, or save time and money? What information do you have that they would want to know and read about in a magazine or hear on the radio or see on TV?

The Direct Response Press Release is not designed to stroke the client's ego or serve some internal requirement to have certain topics covered in releases. It succeeds because it is focused on what will appeal to media people and interest their audiences most.

The third factor that sets the Direct Response Press Release apart from the conventional press release is that there is always an offer. (The term offer, as it applies to a PR promotion, is discussed in detail in chapter 4.) That is, the release always ends with a call to action: The reader is encouraged to call, write, or fax to get a booklet, product sample, videotape, or some similar item being distributed for free or (usually) at nominal cost.

Now, it's true that traditional publicists occasionally do make free offers and put contact information in their press releases, but they do not make a deliberate *practice* of having an offer—a reason for the reader to respond to the article or radio broadcast—in every press release.

In Targeted Public Relations, you do. You simply do not send out a press release without some type of offer and call to action. Your reasoning is that you want, in addition to the usual media pickup, a direct, measurable response to every publicity placement . . . so that it generates not only visibility but leads that convert to immediate new business, revenue, and profits.

THE FIVE TYPES OF PRESS RELEASES THAT GENERATE THE MOST MEDIA COVERAGE AND READER RESPONSE

There are numerous ways to construct a press release that has the characteristics just discussed. You'll probably come up with some innovative ideas that outpull anything I've ever done. However, if you don't feel like reinventing the wheel, you can generate substantial results by using any of a number of formats that have proven successful time and time again.

In my experience, five types of press releases consistently get the most media placement and generate the greatest number of responses from readers:

1. Free booklet or report
2. Telephone hotline
3. Special issue or timely event
4. New literature
5. New product or service

Within these categories, you can have variations. For example, the telephone hotline could be a regular 800 number, an 800 number that spells out a word (800-GAMBLING), a 900 number, or a regular toll number.

Let's take a look at some examples of press releases in these categories. When writing your own release, you can closely copy the format and style of these releases, substituting details specific to your topic. For example, I've used the format for a "free booklet press release" to promote numerous products and services—always with substantial results.

Free Booklet Press Release

This is my "secret weapon" in PR and the single most effective type of release I know of.

It works as follows: You write a free booklet, report, or other giveaway item along the lines described in chapter 4. You then send out a release that (1) announces the publication of your new booklet or report, (2) describes some of the useful information it contains, and (3) offers it free to readers of the publication or to the audience of the radio or TV show.

All three elements are critical. Editors are primarily interested in what's new, so if you are offering a new free booklet on a topic, your headline should always begin NEW FREE BOOKLET . . . followed by a description of the topic, contents, or issue the information addresses.

Next, your press release should repeat (either word for word or edited) some of the key points highlighted in the booklet or report. This is done so the editor can run your release as a "minifeature article" on the topic.

Just saying you have a new booklet available might get you a small mention. But if you allow editors to reprint some of its contents, by putting such material in the release you send, they'll run longer, more in-depth pieces featuring all the useful information you've provided.

"But if all of the information in my booklet is revealed in the article, then people will have no reason to send for my booklet!" you might protest. That sounds like a logical objection. But experience proves the opposite is true: The more the article describes the contents of your booklet, the more people will read the article and send for the booklet. "The more you tell, the more you sell." That's an old saying favored by mail-order ad copywriters, but it also applies to free booklet press releases.

Experience has shown that even if the entire text of a booklet is reprinted in an article (or an ad), people still want to get that text in booklet form. Why? Perhaps people don't like to tear out an ad or article, and find booklets and reports are a more permanent medium.

Remember, *put excerpts from your booklet into your release.* Do not assume that the editor will read your booklet and pull out pertinent material for an article. The press release should be a self-contained miniarticle ready to use "as is," without the editor having to refer to any enclosures or other materials.

Finally, like any DRPR, your free booklet release must call for action. In the last paragraph you say "For a free copy of [title of booklet], call or write [your company name, address, phone]."

Many editors will include that contact information and a call to action when running your release, and you will get many requests. Some editors will not print such contact information. But you have no control over that. However, if you do not put in contact information and a call to action, *no* editors will tell their readers how or where they can request your booklet, and without such information, no one will contact you. So, always close with the call to action.

Finally, should you include a copy of your free booklet with the press releases you mail?

Including a sample of the booklet may be desirable, but it is not necessary. I have had great success mailing press releases that did not include a sample copy of the booklet or report being offered.

The main benefit of leaving out the sample booklet is cost savings: Including a sample booklet can add another 10 to 70 cents or more per release being mailed, depending on the cost to print the booklet and the weight of the booklet (which increases postage). For example, a tip sheet or slim pamphlet will add less cost than a bulky special report, book, or manual.

If the extra 10 cents to 70 cents per piece is significant to you, omit the sample booklet and pocket the savings. Be sure to put a line after the close of your release that says EDITOR: REVIEW COPY OF "[TITLE OF BOOKLET]" AVAILABLE UPON RE-QUEST—CALL JOE JONES AT XXX XXX-XXXX. Some editors may insist on seeing a copy before they'll promote it in their publication, so you should offer to send a copy free to any editor who requests it.

If your free booklet is slim and inexpensive, or if cost is not a factor, include a sample copy with each release you mail. It certainly can't hurt. And some editors may pay extra attention when they open the envelope and see your report or pamphlet.

Some sample new booklet press releases follow.

Sample Release: Free Tip Sheet on How to Market Software

As discussed in chapter 4, your free booklet need not be an actual booklet with cover and staples; you can offer a free report, fact sheet, audiocassette, or other free information in your release.

A release I sent out offering a free tip sheet on how to market and sell software follows. The purpose was to get publicity, establish myself as an authority in software marketing, and get leads from potential clients for my copywriting and consulting services.

The tip sheet was an 8½-by-11-inch sheet of paper printed on two sides; each side contained a reprint of a brief how-to article I wrote on the topic of selling and marketing software.

The press release was sent to fifty advertising and marketing trade journals and several hundred computer magazines and journals. It was picked up as a story by eight or nine of these publications, generating more than a hundred inquiries, resulting in two new clients and consulting assignments.

The cost of printing and mailing the release was less than $200, including postage, and the initial assignments generated amounted to more than $4,000 in revenue from copywriting and consulting fees.

In addition, a number of people requesting the tip sheet ordered more of my tip sheets, books, and reports, resulting in hundreds of dollars in product sales.

FROM: Bob Bly, 174 Holland Avenue, New Milford, NJ 07646
CONTACT: Fern Dickey, 201 385-1220

For immediate release

NEW TIP SHEET SHOWS ESTABLISHED AND START-UP SOFTWARE PRODUCERS HOW TO MARKET AND PROMOTE THEIR PRODUCTS—EFFECTIVELY

New Milford, NJ—With the glut of software products flooding the marketplace, it's essential to produce mailings, brochures, ads, and other printed materials that quickly, clearly, and dramatically communicate the key functions and benefits of your software to potential buyers.

That's the opinion of Robert W. Bly, a New Milford, NJ–based consultant specializing in software marketing and promotion. He is also the author of a new tip sheet, "How to Sell Software," which presents advice on how both established and start-up software producers can effectively advertise, promote, and market software for PC's, mainframes, and minicomputers.

One of the most difficult marketing decisions facing software sellers, says Bly, is whether to use a one-step or two-step marketing approach—that is, whether to sell the product via mail order directly from the ad or direct mail piece, or instead to generate a sales lead which is followed up by mailing a brochure or sending a salesperson for a face-to-face meeting.

"PC software products in the $50 to $299 price range are good candidates for one-step mail order selling," advises Bly. "In the $399 to $899 price range, you may want to test a one-step vs. a two-step approach and see which works best." And at $1,000 and up, says Bly, the two-step lead-generating method is best. "Few people will send payment for a $1,999 software package without some extra convincing by a salesperson, free trial, or demo diskette," he notes.

Some additional software marketing tips from the fact sheet:

- Early in your ad copy, tell the prospective purchaser what type or category of software you are selling. "People are usually in the market for a product to handle one of the known, identifiable, major applications—project management, word processing, accounts payable," says Bly.
- Talk in terms the reader can visualize. Instead of writing "2,400 bps modem," say "The SuperSpeedy modem transmits data at a rate of 2,400 bits per second—about seven seconds for a full page of text."
- The headline or teaser copy should select the right audience for the ad or mailer. For example, if you are selling C compilers, the teaser copy might read "Attention C programmers."
- Product specifications should be scaled down to numbers the reader can relate to. "Stores a mailing list of 50,000 prospects" is better than "stores 5 million

characters" because people have an easier time grasp-
ing the smaller number, says Bly.
- Include testimonials from satisfied users and excerpts
  from favorable third-party reviews.

One of Bly's all-time favorite headlines is from a small
black-and-white display ad for Winterhalter Incorporated,
a manufacturer of coax boards and controllers that enable
micro-to-mainframe communication. The headline reads
"LINK 8 PCs TO YOUR MAINFRAME—ONLY $2,395."
Says Bly, "Computer magazines are filled with 'clever' ad
headlines that give the reader no idea whatsoever what the
product is or who it is for. This headline tells you *exactly*
what the product will do for you and what it will cost."

For a copy of Bly's software marketing tip sheet, "How
to Sell Software," send $1 and a self-addressed stamped
#10 envelope to: Bob Bly, Dept. 105, 174 Holland Avenue,
New Milford, NJ 07646.

Here I requested $1 and a self-addressed stamped enve-
lope from the reader. This was done not to "qualify" the prospect (I don't believe asking for money does this, except if
you're selling mail order information) but to eliminate the labor of addressing envelopes and to cover my costs (I'm a
small-time operator on a limited budget).

If I were doing a similar PR mailing for a corporate client
or entrepreneur, I'd probably advise them not to require a
self-addressed stamped envelope and to send the tip sheet
free of charge—unless they were strapped for cash and
needed a "self-liquidating" promotion (one that pays its own
cost in revenue generated).

Note in the last paragraph of the release my key code
"Dept. 105" in my address. By counting the number of requests for this tip sheet addressed to department 105, I know

exactly how many responses were generated as a result of this PR mailing.

Some practitioners take this a step further and put a different key code on each individual press release; the key code indicates the publication the release was sent to. Therefore the press release on my tip sheet going to *Computer Decisions* would have been key coded "Dept. CD," while the next copy, being mailed to *InfoWorld*, would have been key coded "IW."

The advantage of individual coding of releases keyed to publication is that it lets you know how many responses were generated from each media outlet; you can target those that generate a high level of response for extra promotion or special attention when doing subsequent PR mailings. The major disadvantage of key-coding each release with a different key is that it's time-consuming: You have to do it one release at a time. I personally don't think it's worth the time and trouble, but do whatever seems best for you.

Sample Release: Recession-fighting Business Strategies Booklet

This was one of my more successful new booklet releases, and I think it's a good model for anyone offering free information via press release: The format is easily adapted to any information offer and has worked for everyone who has tried it.

This press release was mailed to 300 business magazines, 50 advertising and marketing magazines, 80 syndicated newspaper columnists who write on business topics, business editors at the nation's 500 largest daily newspapers, and a few other publications. Because I included a sample booklet with the release, total cost for mailing approximately 950 releases was a bit under $1,000.

The release generated dozens of pickups, ranging from brief mentions to magazines that reprinted almost the entire text word for word. I do not know the specific number of pickups since I did not use a clipping service to keep track of all the placements.

Virtually every pickup included information on how the reader could order the booklet. From this press release alone, I sold well over 3,000 booklets at $7 each, for a gross of $21,000. The follow-up sales included several consulting assignments, half a dozen speaking engagements, and additional sales of other booklets and reports.

The release works for two reasons: first, because the topic was timely—the release was issued during the worst of the recession of the early 1990s, so it was a "hot" topic with inherent media appeal; and second, because it precisely follows the three-part formula of (a) announcing the availability of a new booklet, (b) excerpting highlights so editors could run a mini-feature article on the subject, and (c) providing contact information and a call to action.

The only way in which it violates the formula for the free booklet release is that the reader must pay $7. I did this because my primary motivation was to make money selling this booklet as well as a line of related booklets and reports I offer, and I felt the need for such a booklet was so great that charging $7 would not prevent people from ordering.

For a client selling a consulting or advisory service, however, I would probably make the booklet free or ask for a nominal sum if the objective was to generate sales leads for the service.

FROM: Bob Bly, 174 Holland Avenue, New Milford, NJ 07646
CONTACT: Bob Bly, phone 201 385-1220

For immediate release

NEW BOOKLET REVEALS 14 PROVEN STRATEGIES FOR KEEPING BUSINESSES BOOMING IN A BUST ECONOMY

New Milford, NJ—While some companies struggle to survive in today's sluggish business environment, many are doing better than ever—largely because they have mastered the proven but little-known strategies of "recession marketing."

That's the opinion of Bob Bly, an independent marketing consultant and author of the just-published booklet "Recession-Proof Business Strategies: 14 Winning Methods to Sell Any Product or Service in a Down Economy."

"Many businesspeople fear a recession or soft economy, because when the economy is weak, their clients and customers cut back on spending," says Bly. "To survive in such a marketplace, you need to develop recession-marketing strategies that help you retain your current accounts and keep those customers buying. You also need to master marketing techniques that will win you *new* clients or customers to replace any business you may have lost because of the increased competition that is typical of a recession."

Among the recession-fighting business strategies Bly outlines in his new booklet:

- *Reactivate dormant accounts.* An easy way to get more business is to simply call past clients or customers—people you served at one time but are not actively working for now—to remind them of your existence. According to Bly, a properly scripted telephone call to a list of past buyers will generate approximately one order for every ten calls.
- *Quote reasonable, affordable fees and prices in competitive bid situations.* While you need not reduce your rates or prices, in competitive bid situations you will win by bidding toward the low or middle end of your price range rather than at the high end. Bly says that during a recession, your bids should be 15 to 20 percent

lower than you would normally charge in a healthy economy.

- *Give your existing clients and customers a superior level of service.* In a recession, Bly advises businesses to do everything they can to hold onto their existing clients or customers—their "bread-and-butter" accounts. "The best way to hold onto your clients or customers is to please them," says Bly, "and the best way to please them is through better customer service. Now is an ideal time to provide that little bit of extra service or courtesy that can mean the difference between dazzling the client or customer vs. merely satisfying them."

- *Reactivate old leads.* Most businesses give up on sales leads too early, says Bly. He cites a study from Thomas Publishing which found that although 80 percent of sales to businesses are made on the fifth call, only one out of ten salespeople calls beyond three times. Concludes Bly: "You have probably not followed up on leads diligently enough, and the new business you need may already be right in your prospect files." He says repeated follow-up should convert 10 percent of prospects to buyers.

- *Repackage your product line or service to accommodate smaller clients or customers on reduced budgets.* Manufacturers and other product sellers can offer compact models, economy sizes, no-frills versions, easy payment plans, extended credit, special discounts, incentives, and smaller minimum orders to appeal to prospects with reduced spending power. Service providers can be more flexible by selling their services and time in smaller, less-costly increments.

- *Keep busy with ancillary assignments.* Another recession survival strategy is to take on ancillary assignments to fill gaps in your work schedule. For example, a carpenter who normally handled only large, lucrative home remodeling jobs took on lots of smaller jobs and "handyman" work to keep the money coming in when his home renovation work fell off.

- *Add value to your existing product or service.* While prospects may seem reluctant to spend money in a soft economy, their real concern, says Bly, is making sure they get the best value for their dollar. You can retain existing accounts and win new business by offering more value than your competition. For instance, says Bly, a firm selling industrial components added value by computerizing its inventory system so it could give customers faster telephone quotations on the availability and pricing of needed parts.

- *Help existing clients or customers create new sales for you.* Bly advises businesses to call their existing accounts with new ideas that will benefit the client or customer while requiring them to buy more of what the vendor is selling. "It's a win-win situation," says Bly. "They get your ideas, suggestions, and solutions to their problems at no charge, while you sell more of your product or service to help them implement the idea you suggested."

To receive a copy of Bly's booklet, "Recession-Proof Business Strategies," send $8 ($7 plus $1 shipping and handling) to: Bob Bly, Dept. 109, 174 Holland Avenue, New Milford, NJ 07646. Cash, money orders, and checks (payable to "Bob Bly") accepted. (Add $1 for Canadian orders.)

Bob Bly, an independent copywriter and consultant based in New Milford, NJ, specializes in business-to-business, hi-tech, and direct-response marketing. He is the author of 18 books including HOW TO PROMOTE YOUR OWN BUSINESS (New American Library) and SELLING YOUR SERVICES (Henry Holt). A frequent speaker and seminar leader, Mr. Bly speaks nationwide on the topic of how to market successfully in a recession or soft economy.

Sample Release: Free Article Reprint

Here's another variation on the free booklet theme. This company published an article on its specialty, collections, in a trade journal. It made reprints of the article and offered it as a "free special report" in a press release sent to other publications within the same industry. Interestingly, many of these publications used the release, and not one voiced an objection to printing what was essentially an offer to send an article reprint from a competitor's publication.

From this I learned that *any* published article can be offered as a reprint through a free booklet press release and that other magazines will run the offer. You can print somewhere on the booklet cover or at the bottom of the tip sheet that the article was "reprinted with permission from Vol. 5 No. 10 of XYZ MAGAZINE" without fear that this will turn off rival magazines from using it.

In the release, however, call your reprint a "special report" if it's a lengthy article, a "monograph" if it's a scholarly or scientific article, or a "tip sheet" if it's a short (one- or two-page) article. Any of these terms sound more important than an "article reprint," so more readers will write or call you to get it.

FROM: RMCB, 1261 Broadway, New York, NY 10001
CONTACT: Russell Fuchs, 800 542-5025

For immediate release

FREE REPORT FOR DIRECT MARKETERS
PRESENTS 12 NEW WAYS TO COLLECT OLD BILLS

New York, NY, January—A new special report, published by Retrieval-Masters Creditors Bureau (RMCB), a nationwide agency specializing in the collection of low-dollar-amount, high-volume accounts receivables, reveals 12 key strategies for using an outside collection agency to turn past-due accounts into paid-up customers.

The 8-page report, "How an Outside Collection Agency Can Improve Your Conversions," is available free of charge to circulation directors, publishers, direct marketers, business executives, advertising professionals, entrepreneurs, and students. The cost to the general public is $5.

Although the report originally was written to show circulation directors how to improve subscription collections, Russell Fuchs, president of RMCB, says the information is applicable to direct marketers selling virtually any product or service through the mail—including publishers, book clubs, mail order firms, continuity plans, and catalog marketers.

Why should direct marketers, whose invoices typically reflect a low dollar balance, be interested in working with collection agencies to improve collection results? "Whenever you extend credit to the customer and allow him or her to say 'bill me,' you typically have a nonpayment rate ranging from 5 to 35 percent or more," says Fuchs. "Experience shows that a competent collection agency can convert 21 to 25 percent of those delinquent accounts into paid-up customers."

Here are some of RMCB's suggestions on how to use a collection agency to improve collection results:

- *Vary the letterhead.* Fuchs says that sending a dunning letter on a third-party letterhead—either in an internal billing series or the collection agency's billing cycle—lifts response virtually every time.
- *Vary the dunning cycle.* To extend the billing series and

increase net recovery rates, collection agencies will vary the timing between efforts, typically from 14 to 28 days. "This is a proven response-booster," says Fuchs.

- *Make sure "white mail" is given special handling.* "Promptly acknowledge and resolve every nonpayment and partial payment response," warns Fuchs. "Your collection agency should have a special 'correspondence response department' whose job it is to communicate with customers who dispute invoices, make partial payments, or have other responses out of the ordinary."
- *Be aware of the legal requirements for dunning.* For example, the Fair Debt Collection Practices Act requires that specific disclosure copy notifying consumers of their rights appear on each letter sent by any collection agency. (RMCB's report includes the proper wording for this disclosure.)

To receive a free copy of "How an Outside Collection Agency Can Improve Your Conversions," contact: Retrieval-Masters Creditors Bureau, 1261 Broadway, Dept. CM1, New York, NY 10001, phone 800 843-8097, ATT: Ruth Malone.

For a free, no-obligation telephone consultation with expert Russell Fuchs about your direct marketing collection problems, telephone RMCB's "Collections Hotline" at 800 542-5025.

SPECIAL EVENT, "GIMMICK," OR TIMELY ISSUE

The press is always looking for a story that captures the public's imagination. Therefore, if you have a special event, timely issue, or unusual human interest story, or can add some sort of hook or angle to your release, you'll have a better chance of gaining coverage.

Editors are interested in stories that are substantial and of value yet have an unusual twist or gimmick to them. If you can be a bit different (albeit in a relevant way), you will get noticed.

Sample Press Release: Empire State Building Location

Here's a perfect example. This company rents mail boxes—a pretty mundane business. But the "angle" for this story was the unusual, prestigious location of their mail box address: the Empire State Building.

FROM: Empire State Communications, 350 Fifth Ave., New York, NY 10118
CONTACT: Arthur Goodman, phone 800 447-0099

For immediate release

NOW BUSINESSES NATIONWIDE CAN ESTABLISH
A BRANCH OFFICE IN NEW YORK CITY'S
PRESTIGIOUS EMPIRE STATE BUILDING—
FOR AS LITTLE AS $35 PER MONTH

New York, NY—Want to give your company added prestige and impress your customers? NYC-based entrepreneur Arthur Goodman has a suggestion: a "branch office" in New York's most distinguished and memorable location: the Empire State Building.

Goodman's company, Empire State Communications, provides mail receiving, fax, telex, and telephone service for businesses nationwide that want to establish a branch address in New York without physically having an office there. And the price is right: Empire's service starts at $35 per month.

"Our service allows firms nationwide to immediately and inexpensively establish a New York presence at one of Manhattan's most memorable—and impressive—addresses," says Goodman. "The Empire State Building is a status symbol worldwide. And the address is easy for your prospects to remember; no multidigit P.O. box number is necessary."

What types of companies use Goodman's Empire State service? "It's for small out-of-town companies that want to convey an image of a larger, more substantial firm through a prestigious New York City address, as well as large corporations that feel they should have a New York City location but don't want the expense of renting costly office space," he says.

How does Goodman's service work? For a small monthly fee, Goodman's clients obtain the right to use his Empire State Building address as their own in letterhead, business cards, and advertisements. "We act as their New York office," says Goodman. "They can receive mail, phone calls, telexes, and fax transmissions, just as if they were physically located in New York.

"In fact, your prospects and customers will have no way of telling that you don't actually have a big, fancy office in the Empire State Building," he adds.

Mail received at the Empire State location is forwarded daily by Goodman to any location his clients specify—usually their headquarters' corporate mailroom. According to Goodman, the Empire State Building is one of the few buildings in the United States with its own post office branch and private zip code (10118), which results in faster delivery of his clients' mail. Phone calls, telexes, and fax transmissions received are also forwarded immediately, either by mail, phone, fax, or computer modem.

Goodman, in business since 1953, is no newcomer to the mail box industry. One of his other companies, Goodman Communications, offers mail receiving and branch office service in three additional Manhattan locations: midtown, downtown, and the Upper East Side.

"This is the first time that the mailing address of the Empire State Building has been made commercially available to businesses of all sizes here and overseas,"says Goodman, who adds that Empire State Communications is the only company offering mail-receiving service at that address.

For a limited time only, Goodman is making a special offer to entice out-of-town companies to try his Empire State location: one month's service free to people who contact him within the next 30 days.

To receive a free brochure outlining the services offered by Goodman at his Empire State location, call or write: Arthur Goodman, Empire State Communications, 350 Fifth Avenue, Dept. EPR-2, New York, NY 10118, 800 447-0099.

Mentioning that the Empire State Building is one of the few buildings in the country with its own private zip code and post office is a nice added touch, as some editors like to include a bit of trivia or little-known information in their articles.

Sample Press Release: Entrepreneur Seminar

A special event, such as a convention, sale, grand opening, trade show, or seminar, is also a good topic for a press release because it's timely. When Gary Blake and I decided to hold a

seminar on the topic of being an entrepreneur, we sent out
this release to local and national business magazines:

FROM: The Communication Workshop, 217 E. 85th St.,
New York, NY 10028
CONTACT: Gary Blake, 718 575-8000

For immediate release

NEW NYC SEMINAR SHOWS "ORDINARY PEOPLE" HOW TO BECOME SUCCESSFUL ENTREPRENEURS— WITHOUT SPENDING BIG MONEY OR TAKING BIG RISKS

NEW YORK, NY, October 30th—Computer whiz kids,
chocolate-chip-cookie bakers, and other young hot-shot
millionaire success stories have become media darlings.
But what if you're a regular guy or gal, not looking to make
a million but just wanting to make a go of a modest small
business of your own?

Take heart. Two local entrepreneurs—Gary Blake and
Bob Bly, coauthors of the new book OUT ON YOUR OWN:
FROM CORPORATE TO SELF-EMPLOYMENT (New
York: John Wiley & Sons)—have created a new one-day
seminar on BECOMING AN ENTREPRENEUR.

The seminar teaches would-be entrepreneurs that you
don't have to be a Ted Turner or a Victor Kiam to start
your own business. Anybody can do it—and succeed—
without a lot of money, without being a genius, and without
taking big risks.

Says Bly, "Although I always disliked corporate life, I
was the person people would have voted 'Least Likely to
Take a Risk.' But by following a few simple principles, I
successfully made the transition from a 9-to-5 job to self-

employment. I didn't have any money in the bank or a great new product. Yet I quadrupled my corporate salary within 3 years."

Adds Blake, 42, director of The Communication Workshop, a management consulting firm, "It's traumatic to leave the world of weekly paychecks; we know because we've done it. Our seminar on BECOMING AN ENTREPRENEUR helps people progress from just dreaming about quitting to realistically assessing their options, making plans, and then acting on those plans."

The first BECOMING AN ENTREPRENEUR seminar, which costs $85 per participant, will be presented in midtown Manhattan on January 24th. The seminar is aimed at people who are not satisfied with corporate life but may not have the impetus, self-confidence, or focus to break loose. BECOMING AN ENTREPRENEUR gives a blueprint for entrepreneurial success, guiding each participant toward confronting the positive and negative aspects of being your own boss.

The course explores such issues as discovering your values, focusing on what you want to do for a living, weighing the pros and cons of corporate security vs. entrepreneurial freedom, dealing with self-doubt and the criticism of others, coping with solitude, finding a partner, setting fees, setting up a company, getting your first client, managing time, and marketing and advertising for small business. It also gives special strategies for making a smooth, painless transition from corporate employment to self-employment.

For more information on the BECOMING AN ENTREPRENEUR seminar, phone or write The Communication Workshop, 217 E. 85th Street, Suite 442, New York, NY 10028, 212 794-1144.

Although this release was *not* wildly successful, it did catch the attention of a reporter at *Nation's Business*, who featured us prominently in a cover story on entrepreneurism in the United States.

TELEPHONE HOTLINE PRESS RELEASE

Telephone hotlines—numbers people can call to get free advice and information from a live operator, tape recording, or voice mail system—are extremely popular with consumers and therefore with editors.

People like the convenience of being able to dial a phone number and order a product, ask a question, or get free assistance or advice.

There are telephone hotlines on every conceivable topic, from cancer and lawn care, to gambling and auto safety.

While some hotlines are nonprofit, many are sponsored by companies that use them as a way of generating leads, sales, inquiries, visibility, and publicity.

One of the best ways to promote such a hotline is through a press release. Editors will print short blurbs and articles announcing your hotline, describing the information available to callers, and giving the phone number. Such announcements can generate hundreds or thousands of phone calls, plus lots of media coverage.

Sample Press Release: PR Hotline

Alan Caruba, a New Jersey PR counselor, wanted to gain some publicity for his business. The challenge: Caruba is one of hundreds of independent PR counselors, and there is nothing newsworthy about being in the PR business per se.

Alan's solution? Create a "PR Hotline" through which he can offer his consulting service on an hourly basis via telephone to smaller firms that either need quick advice or cannot afford to pay the traditional large monthly retainer most PR firms charge.

Another interesting quirk: Alan accepts MasterCard and Visa, which is an unusual way to charge for professional services. His release on the topic, which gained wide publication and generated many inquiries to the hotline, follows.

THE CARUBA ORGANIZATION
Box 40, Maplewood, NJ 07040
201 763-6392

For immediate release

CHARGE PR ADVICE TO YOUR CREDIT CARD
"PR HOTLINE"—NEW BUSINESS SERVICE

Maplewood, NJ—Mike Wallace of "Sixty Minutes" is at the door with a camera crew! What do you do now?

"Most public relations does not involve a crisis," says PR counselor Alan Caruba of Maplewood, NJ. "In fact, good PR can avert such problems while helping to promote products, services, and causes of every description."

Caruba notes that "many business and professional people neither need, nor want, to retain a full-time public relations agency or counselor. What they need is good advice from time to time." That's why Caruba created the "PR Hotline," a telephone service (201 763-6392) that allows anyone with a PR question or problem to call. One can charge the service to either a MasterCard or Visa.

At $50 for the first forty minutes or $75 for up to a full hour, "a lot of very specific analysis and advice can be provided," says Caruba. "Public relations can be local, regional, or national in scope. It can represent a single project or a long-term program."

Caruba has been dispensing advice and service to corporations, associations, small business operations, and individuals for more than twenty years. He is a member of The Counselors Academy of the Public Relations Society of America and frequently lectures and writes on the subject.

Sample Press Release: The Advertising Hotline

Years ago I wanted to promote myself as an authority in advertising. Unlike the big ad agencies, however, I knew that merely sending a release announcing my latest projects or clients would not be effective. The business of J. Walter Thompson is of interest to the trade press; the business of one lone freelance copywriter is not.

When I asked myself, "How can I create something newsworthy and thus get publicity for myself?" the Advertising Hotline was the answer. The idea is simple: a nationwide telephone hotline businesspeople can call to get quick tips and advice on how to improve their marketing.

To implement the idea was even easier: just set up a phone line in my basement and attach an answering machine with a long outgoing message. Hotline callers were treated to a five-minute prerecorded "miniseminar on tape" on a different topic each week. Here is my release:

FROM: The Advertising Hotline, 174 Holland Ave., New Milford, NJ 07646
CONTACT: Amy Sprecher, 201 385-1220

For immediate release

NEW NATIONAL TELEPHONE HOTLINE
PROVIDES FREE ADVERTISING AND
MARKETING TIPS TO AD AGENCIES,
CORPORATIONS, AND SMALL BUSINESS

New Milford, NJ, December 4th—The "Advertising Hotline," a new nationwide telephone hotline, has been established to provide free advice, information, and tips on advertising, direct mail, publicity, and other forms of promotion to ad agencies, PR firms, large corporations, and small business. The Hotline number is XXX XXX-XXXX.

"Clients and their agencies today need solid, reliable information on what works in advertising—and what doesn't," says Bob Bly, the Hotline's director. "As a free-lance copywriter, I have hundreds of people calling me asking questions such as: 'How can I get more inquiries from my quarter-page trade ad? How can I write a direct-mail package that will get a good response?' I set up the Advertising Hotline to give these folks some of the answers."

Unlike many other information sources, Bly points out, the Advertising Hotline is free. "A lot of companies can't afford to hire consultants, and it takes time to read a book, listen to an audiocassette, or attend a seminar," notes Bly. "The Hotline is free and takes only five minutes of the caller's time."

In the months to come, callers who phone the Advertising Hotline at XXX XXX-XXXX can listen to taped "mini-seminars" on a variety of subjects. Scheduled topics include: "10 Ways to Stretch Your Advertising Budget," "How to Write Winning Sales Letters," "12 Questions to Ask *Before* You Create Your Next Advertising Campaign," "New Ideas for Your Corporate Newsletter," and "Selling Financial Services by Mail." The current topic can be heard right now by calling the Hotline at XXX XXX-XXXX.

The hotline can be reached from any telephone in the world, 24 hours a day, 7 days a week. The taped message usually runs between 3 to 5 minutes in length. The message is changed approximately once a week.

I sent the release to fifty trade publications covering advertising, public relations, promotion, marketing, and sales. Attractively printed Advertising Hotline Rolodex™ cards were mailed with the releases to give editors the impression that the Ad Hotline was a real and ongoing activity.

Eighteen publications ran stories based on the release. At least five ran almost the entire release, practically word for word. This publicity generated thousands of phone calls to the Hotline within twelve months.

Note that it is not necessary to have a hotline number that is a toll-free 800 number or spells out a word (such as 800 AUTO-SAFETY). You can be successful using an ordinary toll number that is staffed by employees or that uses electronic voice mail or an answering machine to deliver its message.

NEW PRODUCT RELEASE

The most popular type of press release is the new product release. This is a simple announcement of a new product. As mentioned, the product need not actually be "new" to qualify for a new product release. Enhancements, upgrades, new models, new features, and new applications can all form the basis for a release of this type.

New product releases are typically featured in the new product sections of trade publications. Editors run short two- or three-paragraph descriptions of the products along with a photo or drawing, if provided along with the release. This type of coverage, while routine in nature, provides additional exposure for your product, builds awareness, and can generate numerous inquiries at low cost.

Here's a typical new product release:

NEWS RELEASE KOCH ENGINEERING COMPANY, INC.

CONTACT: Bob Bly or Mike Mutsakis, 212 682-5755

For immediate release

KOCH ENGINEERING DEVELOPS DRY SO_2 SCRUBBING SYSTEM

Koch Engineering Company, Inc., of Wichita, Kansas, and New York City, has developed a dry SO_2 scrubbing system for cleaning flue gas in coal-fired boilers.

The system uses a lime-based spray dryer and a baghouse for SO_2 and particulate removal. To design dry scrubbing systems tailored to individual applications, Koch Engineering has a fully integrated dry scrubbing pilot plant available for test and evaluation of customer coal and chemicals.

"Koch Engineering is the only manufacturer in the dry scrubbing business that has a dry SO_2 scrubbing pilot plant operating off a dedicated pulverized coal-fired boiler, a large-scale semiworks spray dryer, and a commercial-scale system now in operation," says David H. Koch, president of Koch Engineering. "No company is better equipped to design, scale up, fabricate, and install complete dry scrubbing systems for industrial boilers."

The Koch dry SO_2 scrubbing system, he added, uses a two-fluid nozzle in the spray dryer rather than a rotary or centrifugal atomizer. This results in increased reliability, simpler maintenance, and reduced initial investment.

This release was picked up in more than thirty-five trade journals; many ran the entire three-page release word for word. Result: 2,500 inquiries generated within six months. Total promotion cost: under $500.

NEW LITERATURE RELEASE

The new literature release is used to announce the publication of a new product brochure, capabilities brochure, data sheet, catalog, or any other literature on a product or service.

When you come out with a new product, you can send out a new product release first, then follow up a month or so later with a new literature release (announcing publication of the product brochure or data sheet). In this way, you get two PR opportunities for each new product instead of just one.

If your literature contains how-to or reference information—for example, it tells how to specify a product, select the proper grade, install the right attachment, or the like—your release should highlight that fact.

Here's a sample new literature release:

NEW CATALOG AND REFERENCE MANUAL OFFERS WIDGET BUYERS GUIDANCE IN PROPER SELECTION, INSTALLATION OF WIDGETS

ANYTOWN, USA—Smith Widget Co. announced today the publication of its new 32-page widget catalog and buyer's guide.

The catalog, available free, contains complete specifications for more than 400 grades and models of widgets for standard and custom industrial applications.

It also contains charts, graphs, cross-reference tables, and other technical data enabling engineers to correctly specify, order, and install the right widget for their application, said Joe Smith, president of Smith Widgets.

[List some of the highlights or features of the catalog here.]

For a free copy of the Smith Widget catalog, call or write: Smith Widget, Dept. PRC-1, Anytown, USA, XXX XXX-XXXX.

HOW TO PREPARE A PRESS RELEASE

Preparing a press release is simple and straightforward. Just type your copy double-spaced on regular-size (8½-by-11-inch) sheets of paper.

Press releases can be duplicated by offset at a local "quick copy" printshop or run off on your office copier if the quality of reproduction is good. You can reproduce them on plain paper, business stationery, or special PR letterhead with the words NEWS RELEASE or PRESS RELEASE printed across the top; however, special paper is not necessary, and plain paper is fine.

Follow the format of the samples presented in this chapter. At the top of the first page, put "FROM:" or "SOURCE:" followed by the name and address of your company. Underneath this type "CONTACT:" followed by your name and telephone number.

Note: If you use a public relations agency, it will list its own name and address (under "FROM:" or "CONTACT:") followed by the name and address of you, their client (preceded by the word CLIENT:).

Below this, type "For immediate release." This tells editors that your story is timely, but it doesn't date the release so if you want to keep a supply on hand and send them out to editors as the opportunity arises, you can. If the release is tied to an event that takes place on a specific date, type "For release: Monday, May 22, 1993" (substituting the actual date) instead of "For Immediate Release."

Underneath this comes the headline. It is typed in all caps and can be as short as one line or as long as three lines. Two lines are typical.

Leave some extra space between the headline and the first paragraph of the story. The first paragraph may begin with a dateline, such as "New York, NY, October, 1990—" with the first sentence of the first paragraph coming immediately after that dash.

There are two basic types of leads for press releases: *news* and *feature*.

The news lead is the prototypical "who, what, when, where, why, and how" opening of a straight news story as taught in Journalism 101. The advantage of using the news lead is that, even if the editor chops the rest of your story and prints only the first paragraph—as is frequently done—the gist of your story still gets across.

The sample press release for the Advertising Hotline is an example of a straight news lead. To see more examples of news leads, pick up today's *New York Times* and study the first paragraphs of the stories running on page 1.

The other type of lead is the *feature* lead. The feature lead is written in an entertaining, attention-getting fashion similar to the opening of a magazine feature article. The purpose is to grab the editor's attention by being clever, startling, or dramatic, so that more editors read and use your release.

The press release for the BECOMING AN ENTREPRENEUR seminar is a good example of a feature lead. To see more examples of feature leads, pick up any issue of *Glamour* or *Cosmopolitan* magazine and read the first paragraphs of each of the major articles listed on the contents page.

After the lead comes the body of the story. If you are coming to the end of the page and it looks as if the paragraph will have to continue onto the next page, move the entire paragraph to that page. Do not divide paragraphs between two pages.

Why not? Some editors may want literally to cut up your release into paragraphs with scissors, then tape it together in a different order. (This is how some editors edit.) For the same reason, releases are always printed on one side of a sheet of paper, never on two sides.

You may say at this point, "But I don't want the editor to edit my story. I want it to run as is!" This is an understandable attitude, but it is self-defeating. In public relations, the editor is in clear control, is the "customer" for your stories, and you must meet the editor's needs and standards first if you are to have any chance of reaching your final audience—the readers.

If editors want to edit, make it easy, not difficult. If they want a new angle on your story, don't protest—help them find it. The more you cooperate with editors and give them what they need, the more publicity you will get.

The last paragraph of your press release contains the response information, including name, address, and telephone number. For example, "To get Smith Widget Company's new 32-page Widget catalog, contact: Smith Widget Company, Anytown, USA, XXX XXX-XXXX."

At the end of the story, you can simply type "END" or "XXX" or "-30-". All three symbols let the editor know that this is the end of the story.

FIVE WAYS TO GET YOUR PUBLICITY RELEASES PUBLISHED MORE OFTEN

Copywriter Mike Pavlish offers the following checklist for making sure your press releases get published.

1. *Is the subject of your release important to the publication's readers?* If you were the editor and you had dozens of releases but could only publish a few, would you honestly publish your release? Is the information and story

in your release really important—not to your business, but to the publication's readers? If not, forget it and look for a new angle.

2. *Is it really news or just an advertisement in disguise?* Editors are not in the business of publishing advertising. Almost all will immediately discard publicity that is really advertising in disguise. Of course, most publicity has some advertising value or purpose, but write your publicity to give news or helpful information only.

3. *Is it written so the publication's readers benefit from it?* Your publicity will get published more often if it contains important news that will benefit the publication's readers. This could be new technology the readers will be interested in, helpful information, or a new trend that is emerging.

4. *Is it short and to the point?* Editorial space is very limited, and busy editors don't have the time to sort through irrelevant copy and cut it down to the main points. Write clear and crisp sentences using only the important, relevant information.

5. *Does it include what the editor wants?* That is, facts to back up your statements, plus who, what, when, where, how, and why details.

SIXTEEN ADDITIONAL TIPS FOR IMPROVING YOUR PRESS RELEASES

Don Levin, president of Levin Public Relations, offers these additional tips and tactics on improving press releases:

1. Shorten them. Tighten the writing. Keep paragraphs and sentences concise. Avoid jargon and repetition. Use strong verbs. Create lively—but accurate—text.

2. Use subheads in longer stories, at least one per page.

Help the editor grasp the entire story. Trim sections, or put them in sidebars.

3. Consider adding a fact sheet for details that would clutter your release.

    Example: A New York City restaurant, when sending out a press release announcing its grand opening, included a separate sheet listing five specialty dishes along with the ingredients and recipes.

4. Make the release stand on its own. Do not use a cover letter. If you feel a cover letter is needed to explain why you are sending the release or why an editor should be interested in using it, then your press release is not strong enough. Go back and rewrite until it is irresistible to editors.

5. Get all the facts and establish perspective before starting to write. Adding and rewriting later costs time and money.

6. Keep the news up front, not behind the interpretation or buried in paragraphs of analysis.

7. Cut out puffery; stick to newsworthy information.

8. Put opinion and interpretation in an executive's quotation.

9. Forget the cute headline that forces an editor to dig through a paragraph or two to discover the who, what, when, where, and why. The headline should summarize the release so an editor quickly understands your point.

10. Leave plenty of white space, especially at the top of page 1, because editors like to have room to edit. Double space and leave wide margins. Never use the back of a page.

11. Write for a specific editorial department—up-front news, financial, new products. Similarly, provide separate story slants (in separate releases) for different categories of magazines.

12. Create separate, shorter releases for radio and, at minimum, color slides and scripts for television.

13. End releases with a boilerplate paragraph that explains the organization or division.

14. Consider editing the news release copy for product bulletins, internal publications, and other uses.

15. Write to gain respect for your organization and your next release.

16. Streamline the clearance process so only two or three executives approve each release. This saves time and minimizes the chance to muddy the text.

WHERE AND HOW TO DISTRIBUTE YOUR PRESS RELEASE

Rule of thumb: Your press release should be sent to all of the publications whose readers (or some portion of them) are potential customers for your product or service. This is the opposite of advertising media selection, in which the one or two publications that are most targeted toward our market is focused on.

Why the difference? In advertising, each publication we add to our schedule can cost us thousands or tens of thousands of dollars. But to add a given publication to our press release distribution list costs us only a 29-cent stamp for mailing the release; for this reason, it makes sense to be all-encompassing rather than selective.

For example, if you have a release appropriate to computer publications, don't spend time agonizing over which magazines should get the release and which should not. Instead, just send it to all the publications in the computer and data processing category of your publicity directory automatically. This actually saves time by eliminating a selection process and incurs minimal additional incremental cost ($29 per postage additional one hundred releases mailed).

USING BACON'S PUBLICITY CHECKER

There are many competing directories and services for press release distribution. One of the best-organized, most complete, and easiest to use is *Bacon's Publicity Checker*. It consists of three volumes—newspapers, magazines, and radio—listing thousands of publicity outlets. Listings are organized by category for magazines and geographically for newspapers, with each listing giving names, addresses, and phone numbers of appropriate contacts.

You have three choices for distributing a release via *Bacon's*. The first is to buy or borrow the books and mail out the releases yourself. This involves typing addresses on envelopes, duplicating releases, and stuffing releases into envelopes. It's difficult to get releases out in a timely manner this way unless you have a secretary with time available. One short cut is to enter the publicity outlets once into a computer program, then print labels or envelopes automatically for each subsequent mailing.

The second alternative is to order the names and addresses from Bacon's PR Service on gummed labels. The cost as of this writing is 35 cents per label, which is only $35 for a hundred labels. This eliminates the need to type them yourself. The drawback is that you have to order a fresh set of labels each time you do a mailing.

The third alternative is to send the release to Bacon's and let its staff do the mailing. For a fee, Bacon's publicity distribution service will duplicate and mail your release to publications in select categories from its list.

This is the easiest, most convenient option. All you do is

mail Bacon's one copy of your release. It handles the printing
and mailing. The last time I used the service it charged $143
to send out 300 copies of a two-page press release. There was
a $20 additional charge to insert my brochures (I supplied 300
copies) with the releases.

For information on buying the directories, ordering labels,
or the PR distribution service, contact: Bacon's PR Service
(see appendix).

COMPILING YOUR OWN MEDIA
CONTACT LIST

If you are an active mailer of press releases, you may decide
to create your own customized media mailing list rather than
simply send your release to be mailed by Bacon's or some
other distribution service (see appendix) to a standard list in
a given category.

For convenience, put your list on computer using a database or simple mailing list program capable of generating
mailing labels automatically. You do not need word processing
capability since the press releases themselves will not be personalized; all you need is mailing labels.

Start by checking various media directories listed in the
appendix and putting into your list all the editors at publications and broadcast media relevant to your markets.

Next, add all the editors who have ever interviewed you or
written about you in the past. Because they already know you,
they are more receptive to material from you than editors who
don't know you. (This is discussed in chapter 1.)

Then add any specialized publications or other publicity
outlets not listed in the directories. These can include industry newsletters, trade association newsletters, local ad club
bulletins, and other specialized outlets too small to make it

into the big directories. But even though they are small, they are highly targeted, and often these overlooked outlets are your most productive publicity sources.

Because editors move and publications fold, you must clean out your mailing list frequently. Update it whenever you get a change of address or the name of a new editor. Once a year, have your secretary go through it, call all the publications, and verify that you have the current information.

PR PHOTOS

Photos do not have to accompany press releases. Interesting releases will be picked up and used without an accompanying photograph, and photos are not necessary. On the other hand, if your press release lends itself to photographic treatment, an accompanying photo can only add interest to the article when it is published.

Your PR photo should be black and white, glossy, have sharp contrast, and measure either 5 by 7 inches or 8 by 10 inches.

Photo captions should be typed on a separate sheet of paper and taped to the back of the photo. Do not type or write with ballpoint pen directly on the back of a photo; the impression will come through and show up in reproduction.

What should be in your photo—and when do you need one? Follow these guidelines:

1. A photo of the product should accompany new product press releases. If the product is a prototype or does not yet exist, send a black-and-white photo of a diagram or sketch.
2. Special event, grand opening, seminar, or other time-dated announcements do not require a photograph.

However, a photo never hurts. If you're promoting a free seminar, for example, include a photo of the speaker.

3. New literature press releases do not require a photo. You can mail the release by itself or with a copy of your new brochure or catalog. Some publicists prefer photographing the cover and sending a black-and-white picture for the editor's use.

4. Telephone hotline press releases don't require a photo, and what would you show? I do, however, like to have Rolodex™ cards for the telephone hotline printed and include one or two cards with the press release.

   Sending the Rolodex™ card serves two purposes. First, it adds credibility and gives the editors the impression that yours is a "real" hotline rather than some advertising gimmick.

   Second, editors can put the card in their card files for future reference, and may call your hotline from time to time to get information for additional stories. (You get credit as the source, of course.) This means additional publicity for you at no extra cost.

5. Free booklet press releases don't need to be accompanied by a photo. Send a copy of the booklet, if you wish.

FOLLOW-UP

Generally it is impractical to follow-up on all the press releases mailed because of the time and expense of telephoning. If you have mailed your press release to 100 to 300 publications, you may want to follow up on just the 10 or 12 most important ones.

To follow-up, first, telephone the editor within a week after mailing the release. Say: "We sent you a release about a week ago concerning [topic of release]. Did you get it?" At this point, the editor will probably say she did not get it or doesn't remember it. That's only natural, because so many releases flood her desk.

You reply by explaining briefly what the release is about and then offering to send it again. Out of politeness, most editors will say yes to this offer. Mail or fax the release to them (be sure to get the fax number before you end the call, and ask permission first before faxing), then follow-up again in a day or so, asking if they got it and read it. This time, the answer will be yes.

Your next question is: "Does this seem of interest to your reader?" If the editor answers yes, ask her when she thinks she might run the release. If she gives you an issue date, great! If she has no immediate plans or isn't sure, ask what questions she has or what additional information she needs, and supply it. Or provide even more information that would make her interested in the story.

What happens if the editor is not interested? Find out why not. Say, "Gee, I'm surprised, because I thought [topic of release] would be of great interest to your readers because [reason your product or service is newsworthy]." The editor will probably rethink her position if your argument makes sense.

If not, at least you learn why your item is not of interest to this editor or publication—and you can tailor your next one to better meet the editor's interests. Sometimes, in telling you why your current release is unusable, the editor reveals the nature of the real story she is looking for . . . and if you can help her get that story, favorable publicity may result.

The good news, however, is that if your release is interesting and well written, and the story contains lots of RSI and ESI, follow-up is not necessary. A good release will get attention, be read, and get used, all on its own, without prompting or follow-up on your part.

The advantage of mastering the art of writing a response-getting press release is that it saves you time and effort.

Whether you're a self-employed entrepreneur or a PR manager, you have less and less time nowadays to get on the phone, follow-up with editors, and keep after them until you get a response. When you send out powerful press releases, you eliminate the need for this legwork: Your material "speaks for itself" and gets you results with no further effort on your part.

Many experts advocate including a return postcard with your press release to increase editor response and find out whether editors intend to use your material. These postcards typically have check-off boxes similar to the following:

EDITOR: Please check off your response below and mail this card today. Thank you!

- [ ] We will use your press release in a story to appear in our publication on (date):_____.
- [ ] We may use your information but are not certain at this point.
- [ ] We do not intend to use your release at this time.
- [ ] We would like to interview you; please call to arrange it.
- [ ] Please send a black-and-white photo.
- [ ] Please send us further information including:_____

_____.

I personally do not recommend use of reply cards in press release mailings. Editors work on tight deadlines. If one is interested in doing a story on you and needs more information, he or she will pick up the phone and call you—not mail a reply card.

In addition, if editors are planning to use your material but have no questions, they may resent your asking them to do the extra work of notifying you of their intent. Their job is to put out a magazine or newspaper, not to let you know that your PR is working. One editor at a major magazine told me

he "hates it" when publicists send him a reply card to fill out—
and that he never does it.

Returned reply cards indicating editors are unsure as to
whether they will use your release or are definitely *not* going
to use it can be of some benefit. By phoning these editors, you
can find out what the problem is or what they're looking for.
You can answer their questions or give them the information
they need—and in doing so, you may turn a "no" into a
"maybe," or a "maybe" into a "yes."

However, I do not use reply cards, because the risk of
alienating editors by asking them to do this paperwork out-
weighs the benefits of a response, in my opinion.

WHAT IF THE PRESS RELEASE GETS YOU AN INTERVIEW?

Occasionally editors who receive your press release will call
you up to interview you. This is sometimes done to clarify a
point, or to get you to expand on the information contained in
the release; other times it's done for the purposes of writing a
lengthier article about you.

Giving an interview to reporters and writers should take
priority over everything except the most important work you
are doing for your customers or clients. Journalists are
deadline-pressured, fickle, and have lots of other good story
material to choose from. When they call, answer!

So, when editors or their writers express interest in talking with you, be accessible, pleasant, and cooperative. Don't
put them off or moan about how busy or pressed for time you
are. Instead, act as if the article they are writing is the most
important thing in the world, and that it is your job to help
them complete it—whatever it takes. Be a helpful source
of information, and editors will come back to you, again
and again.

Be as open and forthcoming in the interview as possible. Don't hold back—tell editors everything they want to know about your topic, and answer all questions succinctly but fully.

Businesspeople giving interviews worry too much about making mistakes or accidentally giving away their "trade secrets"; but if you're too tight-lipped and not forthcoming with a free flow of good information, editors may decide there's not enough there to do a story.

About a year ago, a columnist for *USA Today* called to interview me as part of a feature she was writing on careers, job-seeking, and unemployment. She called me because she had read a book I'd written on careers, *Creative Careers* (John Wiley & Sons).

Unfortunately, I'm not a career authority, don't consult in the field, and had written two books on the topic years ago but hadn't kept up. I knew I wasn't giving her what she was looking for when she interviewed me over the phone, and when the article came out, my comments were not included. I was crushed. So don't you make the same mistake.

After the interview, thank editors or reporters for their time. You can politely inquire when the piece will be published, but do *not* ask to be sent a copy. "Can you send me a copy of the finished article?" is an imposition and an annoyance to media people. If you want to see a copy, go out and buy the newspaper or magazine with your story in it. (Of course, if the interviewer *volunteers* to send you a copy, accept graciously.)

Another mistake businesspeople make is to tell a writer, "Please send me a draft so I can review it before the article is published." Do not make this request; it can cause writers to delete you from a story in which you would otherwise be included.

Why don't writers want to give you a draft to review? Several reasons:

1. They're facing a deadline and don't have time to mail you a draft, get your comments, and incorporate them.
2. They view themselves as journalists and believe that journalists don't show copy to sources. (Woodward and Bernstein, for instance, didn't show Nixon a draft before they printed their story on the Watergate break-in.)
3. Some are not overly concerned with accuracy.
4. Some believe that you will take out the "good stuff" (even though you said it) and replace it with safer, blander copy.

    This fear is probably justified. Many people, seeing their words quoted back to them in a story, do not believe they actually said the things they did, and will start rewriting their own quotes.
5. Showing drafts to sources adds to the workload of the already overburdened writer or reporter. It's time-consuming and labor-intensive.
6. They do not want an outside review to hold up a timely piece.

On the other hand, many clients want to see a draft of the story before it sees print because:

1. It is corporate policy to run any copy through layers of management approval before it is printed.
2. They fear the writer will get facts wrong and want to review to correct mistakes and ensure accuracy.
3. They might have said something they didn't want or mean to say, and want a chance to change it.

I know many writers and reporters (and have been in this role myself) and can tell you, from firsthand experience, that most are not willing (or at least not eager) to run their copy by an interview source for corrections and approval.

If you insist on approval rights, or even just that you get a draft copy, editors or writers may decide against going ahead with the story. Therefore, if you want to be sure of getting the story printed, it's best *not* to ask to see a draft. If writers or reporters *volunteer* to show one to you, thank them and say you will review it promptly.

Limit your comments to corrections of factual material. Keep changes to a minimum. If you insist on extensive revisions, or start correcting for tone or style, you will turn off writers, and the story will probably be killed.

CHAPTER 6

CONVERTING THE PLANTED FEATURE STORY INTO A FULL-PAGE DIRECT RESPONSE AD FOR YOUR PRODUCT OR SERVICE

A "planted," or "placed," feature story is an article written and submitted to a publication by a corporation, entrepreneur, or business professional—either directly by the business or on its behalf by its PR firm or consultant. Unlike freelance writers, who write articles because doing so pleases them and because they earn money from it, the company submitting a feature article seeks to gain publicity and exposure for the firm, its ideas, or products and services.

Placing feature articles with appropriate trade, consumer, or business publications is one of the most powerful and effective of all marketing techniques.

- You can get one, two, three or more pages devoted to your product or service without paying for the space. (A paid aid of that length could run you $3,000 to $20,000 or more.)
- Your message has far more credibility as "editorial" material than as a sponsored advertisement.

- The publication of the article results in prestige for the author and recognition for the company.
- Reprints make excellent, low-cost sales literature.

Just one article in a trade journal can bring a company hundreds of leads and thousands of dollars in sales. And with more than 6,000 magazines and trade journals from which to choose, it's a safe bet there's at least one that will be interested in a story from your company.

GETTING ARTICLES PUBLISHED IS NOT DIFFICULT

Getting an article published in a trade journal or local business magazine is not difficult—if you know how. While editors are quick to reject inferior material or "puff" pieces, they are hungry for good, solid news and information to offer their readers. And, unlike newspapers, whose reporters are investigative and frequently antagonistic and adversarial toward business, trade journal editors represent a friendlier audience and are more willing to work with you to get your information to their readers.

One key mistake novices make in placing feature articles is giving up too soon. Your article is probably not going to be accepted by the first editor who sees it, or even the second. But keep trying. Consultant Jeff Davidson, a widely published author, says that to get 400 articles published, he was rejected 8,000 times.

COMING UP WITH IDEAS FOR ARTICLES

The case history or application story is one of the most popular type of articles published by trade and business magazines. This type of story tells how a specific company solved a problem or addressed a need, and usually highlights the product or service the company used to solve its problem. The PR department of the firm whose product or service was used to solve the problem usually suggests case histories to editors; the publication of case histories is an effective marketing tool, because it shows readers how to apply your product and demonstrates its proven success.

Aside from case histories, most planted feature articles are of the how-to variety, aimed at executives, managers, professionals, or technicians in a given field. Editors are also interested in stories on new products, developments, or trends in their industry.

One way to come up with article ideas is to make a list of the ads you would run (and the magazines in which you would run them) if you had an unlimited ad budget, then write articles based on topics related to those ads and place them in those magazines.

For example, if you wanted to advertise your new wood chip stacking system in *Pulp & Paper* magazine but didn't have the budget for it, consider writing an article entitled "A New Way to Stack and Inventory Wood Chips More Efficiently" for that magazine. Writing and placing articles in magazines and for secondary markets in which print advertising is unprofitable or beyond your budget is cost-effective.

STUDY BACK ISSUES TO LEARN WHAT MAGAZINES WANT

Many trade journals will send a sample issue and set of editorial guidelines to prospective authors upon request. These guidelines can provide valuable clues as to style, format, and appropriate topics. They often tell how to contact the magazine, give hints on writing an article, describe the manuscript review process, and discuss any payment or reprint arrangements.

The quickest way to turn off editors is to offer an idea that has nothing to do with their magazines. "My pet peeve with people calling or writing to pitch an idea is that they often haven't studied the magazine," says Rick Dunn, editor of *Plant Engineering*. "If they haven't read several issues and gotten a handle on who we are and who our audience is, they won't be able to pitch an idea effectively."

"There's no substitute for knowing the audience and the various departments within a magazine," adds Jim Russo, editor of *Packaging*. "I'm more impressed by someone who has an idea for a particular section than by someone who obviously doesn't know anything about our format."

EVERY EDITOR HAS UNIQUE NEEDS

Every magazine is a little different in some way from its competitors and from other magazines in general. To increase your chances of getting a placement, you must study tone, style, content, and the quality of a journal's writing and graphics.

Offer an editor the type of article that his or her magazine seems to prefer, and your odds of placing the story increase. If a magazine contains all short articles of one or two pages, don't send a 6,000-word thesis. If it does not run case histories, don't propose one.

Study issues of the magazine to see which topics are covered. The key to success is not to send an idea for an article on something never covered, but to offer an article that presents a new slant or angle on one of the magazine's frequent topics.

TIE IN WITH SPECIAL ISSUES

Companies can increase their chances for coverage by requesting a magazine's editorial calendar and scanning the list of "special issues" to see if there is a possible tie-in between their products and services and any articles to be featured in these issues. Call the magazine's advertising department, say you are a potential advertiser, request a free media kit, and ask for an editorial calendar of special issues along with a sample issue. These items will be sent without charge to potential advertisers.

"If people respond to our editorial calendar with ideas for specific issues, great!" says Dunn. "Or if they can provide background for a story we want to do, they'll have an edge in getting into the magazine."

You may even want to suggest feature story ideas for the next year's calendar. The trick is to do that tactfully. "Don't come across as pushy or demanding," warns Dunn. "Stay away from saying things like 'This is important to your readers' or 'You should run this story.' If someone knows our business better than we do, we'll hire him or we'll go back to school."

However, if you spot a new trend in, say, packaging food in recyclable cardboard containers instead of plastic, and you can provide statistics and information to back up your claim that this trend is important, contact the editor at the appropriate packaging magazine. He or she will probably appreciate your interest and effort.

SELECTING THE RIGHT MAGAZINE

Aside from *Bacon's Publicity Checker* (see appendix), the best source for learning more about magazines and their editorial requirements is a book called *Writer's Market*, published annually by Writer's Digest Books, 1507 Dana Avenue, Cincinnati, OH 45207, 513 531-2222. *Writer's Market* lists more than 4,000 consumer, general, business, and trade publications that accept articles from outside sources. Listings give detailed descriptions of what editors are looking for, along with names, addresses, phone numbers, and other contact information.

The best magazines to target are the ones you are now getting. This is because you read them, are familiar with their editorial slant and style, and are aware of what articles related to your topic they have run recently. However, there may be many magazines in your industry that you don't get and are not familiar with; you can find them in *Bacon's* or *Writer's Market*. Contact each and ask for a sample issue and editorial guidelines. When the sample issue comes, study it and become familiar with the publication.

Timing is important. For a monthly magazine, an article to appear in a special issue should probably be proposed to the editor three to six months in advance of the publication date.

AVOID PUFFERY

Impartiality is a must with many editors. They're not there to praise your company's products.

"We're certainly not prejudiced against articles from PR firms," says Mark Rosenzweig, editor of *Chemical Engineering*. "We just generally have to make more revisions to eliminate their tendency toward one-sidedness. We want all the disadvantages spelled out, as well as the advantages." Adds Rick Dunn: "If an article is about storage methods, we want to see all fifteen methods discussed, not just the ones used by the writer's company or client."

Another issue with editors is exclusivity. Never submit the same idea or story to more than one competing magazine at a time. Only if the idea is rejected should you approach another editor. Most editors want exclusive material, especially for feature articles.

If a story is particularly timely or newsworthy, and has run in a magazine not directly competing with the one you're approaching, however, you may be able to get around this problem by working with the editor to expand or rewrite the piece. But be up-front about it or you will risk losing the editor's confidence and goodwill.

"I'd like everything to be exclusive," says Russo. "That increases its value to us and can sway us toward acceptance if it's a 'borderline' story."

"Exclusivity is a quality consideration for a feature article," adds Dunn. "Editors don't want their readers to pick up their magazine and see something they've already read elsewhere."

MAKING THE INITIAL CONTACT

Should you call or write the editor? Most editors won't object to either method of pitching an idea, but they usually prefer one or the other. It's simply a matter of personal choice and time constraints.

If you don't know how a particular editor feels on the subject, call and ask. An appropriate opening might be: "This is Joe Jones from XYZ Corporation, and I have a story idea you might be interested in. Do you have time to spend a few minutes over the phone discussing it, or would you prefer that I sent you an outline?"

Editors who prefer to get it in writing will tell you so. Editors who prefer a quick description over the phone will appreciate your respect for their time, whether they listen to your pitch on the spot or ask you to phone back later.

But even those editors who will listen to your idea over the phone will also want something in writing. "With a phone call, I can tell someone right away whether he's on the right track," says Rosenzweig. "If I like the idea, I'll then request a detailed outline describing the proposed article." Adds Rick Dunn: "A phone call is all right, but I can't make an editorial decision until I see a query letter."

At *Modern Materials Handling*, assistant editor Barbara Spencer suggests writers send in a letter of introduction, followed by a phone call a week or two later. "We look for someone who knows his field and products, and the letter helps us gauge that expertise," she says. "But call the magazine first and find out which editor handles the type of article you have in mind."

All letters should be addressed to a specific editor by name. A letter that begins "Dear Editor" may not reach the right one and also indicates you were too lazy to find out that person's name.

WRITING THE QUERY LETTER

The best way to communicate an article idea in writing is to send a query letter. A query letter is a miniproposal in which you propose to the editor that you write an article on a particular topic for his or her magazine (and that it be published).

A query letter is, in essence, a sales letter. The "prospect" is the editor. The "product" you want to sell is the article you want to write for his or her magazine.

Here are a few basic facts about query letters.

1. Editors look for *professionalism* in query letters. This means no typos, no misspellings. You address the letter to a specific editor by name. And you spell his or her name right.

2. Editors look for good writing. If you can, write the first paragraph or two of your query so it could be used, as is, as the lead for your article. This shows the editor that you know how to begin a piece and get the reader's attention.

3. Editors hate lazy writers—those who want to see their byline in a magazine but refuse to do research or get their facts straight. Put a lot of hard "nuts-and-bolts" information—facts, figures, statistics—in your letter . . . to show that you know your subject. Most query letters (and articles) are too light on content.

4. Credentials impress editors. State why they should trust you to write the article. If you are an expert in the subject, say so. If not, describe your sources. Tell which experts you will interview, which studies you will cite, which references you will consult. Highlight the breakthrough research your company has done to become a leader in its field.

5. Editors hate to take risks. The more fully developed your idea, the better. If you spell out everything—your topic, your approach, an outline, your sources—editors know what they will get when they give you the go-ahead to write the piece. The more complete your query, the better your chance for a sale.

6. Editors have high standards for article acceptance, no matter who writes the articles. Don't think you can get away with a poorly written query because the editor realizes you're not a freelance writer and are just trying to "get some PR." The editor's readers don't expect PR-placed articles to be inferior, less objective, or less interesting than the other material in the magazine, and neither does the editor.

7. Never state in your query letter "And best of all, you don't have to pay me for this article, because I'm doing

it to publicize my firm." Even though editors know this, it's a breach of etiquette for you to come out and say it. (Why this is I have no idea.)

SOME SAMPLE QUERY LETTERS

Here are some typical query letters you can copy for style and format.

In this first example, note that the article proposal is in two parts: a letter selling the basic idea and an outline listing the details. I used this format simply because it fit the material; the outline can be separate from the "sales pitch," if you wish, but usually is not.

March 5, 1982

Mr. Kenneth J. McNaughton
Associate Editor
CHEMICAL ENGINEERING
McGraw-Hill Building
1221 Avenue of the Americas
New York, NY 10020

Dear Mr. McNaughton:

When a chemical engineer can't write a coherent report, the true value of his investigation or study may be distorted or unrecognized. His productivity vanishes. And his chances for career advancement diminish.

As an associate editor of CHEMICAL ENGINEERING, you know that many chemical engineers could use some help in improving their technical writing skills. I'd like to provide that help by writing an article that gives your readers "Ten Tips for Better Business Writing."

An outline of the article is attached. This 2,000-word piece would provide 10 helpful hints—each less than 200 words—to help chemical engineers write better letters, reports, proposals, and articles.

Tip number 3, for example, instructs writers to be more concise. Too many engineers would write about an "accumulation of particulate matter about the peripheral interior surface of the vessel" when they're describing solids buildup. And how many managers would use the phrase "until such time as" when they simply mean "until"?

My book, TECHNICAL WRITING: STRUCTURE, STANDARDS, AND STYLE, will be published by the McGraw-Hill Book Company in November. While the book speaks to a wide range of technical disciplines, my article will draw its examples from the chemical engineering literature.

I hold a B.S. in chemical engineering from the University of Rochester, and am a member of the American Institute of Chemical Engineers. Until this past January, I was manager of marketing communications for Koch Engineering, a manufacturer of chemical process equipment. Now I'm an independent copywriter specializing in industrial advertising.

I'd like to write "Ten Tips for Better Technical Writing" for your "You and Your Job" section.

How does this sound?

Sincerely,

Bob Bly

Article Outline

TEN TIPS FOR BETTER TECHNICAL WRITING
by Robert W. Bly

1. *Know your readers.*
   Are you writing for engineers? managers? laymen?
2. *Write in a clear, conversational style.*
   Write to express—not to impress.
3. *Be concise.*
   Avoid wordiness. Omit words that do not add to your meaning.
4. *Be consistent . . .*
   . . . especially in the use of numbers, symbols, and abbreviations.
5. *Use jargon sparingly.*
   Use technical terms only when there are no simpler words that can better communicate your thoughts.
6. *Avoid big words.*
   Do not write "utilize" when "use" will do just as well.
7. *Prefer the specific to the general.*
   Technical readers are interested in solid technical information and *not* in generalities. Be specific.
8. *Break the writing up into short sections.*
   Short sections, paragraphs, and sentences are easier to read than long ones.
9. *Use visuals.*
   Graphs, tables, photos, and drawings can help get your message across.
10. *Use the active voice.*
    Write "John performed the experiment," not "The experiment was performed by John." The active voice adds vigor to writing.

With this letter as well as the next one, the first paragraph of the query letter became the lead paragraph of the published article. This is no accident. A catchy lead in the query, one that could logically be used to begin the article, helps grab editors' attention and convince them that you've got something of interest.

Here is a query letter pitching a case history application story. An application story shows the reader how a particular product or system was used in the workplace or home to solve a specific problem. This letter and two follow-up telephone calls gained acceptance from the publication's editor.

date

Joe Smith, Editor
Engineering Trade Journal
Anytown, USA

Dear Mr. Smith:

Attached is a promotional brochure describing our client XYZ INDUSTRIES' High-Flow Lifting System.

I have sent this to you as an initial reference concerning High-Flow use in an industrial situation. The application involves the specialized handling and absolute precision positioning and insertion of TV picture tubes into a console lined with a quick-drying adhesive, thus permitting NO removal or replacement. This custom-designed unit is presently operating at an RCA plant in Pennsylvania.

Because of the unique safety, economic features, and functions of the High-Flow System, I believe you might want to treat the above as a feature article.

I will call within a few days to ascertain your interest. Please know we will cooperate with you or your staff to develop any editorial detail including up to submission of a complete manuscript.

I look forward to talking with you.

Sincerely,

[signature]

The following letter got me the go-ahead to write an article for *Writer's Digest* magazine:

January 3, 1987

Mr. William Brohaugh
Editor
WRITER'S DIGEST
9933 Alliance Road
Cincinnati, Ohio 45242

Dear Mr. Brohaugh:

John Francis Tighe, a soft-spoken, bearded gentleman, modestly refers to himself as "the world's second-most successful freelance direct-mail copywriter."

John's fee for writing a direct-mail package? $15,000.

But that's peanuts compared to the $40,000 Henry Cowan charges. According to WHO'S MAILING WHAT!, a newsletter covering the direct-mail industry, Cowan is the highest paid copywriter in the world. DIRECT MARKETING magazine reports that his income on the Publisher's Clearing House mailing alone (for which he receives a royalty) was $900,000 in a recent year.

Next to the movies and best-selling novels, direct mail is one of the highest-paid markets for freelance writers. Although surprisingly easy to break into, most freelancers don't even know about it, and direct-mail writing is dominated by a few dozen writers who earn lush six-figure incomes writing only a few days a week.

I'd like to write a 3,000-word article on "Making Money as a Direct Mail Writer." The article would tell your readers everything they need to know to start getting assignments in this lucrative but little-known specialty.

Here are the topics I would cover:

1. THE SECRET WORLD OF DIRECT MAIL. What is direct mail? Who is writing direct mail—and how much are they earning? Why has this market been a secret until now? I would interview some old pros as well as some new writers to get their perspective.

2. A LOOK AT THE MARKET. What are the various uses of direct mail (mail order, fund-raising, lead generation, cordial contact)? Types and formats of direct-mail packages you might write. Types of organizations that hire freelance direct-mail writers (publishers, catalog houses, fund-raisers, insurance companies, banks, manufacturers, ad agencies) . . . and how (and where) to find them.

3. GETTING STARTED. Learning about direct mail. Studying the market. Building your swipe files. Getting your first assignments.

4. HOW TO WRITE DIRECT-MAIL COPY THAT SELLS. Understanding the mission of direct mail. Tips for writing copy that will get results. How to present your copy to clients. Graphics and layouts for direct-mail copy. Differences in sales copy (direct mail) vs. editorial copy (magazine writing).

5. MARKETING YOUR SERVICES. Getting and keeping clients. How to market your services using: Portfolios.

Meetings. Telephone calls. Letters. Advertising. Publicity techniques.

6. FEES. How to set fees. Table of typical fees. What others charge.

7. KEEPING UP WITH THE FIELD. Books. Publications. Professional organizations. Courses. Seminars.

This article will draw both from my own experience as a successful direct-mail copywriter (clients include Prentice-Hall, New York Telephone, Hearst, Chase Manhattan, Edith Roman Associates) and from interviews with top pros in the field—including Milt Pierce, Sig Rosenblum, Richard Armstrong, Don Hauptman, Andrew Linick, and others. I know these people personally, so getting the interviews is no problem.

Also, I am a member of the Direct Marketing Club of New York and author of the forthcoming book DIRECT MAIL PROFITS (Asher-Gallant Press).

May I proceed with the article as outlined?

An SASE is enclosed. Thanks for your consideration.

Regards,

Bob Bly

NOTE:

The term SASE in the last sentence stands for "self-addressed stamped envelope." It's generally a good idea to include an SASE when writing to editors because it makes it easy for them to respond to your letter. I always include an SASE with all my queries.

The editor most likely to be receptive to your queries is one you have written for successfully in the past. When you sell one article to an editor, it makes sense to fire off a second letter immediately if you have another good idea that might be right for him or her. A sample of such a follow-up query follows.

Ms. Kimberly A. Welsh
Editor
CIRCULATION MANAGEMENT
859 Willamette Street
Eugene, Oregon 97401-2910

Dear Kimberly:

Thanks for publishing the article on mailing lists so quickly. I hope you get good reader response to it.

I'm writing because I have another idea that might be right for CIRCULATION MANAGEMENT.

How about an article—"Do Premiums Work?"

Background: As you know, response rates are down all over. In an attempt to combat this, publishers are offering more and more expensive premiums to attract first-time subscribers. SPORTS ILLUSTRATED, for example, is offering a videocassette on great sports flubs. TIME recently offered a camera. And then there's NEWSWEEK's successful free telephone offer.

Questions: Is there some point at which a premium ceases to be an added inducement and actually becomes a "bribe," overshadowing the primary offer and becoming the key reason why people respond to a mailing? If so, how does that affect the quality the subscriber-base circulation is delivering to the publication's advertisers?

This would be the basis of my article, which would attempt to answer these specific questions:

- Do premiums still work? Are they still profitable? Or is their effectiveness declining as more and more publications jump into premium offers?
- Is there any limit to premium cost in relation to the cost of a one-year subscription? What is this limit? What's the "average" premium cost in publishing today?
- What works best—an information premium (printed report or book) or tangible item (telephone, clock-radio, etc.)?
- Must the premium be related to the publication, the market, or the theme of the mailing? Or do totally unrelated premiums work well as long as they have high perceived value?
- Once a subscriber is sold through a premium offer, must renewals also offer a premium?
- How do advertising managers feel about subscribers generated through premium offers? Is there a perception that a subscriber generated through a premium offer is worth less to an advertiser than someone who buys the magazine without such a bribe? Any proof to back up this feeling?

To get the answers to these questions, I will interview circulation directors, advertising managers, direct-response agencies, DM consultants, and freelancers responsible for creating and testing premium-based packages. I see this as a feature article running 3,000+ words.

Kimberly, may I proceed with this article as outlined?

Thanks for your consideration. An SASE is enclosed.

Regards,

Bob Bly

P.S. By way of background: I'm a freelance copywriter specializing primarily in business-to-business direct mail. Publishing clients include Thomas Publishing, Hearst, Prentice-Hall, and EBSCO. My most recent book is DIRECT MAIL PROFITS: HOW TO GET MORE LEADS AND SALES BY MAIL (Asher-Gallant Press). Magazine credits include contributions to DIRECT MARKETING, WRITER'S DIGEST, COSMOPOLITAN, COMPUTER DECISIONS, and NEW JERSEY MONTHLY.

You may wonder why I gave my background in the P.S. when the editor has already done business with me. She had bought only one previous article and didn't know me all that well, so I felt it would be beneficial to remind her of why I was exceptionally well qualified to write this particular article for her. It couldn't have hurt, because I got the assignment.

Also, note that the query letters shown are detailed, not superficial. You may object, "But that's a lot of work to do with no show of interest or commitment from an editor." Yes, it is. But that's what it takes to get published, and there's no way around it.

Finally, here is a query letter that was successful in getting an editor to request an article on a new product. (A PR firm wrote and sent this letter to place a story about a new product developed by the firm's client.)

February 27, 19XX

RE: Article on synthetic cork

Dear Mr. Hiaring:

This is to propose an editorial feature on the subject of a new synthetic cork as it relates to traditional wood bark cork for wine bottles.

Despite the numerous disadvantages of natural corks, consumers associate them with quality wines, both correctly and incorrectly. Correctly because wineries have only resorted to screw cap closures for lower-priced wines, thereby establishing a correlation for the consumer. Incorrectly because wood bark wine cork is responsible for wine taint and leakage, resulting in off-flavor in a minimum of every three bottles per hundred on average.

Rising unit costs and processing costs of wood bark cork have compounded the wineries' problems.

The synthetic cork products are entirely uniform, are manufactured by Lermer Packaging in Southern California, and are the first wine closures to satisfy the needs of the winery and the demands of the consumer virtually without compromise. The enclosed comparison chart outlines all important characteristics of both closures.

After several years of intensive testing confirming the product's performance, a massive sampling campaign was launched this month with overwhelming results thus far. (Wineries exposed to Cellukork immediately prior to this sampling program have already placed orders for the new cork substitute.) A major advertising program should also break by July of this year.

We sincerely feel that Cellukork is such a major trade development, it is likely to revolutionize one important aspect of a most traditional industry.

As such, we believe that an editorial article on the subject will be of great interest to the vast majority of winery publication readers worldwide.

We would be gratified to have this news appear in your respected publication on an exclusive basis.

We would of course be flexible about the article's preparation by providing complete copy and photographs, photographs only, or reference materials to assist your staff.

Because the news and acceptance of Cellukork is spreading more quickly than anticipated, I would greatly appreciate your reply by March 20.

Thank you in advance for your consideration.

Sincerely,

[signature]

MUST YOU QUERY?

Many businesspeople ask me, "Why bother with a query? It seems to slow things down, creates an extra step and more work. Why not just write and send the full article?"

In my opinion, you should always query. Ninety-five percent of editors prefer a query and will not look at a full manuscript they did not request.

In *The Query Letter Book* (Communication Unlimited), Gordon Burgett, author of more than 1,000 magazine articles, says the reason to query is that it raises odds of acceptance. Burgett says the chances of getting an unsolicited manuscript into print are slim to none, but when you send a manuscript an editor has asked to see after reading your query letter, the odds of publication increase to 50 percent or higher.

Submitting unsolicited manuscripts is an iffy proposition—except for very short news pieces and case histories. Most editors do not want to see an unsolicited manuscript; only a few are willing to review and publish them.

Barbara Spencer says she never uses unsolicited manuscripts, and Jim Russo can't remember the last time his magazine used an unsolicited piece as a major story.

Most editors prefer to be asked about story ideas before you write the article. A query saves them the time it takes to read a lengthy manuscript to determine whether the subject is right for the magazine. And querying saves you, the publicist, the time and trouble of researching and writing an article that might never get accepted anywhere.

TIP

Even if you have already written the article, it's better to condense and summarize it in a query, and send the query first—acting as if you have not yet written the article. Only when the editor reads the query and says "let me see the article" should you send the story.

VISUAL MATERIALS

Do you need to offer photos or drawings to get your article run? It depends on the publication. The vast majority require only text for the article and will design graphics to go with it in-house.

Other magazines do not require, but certainly prefer to get, good photos or illustrations to run with articles. The availability of such material can sometimes be the deciding factor in choosing one story over another. Even though the larger journals have illustrators on staff to produce high-quality finished drawings, they often work from materials supplied by the article contributor.

You can get a good idea of how important visuals are to a particular magazine by scanning a couple of issues. Note whether there is no, little, moderate, or heavy use of photos and drawings to accompany articles. If photos are used, are they black and white or color? How many visuals are there per magazine page? You should prepare and supply the quantity and quality of visual material the editor desires. Otherwise, your article may have a lesser chance of publication.

Professional photographs, while nice, are not necessary for most trade journals. Straightforward, good-quality 35-mm color slides satisfy most trade editors. Some magazines will also take black-and-white glossies or color prints. An editor will be happy to tell you what's acceptable.

FOLLOWING UP YOUR QUERY

One of three things will happen after you mail your query letter:

- The editor will accept your article "on spec" (on speculation). This means the editor is interested and wants to see the completed manuscript, but is not making a firm commitment to publish. This is the most positive response you are likely to get, and unless the article you write is terrible, there is a better than 50 percent chance it will get published.
- The editor will reject your query. The next step is to send the query to the next editor and magazine on your list.
- The third and most likely alternative is that you will not hear one way or the other. There are several reasons for this. The editor may not have gotten around to your query. She may have read it but not made a decision. Or she didn't receive it, or she lost it.

The follow-up should be a polite note asking editors (a) whether they received the article proposal, (b) whether they had a chance to look at it yet, and (c) whether they're interested. You can enclose a reply card editors can use to check off their response:

☐ YES, we're interested. Please submit manuscript (on spec, of course).

☐ NOT for us. Sorry.

☐ MAYBE. We haven't made a decision but will let you know shortly.

☐ DIDN'T receive your query. Send another copy.

Many professional writers use such a system for making it easy for editors to respond. I personally do not use a reply card but enclose a self-addressed stamped envelope so editors can jot replies on my letter and mail it back to me in my envelope.

If I do not get a reply to my query after four weeks, I send a follow-up letter asking if editors received the original query (copy of which I enclose), and whether they are interested.

If there is no reply to the follow-up letter, I make a phone call. If I do not get through after three or four calls, I move on and submit the proposal to the next magazine on my list.

You may be thinking, "If it takes four to six weeks to get an answer from each publication, it might take many months to get my story into print." The answer is to have multiple press releases and query letters in the mail simultaneously. Doing so ensures a steady stream of media pickups and makes the results of any individual query much less critical in terms of your overall PR success.

GETTING THE GO-AHEAD

An editor is interested. Hurrah! You've passed the first step. Now the real work begins.

Once you've gotten your idea accepted, you'll need to know the length and deadline requirements. If the editor doesn't volunteer this information, ask. The answers may avoid misunderstanding later on.

As a rule, be generous with length. Include everything you think is relevant, and don't skimp on examples. Editors would rather delete material than have to request more.

While a few magazines are flexible on length, most give authors specific word lengths to shoot for. Ask how long your article should be. To translate this to typed pages, every 500 words is equivalent to two double-spaced typewritten manuscript pages. In its final printed form, a "solid" page of magazine copy (no headlines, photos, or white space) is, on average, 800 to 1,000 words for a magazine with a standard 7-by-10-inch page size. The first page, which has to leave room for a headline and byline, is approximately 700 words. Table 6.1 can help you translate word length and magazine page length to typed manuscript pages.

Table 6.1. Guide to Article Length

Number of Words	Number of Magazine Pages	Number of Manuscript Pages
800–1,000	1	3–4
1,500	2	6
2,000	2–2½	8
2,500	3	10
3,000	3½–4	12

Deadlines also can vary considerably among journals. Some don't like to impose any deadlines at all, especially if they work far enough in advance that they are not pressed for material. But if the article is intended for publication in a special issue, the editor will probably want the finished manuscript at least two months before publication date. This allows time for revisions, assembling photos or illustrations, and production.

Rule of thumb: Don't put an editor's patience to the test. Missing a deadline may result in automatic rejection and waste the effort you spent making the placement and writing the article. Hand in every article on the deadline date, or sooner. If you cannot, advise the editor well in advance and request a reasonable extension. Editors dislike late copy, but they hate surprises.

THE PITCH LETTER

An alternate method of getting feature story placement is to get stories written *about* you and your product rather than place stories written *by* you.

How do you get the press to write about you? Sending press releases, as described in chapter 5, is one method. If an editor receives a release related to an article he is planning, he may contact you to interview people in your company even if the material in the release isn't exactly what he needs.

TIP

Whenever editors respond to a press release or query, or call to interview someone in your company, put them on your media list to ensure they receive all future news you issue.

Another way to get articles written about you—or at least get your company mentioned in articles—is to send a *pitch letter*. Unlike the query letter, which proposes that you write a specific article, the pitch letter simply offers your company as an expert source for interviewing purposes. The following is a typical pitch letter I received from a public relations firm on behalf of its client. (I am listed in some directories as a magazine writer and therefore receive many such letters from PR departments and firms.)

January 13, 19XX

Dear Robert:

Compact disc (CD) sales are booming. In fact, some music industry executives are projecting disc sales will surpass album sales by the end of the year.

The first "compact disc only" retail store, Compact Disc Warehouse, in Huntington Beach, California, opened in November, 19XX. It grossed nearly $1 million in sales in just 18 months operating out of a 1,200 square foot store.

Now Compact Disc Warehouse, Inc. is launching the first CD franchise offering to meet the national demand for the hottest home entertainment product in the music industry today.

Edward Dempsey, president of CD Warehouse, is an expert on why CDs are changing an industry that has been dominated by record albums for decades and how the retail world is gearing up to meet the CD demand.

If you would like to arrange an interview, please call our offices.

Sincerely,

Mitch Robinson, Account Executive
S&S Public Relations, Inc.

Sending pitch letters is effective because editors and re-porters are constantly on the lookout for accessible sources of

expert information they can call to get a quote or fill in a missing fact for a story when on deadline.

It pays to include a Rolodex™ card with your query letter
that reporters or editors can file under the appropriate category. That way, when a reporter is working on a story on CDs,
she turns to her card file, finds Edward Dempsey's name, calls
him for a quote, and quotes him in her story. Edward Dempsey, then, and not his competition, becomes known as the industry leader because he is constantly quoted in the press.

I'm sure you've noticed that within your own industry, the
same spokespeople are quoted again and again. Well, it's not
by accident. Diligent public relations efforts—not fate—ensure that one person or company is publicized while others
wallow in obscurity.

HOW TO MAKE YOUR PLANTED ARTICLES
GENERATE DIRECT RESPONSE

In addition to building image, increasing visibility, and serving as low-cost article reprints, you can also turn planted feature stories into direct-response tools. How is this done? With
a resource box.

A resource box—a term invented by Dr. Jeffrey Lant—is
a box that appears at the end of your article. Instead of the
usual brief author bio ("Bob Bly is a consultant whose articles
frequently appear in *Business Marketing*"), the resource box
gives complete information on who you are, what your company offers, and how readers of the article can reach you. A
sample resource box is shown on page 189; feel free to adapt
the format to your own company:

"I swap the articles I write in return for resource boxes in
those publications," explains Lant. "Publications run the article. I get the resource box.

"Some of these publications swap for outright ad space—that is, they will *not* let my resource box run along with the article. One publication, with a readership of more than 75,000 financial planners, gives me both the resource box *and* an ad. I therefore have a very good sense of which draws better.

"The resource box ALWAYS wins. There are several reasons for this. First, the article acts as a qualifying device. If you're not interested in copywriting, you probably won't read an article on the subject. If you're interested, you may have a need. And if you have a need, you'll be more receptive to filling it.

"Second, the article plus the resource box is several times larger than the ad.

"Third, the article gives the product credibility. The buyer reasons that the publication wouldn't publish the article—and as a result 'recommend' the product—if it wasn't good. The article and the resource box lower the buyer's suspicion.

"Fourth, the words resource box are far superior to ad. This helps sales. The resource box looks like a public service, which, of course, it is. For these reasons, the resource box always draws substantially better than the same product or

---

Robert Bly is a freelance copywriter specializing in business-to-business and direct response advertising. He writes ads, brochures, direct-mail packages, and sales letters for more than 75 clients nationwide including Prentice-Hall, Grumman Corporation, Sony, On-Line Software, Philadelphia National Bank, and Associated Air Freight. He is also the author of 20 books including THE COPYWRITER'S HANDBOOK (Henry Holt). Mr. Bly can be reached at 174 Holland Avenue, New Milford, NJ 07646, 201 385-1220.

service featured in an ad, no matter how well written and complete the advertisement."

How do you get a resource box printed with your article? Don't ask editors outright. Instead, simply type in the resource box at the end of your manuscript and submit it along with your article. I find that 10 to 20 percent of the time, editors will print it as is without questioning you. Another 10 to 20 percent of editors will object initially but relent after some discussion.

The remainder will refuse you, because they see the resource box as too blatantly promotional and somehow compromising standards of journalistic integrity. But with my method you will have resource boxes running with at least 10 percent and up to 30 to 40 percent of all feature stories you place—significantly increasing the effectiveness of these articles.

HOW TO RECYCLE YOUR PUBLISHED ARTICLES

Don Hauptman, a New York City–based direct marketing copywriter and consultant, says that just publishing any article once does not take advantage of its full potential as a marketing tool. "Most professionals who write for publication stop at this point," says Hauptman. "But for the aggressive, savvy self-marketer, the first publication of the article is only the beginning."

Why recycle your article? Because, as Hauptman notes, "The lifespan of any magazine, newsletter, or newspaper is limited. You want to get as much mileage as possible out of your effort." Here are Hauptman's suggestions:

1. When you sell the article initially, make sure the publication gets one-time publication rights (known as

"first rights" only). You, the author, retain all other rights. Ideally, try to have a copyright line printed at the end of your article (© 19XX Jane Doe). Reason: You have plans for the article, and you don't want to have to beg for permission to use your own work.

2. Be sure to get several copies of the issue as soon as it's off the press. When you receive them, cut apart one copy and paste it up for duplication.

3. For its new incarnation, the article may require some creative rearrangement. You will probably want to delete surrounding ads. Cut the publication's logo from the cover, masthead, or contents page and place it at the top. This step is important—it gives your words the imprimatur of a known (and presumably respected) medium. At the end, tack on your firm's name, address, and phone number . . . easily obtainable from your letterhead or business card.

4. Send the resultant mechanical or paste-up to a quickprint shop. Or simply run it through your office copier. Watch out for problems that might make your new publicity piece appear unattractive or unprofessional: dirt, skewed paragraph, or cut marks (stray lines created by the edge of the pasted-up article—they'll disappear with the help of typewriter correction tape or fluid).

5. For maximum readability, print the article in black on white or light-colored paper. Your name or your firm's name can be highlighted using a second color ink. Or save the extra expense by circling your name or byline on each printed copy with a contrasting color fiber-tip pen.

6. Distribute copies of reprints to current, past, and potential clients. Include the reprints in your literature package or press kit, leave them in your reception area or lobby, hand them out at conferences and speaking

engagements, and enclose them in a direct-mail package. The possibilities are endless.

7. Since you own all rights to the article, you are free to publish it elsewhere. Other publications might want to run the article in its entirety, or excerpt or quote from it. Or an editor may ask you to revise the article for his or her particular publication. Such adaptation is usually easy; the hard work has been done. You can even use the article as part of a book, either your own or perhaps an anthology by someone else.

CHAPTER 7

SPEECHES AND PRESENTATIONS THAT BRING YOU BUSINESS

PUBLIC SPEAKING AS A PR TOOL?

Public speaking—giving speeches, lectures, talks, papers, and presentations at public events, industry meetings, conventions, and conferences—is a PR technique that businesses use widely to promote their products or services.

Why is public speaking so effective as a promotional tool? When you speak, you are perceived as the expert. If your talk is good, you immediately establish your credibility with the audience so that members want *you* and your company to work with them and solve their problems.

Unlike an article, which is somewhat impersonal, a speech or talk puts you within hand-shaking distance of your audience. And, since in today's fast-paced world more and more activities are taking place remotely via fax, computer modem, and videoconferencing, meeting prospects face to face firmly implants an image of you in their minds. If that meeting takes place in an environment where you are singled out as an expert—as is the case when you speak—the impression is that much more effective and powerful.

WHEN TO USE SPEAKING

Speaking is not ideal for every product or marketing situation. If you are trying to mass-market a new brand of floppy disk on a nationwide basis to all computer users, television and print advertising is likely to be more effective than speaking, which limits the number of people you reach per contact. On the other hand, a wedding consultant whose market is Manhattan would probably profit immensely from a talk on wedding preparation given to engaged couples at a local church.

In his book *Effective Communication of Ideas* (Van Nostrand Reinhold), George Vardaman says speaking should generally be used when:

1. Confidential matters are to be discussed.
2. Warmth and personal qualities are called for.
3. An atmosphere of openness is desired.
4. Strengthening of feelings, attitudes, and beliefs is needed.
5. Exactitude and precision are *not* required.
6. Decisions must be communicated quickly or important deadlines must be met rapidly.
7. Crucial situations dictate maximum understanding.
8. Added impact is needed to sustain the audience's attention and interest or get them to focus on a topic or issue.
9. Personal authentication of a claim or concept is needed.
10. Social or gregarious needs must be met.

Speaking is also the promotional tool of choice when targeting your PR efforts to a highly specific, narrow vertical market in which many of your best prospects are members of one or more of the major associations or societies in that market. For example, in the widget industry, if you wanted to reach widget buyers, you might run ads or write articles for the large-circulation magazines going to all widget people. But if your company specialized in widget polishing, you might be better off getting involved in a variety of ways, including speaking engagements or presentation of papers, at meetings of the Society for Widget Polishers and the National Association for Widget Cleaning and Polishing, if two such organizations existed.

FINDING SPEAKING OPPORTUNITIES; SELECTING A TOPIC

Unless you are sponsoring your own seminar, as is discussed in chapter 8, you will need to find appropriate forums at which your company personnel can be invited to speak. How do you go about it?

First, check your mail and the trade publications you read for announcements of industry meetings and conventions. For instance, if you sell furnaces for steel mills and want to promote a new process, you might want to give a paper on your technique at the annual Iron and Steel Exposition.

Trade journals generally run preview articles and announcements of major shows, expos, and meetings months before the event. Many trade publications also have columns that announce such meetings on both a national and a local level. Make sure you scan these columns in publications aimed at your target market industries.

You should also receive preview announcements in the

mail. If you are an advertising manager or the owner of your own small business, professional societies and trade associations will send you direct-mail packages inviting your firm to exhibit at their shows. That's fine, but you have another purpose: to find out whether papers, talks, or seminars are being given at the show, and, if so, to get your people on the panels or signed up as speakers. If the show mailing promotion doesn't discuss papers or seminars, call up and ask.

Propose some topics with your company personnel as the speakers. Most conference managers welcome such proposals, because they need speakers. The conference manager or another association executive in charge of the "technical sessions" (the usual name for the presentation of papers or talks) will request an abstract or short 100- to 200-word outline of your talk. If others in your company will be giving the talks, work with them to come up with an outline that is enticing— so as to generate maximum attendance—but also reflects accurately what the speaker wants to talk about.

Because many advertisers will be pitching speakers and presentations at the conference manager, the earlier you do it, the better. Generally, annual meetings and conventions of major associations begin planning eight to twelve months in advance; local groups or local chapters of national organizations generally book speakers three to four months in advance. The earlier you approach them, the more receptive they'll be to your proposal.

You can "recycle" your talks and give them to different groups in the same year or different years, tailoring them slightly to fit current market conditions, the theme of the meeting, or the group's special interests. When you create a description, outline, or proposal for a talk, keep it on computer disk. Then, when other speaking opportunities come your way, you can quickly edit the file and print out a customized proposal or abstract you can fax or mail to the person in charge of that meeting.

Since your goal is to sell your product or service, not educate the audience or become a professional speaker, you want to pick a topic that relates to and helps promote your business but is also of great interest to the group's audience. Importantly, the presentation does not sell you directly, but sells you by positioning you and your company as the expert source of information on the problem your product or service addresses. As such, it must be objective and present how-to advice or useful information; it cannot be a sales or product presentation.

For example, if you sell computer-automated telemarketing systems, your talk cannot be a sales pitch for your system. Instead, you could do something such as "How to Choose the Right Computer-automated Telemarketing Software" or "Computer-automated vs. Traditional Telemarketing Systems—Which Is Right for Your Business?" Although you want people to choose your system, your talk should be (mostly) objective and not too obviously slanted in favor of your product; otherwise, you will offend and turn off your audience.

I once spoke at a marketing meeting where one of the other presenters, a manufacturer of such computerized telemarketing systems, was giving a talk. Although he was supposed to talk about how to improve telemarketing results with software, he proceeded to haul in his system and give a demonstration. The comments from attendees were openly hostile and negative. I'm sure he didn't get any business, and this did not enhance his reputation either.

For more details on how to pick a topic and structure its contents, follow the same basic guidelines for producing informational bait pieces as outlined in chapter 4. Only keep in mind that this presentation is spoken, not written, so it must appeal to the ear, not the eye.

One last tip: If you are not on the mailing list to receive advance notification of meetings and conventions of your industry associations, write to request that they place you on such a list. Their names and addresses are listed in *The Encyclopedia of Associations*, published by Gale Research and available in your local library.

SCREENING SPEAKING OPPORTUNITIES

On occasion, meeting planners and conference executives may call you up and ask you (or a representative from your firm) to speak at their event, rather than you having to seek them out and ask them.

This is flattering. But beware. Not every opportunity to speak is really worthwhile. Meeting planners and committee executives are primarily concerned with getting someone to stand at the podium, and do not care whether your speaker or your firm will benefit in any way from the exposure. So, before you say yes to an opportunity to speak, ask the meeting planner the following questions:

- What is the nature of the group?
- Who are the members? What are their job titles and responsibilities? What companies do they work for?
- What is the average attendance of such meetings? How many people does the meeting planner expect will attend your session?
- Do they pay an honorarium or at least cover expenses?
- What other speakers have they had recently and what firms do these speakers represent?
- Do they pay those other speakers? If so, why not you too?

If the answers indicate that the meeting is not right or worthwhile for your company, or if the meeting planner seems unable or unwilling to provide answers, thank him or her politely and decline the invitation.

NEGOTIATING YOUR "PROMOTIONAL DEAL"

Since your goal is not to make money as a speaker but to promote your product or service, you can use the group's lack of payment for your talk as a weapon in negotiating for concessions—extra things it gives you that can help maximize the promotional value of your talk for your firm.

Here are some things you can ask for. You should get all or at least some of them, in addition to the opportunity to address the group:

- Tell the meeting chairperson you would be happy to speak at no charge, provided you receive a list of the members. You can use this list to promote your company via direct mail before as well as after your presentation.

  A pretalk mailing can let people know about your upcoming talk and be a personal invitation from you to them to come. A posttalk mailing can offer a reprint or audio recording of your presentation to those who missed it.

- At larger conferences and conventions, the conference manager provides attendees with show kits including a variety of materials such as a seminar schedule, passes to luncheons and dinners, maps, tourist sights of interest to out-of-town visitors, and the like. These kits are either mailed in advance or distributed at the show.

  You can tell the conference manager, "I will give the presentation at no charge, but in exchange, we'd like to have you include our company literature in the conference kits mailed to attendees. Is that possible? We will supply as many copies of our literature as you need, of course." If he or she agrees, then you get your promo pieces mailed to hundreds, even thousands, of potential clients *at zero mailing cost.*

- A speech is an effective way of getting known to a particular audience (the members of the organization and, more specifically, those members who attend your presentation). But as you know, making a permanent impression on a market segment requires a series of contacts, not a single communication.

  You can easily transform a one-shot speaking engagement into an ongoing PR campaign targeted to the membership of this particular group. One way, already discussed, is to get the mailing list and do your own mailings, plus have the sponsor include your literature in their mail-out kit.

  Another is to get one or more PR placements in the organization's newsletter or magazine. For instance, tell the meeting planner you will supply a series of articles (your current press releases and feature articles, recycled for this particular audience) to run in the organization's newsletter before the talk; this makes you known to the audience, which is good PR for your firm but also helps build interest in attending your program.

  After your talk, give the editor of the organization's newsletter the notes or text of your speech, and encourage him or her to run all or part of it (or a summary) as a posttalk article, so those who could not attend can benefit from the information. Additional articles can also be run as follow-ups after the talk to reinforce your message and provide additional detail to those who want to learn more, or to answer questions or cover issues you didn't have time to cover.

- If the editor will not run a resource box with your phone

number with the articles, talk to the meeting planner about getting some free ads for your product or service. For a national organization that actually charges for ads in its magazine, the value of your free ad space should be approximately twice what your fee would be if you were charging for your talk.

- The organization will do a program or mailing (or both) with a nice write-up of you and your talk. Usually it prints more than it ends up using, and throws out the extras. Mention that you would be glad to take those extra copies off its hands. Inserting those fliers is a nice touch in press kits and inquiry fulfillment packages.

- A professionally done audiotape or video of you giving a seminar can be a great promotional tool and an attention-getting supplement to printed brochures, direct mail, and other sales literature. But recording such presentations in a studio can be expensive.

One way to get an audio or video produced at low cost is to have someone else foot the bill for the taping. If an organization wants you to speak but cannot pay you, and especially if its audience is not a prime market for you, say, "I'll tell you what. Normally I charge $X for such a program. I will do it for you at no charge, provided you can arrange to have it professionally videotaped (or audio recorded, or both) and give me a copy of the master." If the organization objects to the expense, say, "In exchange, you can copy and distribute the video or audio of my speech to your members, or even sell it to those who attend the meeting or belong to your group or both— and I won't ask for a percentage of the profits. All I want is the tape master when you are through with it."

At many major meetings, it is standard practice for sponsoring organizations to audiotape all presentations and offer them for sale at the conference and for one year thereafter in promotional mailings. If you are being

taped, tell the sponsor you normally do not allow it but
will as long as you get the master. (Also make clear that,
while you will allow the sponsor to sell it and will waive
any percentage of the profits, the copyright is to be in
your name.)
- If the group is a local chapter of a national organization,
ask the meeting chairperson for a list of the other state
or local chapters, along with addresses, phone numbers,
and the names of the meeting organizers for each of
those chapters. Then contact these chapters and offer to
give the talk to their members.

PLANNING YOUR OBJECTIVE; PREPARING
YOUR PRESENTATION

Of course, your objective is to sell. But be careful. People attending a luncheon or dinner meeting aren't there to be sold.
They want to be entertained. Informed. Educated. Made to
laugh or smile. Selling your product, service, or company may
be your goal, but in public speaking, it has to be secondary
to giving a good presentation, and a "soft-sell" approach
works best.

Terry C. Smith, author of *Making Successful Presentations*
(John Wiley & Sons), lists the following as possible objectives
for business presentations:

- Inform or instruct
- Persuade or sell
- Make recommendations and gain acceptance
- Arouse interest
- Inspire or initiate action
- Evaluate, interpret, clarify
- Set the stage for further action

- Gather ideas and explore them
- Entertain

I'd add "establish credibility" to this list; a good talk can go a long way toward building the image of the speaker and his or her firm as authorities in the field.

"Perhaps you are aiming for a combination of these," says Smith. "For example, there is nothing wrong with being both informative *and* entertaining—the two are not mutually exclusive. In fact, the two may complement one another."

Let's say your talk is primarily informational. You could organize it along the following lines: first, an introduction that presents an overview of the topic; next, the body of the talk, which presents the facts in detail; finally, a conclusion that sums up for the audience what they have heard.

This repetition is beneficial because, in a spoken presentation, unlike an article, listeners cannot flip back to a preceding page or paragraph to refresh their memory or study your material in more detail. For this reason, you must repeat your main point at least three times to make sure it is understood and remembered.

And what if your talk is primarily persuasive or sales oriented? In their book *How to Make Speeches for All Occasions* (Doubleday), Harold and Marjorie Zelko present the following outline for a persuasive talk:

1. Draw attention to the subject.
2. Indicate the problem, need, or situation.
3. Analyze the problem's origin, history, causes, manifestations.
4. Lead toward possible solutions, or mention them.
5. Lead toward most desired solution or action.
6. Offer proof and values of solution proposed.
7. Prove it as better than other solutions. Prove it will

eliminate causes of problems, will work, and has value.

8. Lead toward desired response from audience.
9. Show how desired response can be realized.
10. Conclude by summary and appeal as appropriate.

Janet Stone and Jane Bachner present a similar outline for persuasive organization in their book, *Speaking Up* (McGraw-Hill):

1. Secure attention of audience.
2. State the problem.
3. Prove the existence of the problem.
4. Describe the unfortunate consequences of the problem.
5. State your solution.
6. Show how your solution will benefit the audience.
7. Anticipate and answer objections you know are coming.
8. Invite action.

Many other organizational schemes are available to speakers. For instance, if you're describing a *process*, your talk can be organized along the natural flow of the process or the sequence of steps involved in completing it. This would be ideal for a talk entitled "How to Start Your Own Collection Agency" or "How to Design Mixers for Viscous Fluids."

If you're talking about expanding a communications network worldwide, you might start with the United States, then move on to Asia, then cover Europe. If your topic is vitamins, covering them in alphabetical order—from vitamin A to zinc—seems a sensible approach.

I allow at least one full day for preparation and rehearsal of any new short (twenty- to thirty-minute) talk. Terry Smith says that for every brand-new presentation, his ratio is one hour of preparation for every minute he plans to speak. "This is the preparation level at which I feel comfortable that I'm giving my very best," says Smith.

TIP

The trick to reducing preparation time is to have two or three "canned" (standard) talks that you can offer to various audiences. Even with a canned presentation, you'll need at least several hours to analyze the audience, do some customizing of your talk to better address that particular group, and rehearse once or twice.

THE MOST IMPORTANT PART OF
YOUR TALK

A talk has three parts: beginning, middle, and end. All are important. But the beginning and ending are more important than the body. Most people can manage to discuss a topic for fifteen minutes, give a list of facts, or read from a prepared statement. And that's what it takes to deliver the middle part.

The beginning and ending are more difficult. In the beginning, you must immediately engage the audience's attention *and* establish rapport. Not only must members be made to feel that your topic will be interesting, but they must be drawn to you, or at least not find fault with your personality.

To test this theory, a well-known speaker put aside his usual opening and instead spoke for five minutes about himself—how successful he was, how much money he made, how in demand he was as a speaker, why he was the right choice to address the group. After his talk, he casually asked a member, "What were you thinking when I said that?" The man politely replied, "I was thinking what a blowhard you are."

How do you begin a talk? One easy and proven technique is

to get the audience involved by asking questions. For example, if addressing telecommunications engineers, ask: "How many of you manage a T1 network? How many of you are using 56 K DDS but are thinking about T1? And how many of you use fractional T1?"

If you are speaking on a health topic, you might ask, "How many of you exercised today before coming here? How many of you plan to exercise after the meeting tonight? How many of you exercise three or more times a week?"

Asking questions like these has two benefits. First, it provides a quick survey of audience concerns, interests, and levels of involvement, allowing you to tailor your talk to their needs on the spot. Second, it forces the audience to become immediately involved.

After all, when you are in the audience, and the speaker asks a question, you do one of two things—you either raise your hand or don't raise it, don't you? Either way you are responding, thinking, and getting involved.

ENDING YOUR TALK

While the beginning is important, don't neglect a strong closing, especially if you are there not just for the pleasure of speaking but to help promote your company or its products. As Dorothy Leeds observes in her book *PowerSpeak* (Prentice-Hall):

> Speakers, as you now know, are also in the selling business, and the conclusion is the time to ask for the order. Nothing will happen if you don't ask. And you ask by telling the audience what you want it to do with the information you've presented and *how* they can take that action. An effective speaker presenting a central idea ends by pointing out to those in his audience exactly what is needed from

them to put that idea to work. For example . . . if you've been persuading them to give blood, tell them where. And make it sound easy to get there.

Action doesn't always have to be literal. If you simply want the people in your audience to mull over your ideas, tell them this is what you want them to do.

Although you want a great opening that builds rapport and gets people to listen, and an ending that helps "close the sale," don't neglect the body or middle of your talk. It's the "meat"; it's what your audience came to hear. If your talk is primarily informational, be sure to give inside information on the latest trends, techniques, and product developments. If it's motivational, be enthusiastic and convince your listeners that they *can* lose weight, make money investing in real estate, or stop smoking.

If your talk is a how-to presentation, make sure you've written it so your audience walks away with lots of practical ideas and suggestions. As actor and Toastmaster George Jessel observes, "Above all, the successful speaker is sincerely interested in telling his audience something they want to know."

When speaking to technical audiences, tailor the content to listeners' expertise. Being too complex can bore a lot of people. But being too simplistic or basic can be even more offensive to an audience of knowledgeable industry experts.

MATTERS OF LENGTH AND TIMING

Talks can vary from a ten-minute workplace presentation to a two-day intensive seminar. How long should yours be? The event and meeting planner often dictate length. Luncheon and after-dinner talks to local groups and local chapters of professional societies and business clubs usually last twenty to thirty minutes, with an additional five to ten minutes allotted for questions and answers.

For technical sessions at major conferences and national expositions, speakers generally get forty-five to seventy-five minutes. For a one-hour talk, prepare a forty-five-minute talk. You'll probably start five minutes late to allow for late arrivals, and the last ten minutes can be a more informal question and answer session.

The luckiest speakers are those who get invited to participate in panels. If you are on a panel consisting of three or four experts plus a moderator, it's likely that you'll simply be asked to respond to questions from the moderator or the audience, eliminating the need to prepare a talk.

Richard Armstrong, a freelance corporate speechwriter, says most of the speeches he writes are twenty minutes in length. James Welch, author of *The Speech Writing Guide* (John Wiley & Sons), says that a typed double-spaced page of manuscript should take the speaker two and one-half minutes to deliver. This means an eight-page double-spaced manuscript, which is about 2,000 words, will take twenty minutes to deliver as a speech.

That's about a hundred words a minute. Some speakers are faster, talking at 120 to 150 words a minute or more. So the twenty-minute talk can really be anywhere from eight to ten typed pages.

The most important thing is to not exceed the allotted time. If you are given twenty minutes with an additional ten minutes for questions and answers, stop after twenty minutes. People won't mind if you finish a bit early, but they will become fidgety and start looking at their watches if your time limit is up and you don't seem even near finished.

Since most of us cannot concentrate on two things at once—giving a talk and watching a clock—I ask someone in the audience to be the timekeeper, to keep me on track. For example, if giving a forty-five-minute talk, I ask him to shout

out "TIME!" every fifteen minutes. The first two interruptions tell me where I am and how closely I'm on track; the last tells me to stop and shut up.

Incidentally, rather than finding this shouting of the word time annoying, audiences like it. I make it fun, telling the timekeeper, "You must shout out 'time' in a loud, obnoxious voice!" Then when he or she does, and the audience laughs, I ask them to rate, in a tongue-in-cheek way, whether the timekeeper was indeed loud and obnoxious enough. It gets a laugh every time.

DR. ROB GILBERT ON HOW TO GIVE A SPEECH

Professional speaker Rob Gilbert charges $3,000 to $7,000 to give a speech or presentation. Here are forty-one of Gilbert's most effective techniques:

1. Write your own introduction and mail it to the sponsoring organization in advance of your appearance. (Also bring a copy with you for the master of ceremonies in case he lost your original.)
2. Establish rapport with the audience early.
3. What you say is not as important as how you say it.
4. Self-effacing humor works best.
5. Ask the audience questions.
6. Don't give a talk—have a conversation.
7. Thirty percent of the people in the audience will never ask the speaker a question.
8. A little bit of nervous tension is probably good for you.
9. Extremely nervous? Use rapport-building, not stress reduction, techniques.
10. The presentation does not have to be great. Tell your

audience that if they get one good idea out of your talk, it will have been worthwhile for them.

11. People want stories, not information.

12. Get the audience involved.

13. People pay more for entertainment than education. (Proof: The average college professor would have to work ten centuries to earn what Oprah Winfrey makes in a year.)

14. You have to love what you are doing. (Dr. Gilbert has 8,000 cassette tapes of speeches and listens to these tapes three to four hours a day.)

15. The first time you give a particular talk it will not be great.

16. The three hardest audiences to address: engineers, accountants, and high school students.

17. If heckled, you can turn any situation around ("verbal aikido").

18. Communicate from the Heart + Have an Important Message = Speaking Success.

19. You can't please everybody, so don't even try. Some will like you and your presentation—and some won't.

20. Ask your audience how you are doing and what they need to hear from you to rate you higher.

21. Be flexible. Play off your audience.

22. Be totally authentic.

23. To announce a break say: "We'll take a five-minute break now, so I'll expect you back in ten minutes." It always gets a laugh.

24. To get them back in the room (if you are the speaker), go out into the hall and shout, "He's starting; he's starting."

25. Courage is to feel the fear and do it anyway. The only way to overcome what you fear is to do it.

26. If panic strikes: Just give the talk and keep your

mouth moving. The fear will subside in a minute or two.

27. In speaking, writing, teaching, and marketing, everything you see, read, hear, or do is grist for the mill.

28. Tell touching stories.

29. If the stories are about you, be the goat, not the hero. People like speakers who are humble; audiences hate bragging and braggarts.

30. Join Toastmasters. Take a Dale Carnegie course in public speaking. Join the National Speakers Association.

31. Go hear the great speakers and learn from them.

32. If you borrow stories or techniques from other speakers, adapt this material and use it in your own unique way.

33. Use audiovisual aids, if you wish, but not as a crutch.

34. When presenting a daylong workshop, make the afternoon shorter than the morning.

35. Asking people to perform a simple exercise (stretching, Simon Says, etc.) as an activity during a break can increase their energy level and overcome lethargy.

36. People love storytellers.

37. Today's most popular speaking topic: change (in business, society, lifestyles, etc.) and how to cope with it.

38. There is no failure—just feedback.

39. At the conclusion of your talk, tell your audience that they were a great audience—even if they were not.

40. Ask for applause using this closing: "You've been a wonderful audience. [pause] Thank you very much."

41. If you want to become a good speaker, give as many talks as you can to as many groups as you can. (Dr. Gilbert has some speeches he has given more than 1,000 times.)

Do not be upset if this list seems daunting or you think, "I'm not a professional speaker—I can't do all that!" You don't have to. Just using *one* of these techniques will give you significant improvement, raising the audience's enjoyment of your presentations and making you more memorable than most of the other businesspeople who lecture to them for purposes of publicity and promotion (90 percent of whom rate mediocre to awful as speakers).

The most important tip? Just be yourself. Talk to the audience. Don't worry about being smooth, or polished, or funny or clever, or dynamic or dramatic. Since you are not expected to be a professional speaker, coming off as a bit amateurish and inexperienced can even endear you to the crowd and get them "on your side."

SHOULD YOU USE AUDIOVISUAL AIDS?

When I was a marketing trainee at Westinghouse in the late 1970s, slides were all the rage in the corporate world. Nearly every presentation was an audiovisual presentation. Two managers could literally not get together for an informal chat without one pulling out a slide projector and dimming the lights.

Slides are still popular today, as are overhead projectors, but in my opinion, audiovisual aids are not necessary for most presentations. Most corporate presentations are dependent on slides or overheads and they are boring.

Most professional speakers—people who earn thousands for a brief talk—do *not* use audiovisual aids. I feel that businesspeople, especially in the corporate world, become dependent on the visuals and lose the spontaneity and relaxed manner that come with "having a conversation" rather than "making a presentation."

The problem with the corporate approach to visuals is that the audiovisual aid is seen as something that must run continuously and concurrently with the talk. So, although only 10 percent of the presentation requires visuals, the slide projector runs for 100 percent of the time, and the speaker fills in with stupid "word slides" that are wasteful and silly.

For instance, if the speaker is going to talk for three or four minutes on quality, she hits a button, and the word QUALITY appears on the screen in white against a black background. Such a visual adds nothing to the talk and is in fact ridiculous.

A better approach is to have visuals you can use when appropriate, then deliver the rest of your talk unaided. When I speak, I use flip charts and Magic Markers™, and I don't prepare them in advance. Rather, I draw as I speak, which adds excitement and motion. It also creates anticipation: The audience becomes curious about what is being created before their eyes.

Slide projectors and overhead projectors are prone to mechanical failure. Errors in presentations, such as difficulty sorting through a pile of overhead transparencies, or slides that are upside down or out of order, confuse and embarrass the speaker; they also cause the audience to snicker or lose interest.

I have seen speakers who, interrupted by a jammed slide tray, lose their train of thought and never fully recover. Errors or mishaps with audiovisual support can be extremely disconcerting, especially when making a good impression is important or the presenter is not comfortable with public speaking in the first place.

At times, high-quality visuals are needed—to demonstrate how a product works, explain a process, show the components or parts of a system, or graphically depict performance, perhaps. For instance, if you are trying to promote your landscape design practice by giving a talk entitled "How to Design a Beautiful Front Yard," you want to show pictures of attractive front yards you have designed. If your speech is entitled "Advancing Science Using Supercomputer-Generated Images," people will want to see color slides of those images.

In such cases, I suggest you prepare overhead transparencies, a videotape, flip charts, or similar displays that can be shown for a brief period and then put away. If you use slides, turn the projector off and the lights up when the visuals are not in use.

According to a research study from 3M, it's estimated that we retain only 10 percent of what we hear; by adding visual aids, the retention rate increases to 50 percent. And a report from Matrix Computer Graphics notes that 85 percent of all information stored in the brain is received visually.

Actually, I'm not convinced they're right. I can recall a number of memorable presentations—the speaker, the delivery, and many of the ideas—but I can't recall a single slide or visual from those talks.

If you do use slides, make them bold, bright, colorful, and easy to read. Slides and overheads are used to show, demonstrate, create excitement. They are not a good medium for transmitting complex detail. Too much detail in a slide or overhead makes it unclear. To test the readability of a slide: Hold it at arm's length. If you can't read the text, your audience won't be able to either.

WHY YOU *MUST* HAVE A HANDOUT

The leave-behind can take one of several formats: hard copy of the slides or overheads, brochures, article reprints, or reprints of the narration (with visuals incorporated, if possible).

It can be the full text of your talk, an outline, just the visuals, or a report or article on a topic that is either related to the presentation topic or that expands on one of the subtopics you touched on briefly in the talk.

Every handout should contain your company name, address, phone, and fax, and if possible a full resource box with a brief summary of who you are and what you do—as should *every* marketing document you produce.

If the handout is the full text of your talk or a set of fairly comprehensive notes, tell the audience before you start: "There's no need to take notes. We have hard copies of this presentation for you to take home." This relieves listeners of the burden of note-taking, freeing them to concentrate on your talk.

Handouts such as transcripts of a speech, articles, reports, or other materials with lots of copy should be handed out *after* the talk, not before. If you hand them out before you step up to the podium, the audience will read the printed materials and ignore you. You can hand out reproductions of visuals or pages with just a few bullet points in advance, so attendees can write notes directly on them.

Why do you need handouts? They enhance learning. But the main reason to give handouts is to ensure that every attendee (most of whom are potential customers, or you wouldn't be addressing the group) walks away with a piece of paper containing information on what you offer and how to contact you. That way, when the person goes to work the next morning and thinks, "That was an interesting talk; maybe I should contact them to talk about how they can help us," he or she has your phone number in hand. Without it, response to your talk will be zero or near zero; most people are too busy, lazy, or indifferent to start tracking you down if they don't have immediate access to your contact information.

HOW TO MAKE SURE MOST AUDIENCE MEMBERS TAKE YOUR HANDOUT MATERIAL

It is most important to give a useful, interesting, information-packed talk that convinces prospects you know what you are talking about and makes them want to talk with you about doing work for them. But without the contact information immediately in hand, the prospect's interest and curiosity will quickly evaporate.

Since you cannot tell in advance who in the audience will want to follow up with you and who will not, your goal is to get everybody—or as many people as possible—to pick up and take home your handout material.

There are several ways to distribute handouts at your talk. The most common is to leave the materials on a table, either in the back of the room or at the registration table where people sign in for the meeting or your session.

But this is not effective. Most people will walk right by the table without picking up the material. Many won't even notice the table or stack of handouts. Even if you point out the table and say that reprints are available, many won't take one. And you might feel embarrassed at the silence that follows your announcement; it makes you seem less authoritative, more of a promoter.

Another technique is to put a copy of your handout on each seat in the room about a half hour before the start of your presentation. Most people will pick it up, look at it; about one-quarter to one-half will take it with them when they leave and half or more will leave it on the chair. Disadvantages? People may read the handout and not pay attention to your presentation. Also, some people resent this approach, seeing it as being too pushy and too salesy.

USING THE GREEN-SHEET METHOD TO
MAXIMIZE HANDOUT DISTRIBUTION

The most effective method of distributing handouts is the "green sheet" method. It maximizes the number of attendees who take handouts, increases their desire to have the material, and importantly, eliminates any hint of self-promotion or salesmanship.

Here's how it works. Prepare a handout that expands on one of the points in your talk, covering it in more detail than you can in a short presentation. Or make the handout a supplement, covering additional points not discussed but related to the topic.

Another option is to do a handout that's a resource guide; for example, a bibliography of reference books on your topic, tables of technical data, a glossary of key terms, a series of equations or examples of calculations, and the like. The important point is that the handout relates to *but does not merely repeat* information covered in your talk; instead, it *expands* on it.

When you get to that topic in your talk, which should be about halfway or three-quarters through the talk, discuss the point, then say something similar to the following (adapting it to your topic and handout, of course): "I really can't cover in this short talk all of the techniques related to this, so I've prepared a checklist of twenty-five points to consider when planning this type of project, and reprinted it on this green sheet." Pause, hold up the sheet for everyone to see, then continue: "I have plenty of copies, so if you want one, come up to me after the talk and I'll give you a copy."

After your talk, you will be surrounded at the podium by a large crowd of people with their hands out to get the free green sheet. Try it—it works. Oh, and why a "green sheet" rather than copying it on plain white paper? Doing it on colored paper and calling it a green sheet just seems to make it more special; also, instead of having to remember what's actually in the sheet (many people would not and therefore would hesitate to ask for it), people can just come up and say, "May I have a green sheet please?"

USING HANDOUTS TO CAPTURE NAMES OF POTENTIAL CUSTOMERS

Let's say the conference organizer will not release a list of attendees or those who go to your specific session, but you want to capture as many of those names as possible for marketing follow-up. In that case, offer your handout as a bait piece rather than giving it out at the session.

At the conclusion of your talk, discuss your handout and what it covers, and say, "So if you would like a free copy of our free telecom security checklist, just write 'TSC' on the back of your business card and hand it to me. I'll mail a free copy of the checklist to you as soon as I get back to the office." The more enticing and relevant your bait piece, the more business cards you will collect. A really strong bait-piece offer can get you the business cards of 25 to 75 percent of attendees or more.

CHAPTER 8

SEMINARS, DEMONSTRATIONS, AND TEACHING: SELLING THROUGH EDUCATION

WHY SEMINARS CAN BE USED AS A MARKETING TOOL

Seminars, once thought of as strictly a means of training, educating, or informing an audience, have become effective marketing tools for both business and consumer marketers.

On the high-tech end, mainframe software vendors hold half-day product demonstrations/education sessions to educate IS (information systems) directors and systems analysts on how the software can fit into the corporate data center. On the consumer side, a producer of baby toys and products recently invited me and my expectant wife to a seminar on child care. The seminar is free, and we also get a free baby toy worth $35.

"Seminars can be effective marketing promotions," writes Herman Holtz in his book *Expanding Your Consulting Practice with Seminars* (John Wiley & Sons). "The Evelyn Wood speed reading school advertised weekly free seminars for a number of years, offering a demonstration lesson along with a sales presentation. Albert Lowry, the butcher turned real estate tycoon, has used many free seminars to promote his $500 weekend seminar on how to make money in real estate."

Why are seminars so effective? Because they fit in nicely with the transition sellers and consumers have undergone over the past two decades.

Twenty years ago, consumers were more open to traditional advertising messages. Salespeople were perceived as peddlers whose job it was to "move merchandise"—regardless of whether that merchandise was right for the customer. "Pressure selling" was the predominant technique. We tended to feel an adversarial relationship with salespeople while believing much of what was force-fed us through TV commercials and magazine ads.

Today's consumers are more educated, more savvy, and more skeptical of advertising in all its forms. Consumers know what they want and are not afraid to question authority. That's why so many companies are putting more effort in their public relations. As we've discussed, when your message is carried by the media as editorial material, readers will not react with skepticism or scrutinize it as carefully as they would a paid ad.

I recently read an article that offers proof of the power of publicity and other "editorial" forums (I'd include seminars) versus paid advertising (I'd include sales presentations):

A couple noticed that many people holding garage sales were inadvertently selling, at low prices, items that had much greater value. They realized people did not know how to go through a garage or attic and separate the junk from the "hidden treasures"—antiques, collectibles, and other items that could fetch a high price if sold to dealers or collectors.

The couple wrote and self-published a book called *I'll Buy That!* on how to find a profit from such hidden treasures and sent a press release to a number of magazines. *Family Circle* picked up the release and ran a half-page article, giving information on how to order the book, which cost $12.95 or so. The article generated *180,000 orders* and more than $2 million in revenue!

The couple thought a natural follow-up would be to have the article repeated. Since the editor would not run it twice, they bought a half-page ad and reprinted the article in that space; the only difference was that it had the word ADVERTISEMENT above it. Want to guess the results? That second run of the article as an ad generated fewer than *20 orders*—testimony to the power of "neutral" or editorial forums versus paid ads.

As the consumerism movement grows, consumers shift from being passive buyers to informed buyers. And to be informed buyers, they need information: information on products, information on trends, information on the very problems and applications the products address. This is where seminars come in.

ADVANTAGES OF USING SEMINARS AS A PR TOOL

Publicizing and marketing your product or company by giving a seminar offers a number of advantages.

1. Seminars are, by nature, educational, so they fill the consumer's need and desire to be better educated.
2. Presenting a seminar, or being a seminar sponsor, positions you and your company as expert sources of information. It in essence lets you make your "sales pitch" in a forum where you won't be perceived as a salesperson.
3. Getting a group of good prospects in a room for a seminar gives you a "captive" audience for making a sales pitch or giving some "commercials" before and after the seminar, as well as during the breaks.

4. Your product can be demonstrated at the seminar, and demonstrations are a proven, powerful sales tool.

5. Seminars enable you to reach many prospects who skip over your ads, throw away your direct mail, and don't attend trade shows at which you exhibit.

6. Done right, the seminar gives attendees useful information. You will have done a service for your prospects, and their appreciation can translate into greater receptiveness to any follow-up selling you do, either in person or by mail or phone.

7. Seminars hold the prospects' attention and get them listening longer than they would listen to something that was pure sales presentation.

8. In fields where giving seminars is not a common PR tool, a seminar makes you stand out from the crowd and is more memorable than traditional ads, brochures, direct mail, and the like.

9. Because seminars, by definition, are local events, local media outlets are inclined to print publicity releases announcing your seminar.

10. Since most seminars focus on interesting topics, or at least on topics of interest to a certain group of people, many editors will use the seminar press release as the basis of an article. The article is typically a short feature on the topic addressed by a seminar, with some mention at the beginning and end of the seminar itself.

SIX OPTIONS FOR PROMOTING YOUR BUSINESS THROUGH SEMINARS

If you decide to try a seminar to promote your product, you have six options available to you:

1. Giving a free "tutorial" seminar.
2. Giving a promotional or "product" seminar.
3. Giving a self-sponsored fee-paid public seminar.
4. Giving a seminar for a seminar company.
5. Giving a short presentation at an association meeting or industry event.
6. Teaching a college or adult education course.

Let's explore each of these options.

Option 1: Free Tutorial Seminar

The free tutorial is a short morning, afternoon, or evening seminar presenting useful advice, suggestions, recommendations, or tips on a particular topic. The topic is one that would be of interest to potential clients of the seminar sponsor and relates to services offered by the sponsor. Length is usually one or two hours.

For example, a local financial planning firm offers a free seminar on retirement and estate planning. It attracts people, usually thirty and older, who want to build a "nest egg" for a comfortable retirement and leave a large estate for their dependents should they pass away. Subjects discussed include retirement investments, life insurance, pension plans, and wills.

Why give this seminar for free instead of charging a fee? The goal is not to make money on the seminar, but to attract the maximum number of prospects. Logic dictates that anyone attending a basic seminar on retirement planning and estate planning is interested in the topic, needs to do this planning, but probably is not an expert and needs help—the kind of help the financial planning firm, the sponsor of the program, can provide.

At such a seminar, the emphasis is on giving the audience useful, objective information—or at least information that the audience will perceive as helpful and objective. Actually, the content may be "slanted," subtly leading attendees to become more interested in certain types of investments than in others . . . investments that the sponsor just happens to specialize in selling.

Free tutorials are used most commonly by service firms, but they can be successful for other types of businesses too. For example, as I write this in 1992, the drinking of vegetable and fruit juice as an aid to health is a hot trend. A big department store or small health food store could hold a free seminar on the health benefits of juice, which juices to drink, recipes, how to make juice in a juicer, and so on. Do you think the store could sell a lot of juicers to attendees after such a free seminar? Of course.

Remember in chapter 2 the discussion of the seven key themes that appeal to editors? Virtually every seminar contains at least three of the seven: timeliness (because the event is tied to a specific date), interesting information, and useful advice. Therefore seminars are inherently promotable via free publicity.

Want to increase attendance dramatically at your free tutorial seminar and get much wider publicity as well? Hire a local celebrity to be one of the speakers.

In our area, for example, several financial planning firms fill large auditoriums to standing-room-only capacity by featuring the hosts of local radio talk shows dealing with money matters. Radio show hosts, TV personalities, authors, athletes, and other celebrities can pull in the crowds at free seminars, doubling or tripling attendance—or better. And if your celebrity is a radio or TV personality, you will get lots of free press as he or she plugs the upcoming appearance at your seminar on their show.

Option 2: Promotional or "Product" Seminar

A promotional or "product" seminar—one designed ulti-mately to sell a product or service rather than be a profit cen-ter in itself—helps move consumers one step closer to a purchase decision. It does so by providing the knowledge con-sumers feel they need to make an intelligent buying decision.

Unlike a tutorial, which is more of a "pure" informational seminar, with the "pitch" for the service limited to the begin-ning, the end, and the coffee breaks, a product seminar usu-ally combines advice on how to do something (such as how to stay fit and trim) with a lengthy demonstration of a specific product (how to use Brand X rowing machine).

Length of program is typically two or three hours. For groups of business prospects, breakfast is usually provided at morning seminars; lunch at afternoon programs. Evening ses-sions are usually followed by an open bar and light snacks.

Seminars help promote products and services in three ways: by establishing the seminar giver as the authority, dem-onstrating the product, and "setting the specs" for a product purchase.

ESTABLISHING THE SEMINAR GIVER AS
THE AUTHORITY

Even if your seminar does not promote your product directly, just the mere fact that *you* and not your competitor is giving the seminar establishes you as the authority in your field, put-ting you in a superior position to make the sale to your atten-dee/prospect. Those who write books, publish articles, make speeches, or give seminars are perceived as experts, as au-thorities, as leaders in their field. And whom do you want to buy from? An expert, of course. The seminar giver is per-ceived as more knowledgeable and better able to solve prob-lems, and therefore is more likely to get the order.

DEMONSTRATION

For many, many products, the best way to sell the product is to demonstrate it. (Two examples that come immediately to mind are computer software and exercise equipment.) The seminar gives you a captive audience of prospects who will sit still for a lengthier demonstration than they might agree to in a store, at home, or in their office. And the more you show, the more you sell.

SETTING THE SPECS

A common technique in a seminar is "setting the specs." In plain English, this means using the seminar to educate prospects on what they should be looking for in your type of product—the specifications to include in their request for proposal (RFP), the features they should want, the questions they should ask. Of course, you set these specs in such a way that *your* product satisfies them best. Your seminar tells prospects, "This is how you should shop for [name of product or service.]" Of course, when they follow your shopping guidelines, your product or service clearly emerges as the logical choice.

Like the tutorial, the product seminar is free. The reason is simple: You are going to demonstrate and sell a product; attendees know it; and you can't ask someone to *pay* to hear your sales pitch. Since the seminar is free and openly billed as a seminar on a specific product, attendees expect some selling and won't resent it.

Because product seminars are openly promoting a product, editors are somewhat less likely to publicize them than they are tutorials, which operate under the guise of pure "information dissemination." One solution is to position the main topic as an issue or problem ("computer security"), then spend half the seminar addressing the problem and half demonstrating how your product or service ("OmniGuard Computer Security System") solves it. Stress the problem or topic in the release; keep mention of product selling to a minimum. That will increase pickup.

Option 3: Fee-paid Self-sponsored Public Seminar

If you work in a corporation, you probably get many invitations to public seminars on topics ranging from stress management and self-esteem building, to newsletter design and desktop publishing. These seminars are typically one or two days, with the fee ranging from $99 to $295 for a full-day program, $495 to $795 for a two-day program.

Although most of these seminars are done as a profit-making venture in themselves, some people do them primarily to promote their product or service, with revenue from the seminar being a secondary goal or by-product. The theory is that if people are interested enough to attend a full-length seminar on a topic that addresses a problem or need your product or service solves, then they are ideal prospects for buying that product or service.

A self-sponsored fee-paid seminar has several advantages over the product seminar or tutorial. First, it is the most impressive, offering intense education with no hint of sales hype.

Second, you can include mention of your products or services in the seminar mailing, or at least a description of what your company does (in an "about the sponsor" section) in the seminar brochure. Let's say you mail 5,000 brochures and that gets 75 people to attend. By putting a description about your company's capabilities in the brochure, you have promoted yourself to the 4,925 who did not respond as well as the 75 who do come.

Disadvantages of a public seminar are twofold. First, because people are paying, it is inappropriate to do promotion or self-selling. You have to let the seminar "sell itself"; that is, you and your firm gain credibility and generate interest simply by virtue of being the seminar sponsor and leader.

Second, fee-paid public seminars are a business in themselves, and your company may not want to get into this business. It's time-consuming and a logistics challenge to coordinate and put on such events. Also, unless you are experts in direct-mail seminar promotion, you could easily spend thousands of dollars putting together and mailing a brochure, and then get virtually no response. So it's risky.

Option 4: Seminar Sponsored by a Seminar Company

You can be a seminar leader without sponsoring your own seminar. This eliminates the time, expense, and risk of promoting your own self-sponsored seminar, while providing the same forum for positioning yourself and your company as the experts in a particular field or topic.

There are many public seminar companies whose only business is to sponsor and promote, for a profit, public seminars on a variety of topics. You can write a letter to these companies explaining who you are, your qualifications, and the subjects you are interested in teaching. These subjects should either be topics they are already offering or related ones that would appeal to the same audience. Don't suggest a seminar on interpersonal skills to a public seminar company whose other programs are titled "LAN/WAN Internetworking" and "Troubleshooting T1 Networks."

A fairly comprehensive list of public seminar companies, including their addresses, a contact person, and the topics they specialize in, can be found in the book *How to Make It Big in the Seminar Business* by Paul Karasik. This book and other information on how to present and market seminars is available from the American Seminar Leaders Association,

899 Boulevard East, Suite 6A, Weehawken, NJ 07087, 201 864-9149.

As stated, the advantage of teaching a public seminar sponsored by a seminar company is that the company does all the marketing and arranging. All you have to do is show up and deliver the program. And if the seminar mailing doesn't generate registrations, it's the seminar company's money that has been spent, not yours.

You and your firm are promoted because the seminar company gives you the opportunity to lead the seminar and to provide your biography to thousands of people on the direct-mail invitation.

The disadvantage is that you are more restricted in your ability to sell your product, mention what your company does, and even in the information you present in the program. Some sponsors might encourage you to let the audience know about your products and services, while others have strict rules limiting such self-promotion. Some let you mix your information with theirs; others insist you present a program of their design as-is.

The other disadvantage is that there is a limited number of public seminar companies, and an even smaller number giving seminars on a topic that would be beneficial for you to present. If no company is interested in having you present a seminar, you'll have to pursue one of the other five options discussed in this chapter.

Option 5: Speech or Presentation at an Association Meeting or Industry Event

Another way to find a "sponsor" for your program is to present it as a talk or speech, rather than a longer seminar, at an association meeting or an industry convention or trade show. This option is discussed in detail in chapter 7.

Option 6: Teaching a College or Adult Education Course

The sixth option is to give your seminar or lecture as a college course. Businesspeople who teach do so primarily at adult education programs sponsored by local universities, colleges, and high schools.

This would be my last choice because of its many disadvantages:

1. *Significant time commitment.* A typical course might be held in the evening from 6 P.M. to 8 P.M. every week for ten or twelve consecutive weeks. That's a three-month commitment and more than twenty hours of your time.

2. *Low return.* During those twenty hours you'll only be addressing a single group: your students. And class sizes are usually small—ten to twenty students.

3. *Wrong audience.* I taught adult education programs in topics related to my consulting practice (advertising and technical writing) for seven years at New York University's School of Continuing Education. While every class had several good prospects in it, most of the students (all working adults, by the way) did not hold positions that would make them potential clients.

4. *Not a selling forum.* I think it is inappropriate to take as a customer or client any student in your adult education class until the class is over. Reason: You must assign a grade to each student, and other students could claim you were favoring a student who was also a customer with a better grade.

The main *advantage* of teaching adult education at a local college or university is prestige. Especially for a service provider, it doesn't hurt to add to your brochure "Professor of Accounting at Andover College."

Another small advantage is that teaching adult education pays; however, the pay is usually low: $20 to $30 or so per hour of class time. A ten-week, twenty-hour class might pay $600 to $800 but not much more.

DETERMINING WHETHER YOU CAN USE A SEMINAR TO PROMOTE YOUR PRODUCT OR SERVICE

Whether a seminar is a useful way for you to promote your product or service depends on your marketing situation. Product seminars work well when introducing new products or technologies. They are also ideal for products that require an in-person demonstration, such as software or computer systems.

Seminars are also effective for introducing new *concepts*, new approaches to business, and professional and consulting services. For service firms, the seminar is the first opportunity to allow prospects to "sample" the service before they make a commitment to buy a larger chunk of it. Also, if your product or service solves or addresses a major business problem or issue (such as plant safety, computer security, employee benefits planning, life insurance), a seminar is a good place to educate your prospects on the subject.

Price is another factor. In most cases, seminars are appropriate only for expensive items, since it doesn't pay to rent a hotel room, mail invitations, and spend staff time presenting a seminar to people in the hopes of selling them a single product that only costs $10. However, there are exceptions. "Tupperware" parties, in a sense, miniseminars on how to store food in the home, and the unit of sale at such events is typically small.

SEMINAR OR SALES PITCH?

At this point, you might ask, "Aren't most product seminars thinly disguised sales pitches for a specific product and not really seminars?"

Yes, and that's why they fail. Obviously, your purpose in presenting the seminar is to convince people to buy your product. But if the seminar is a blatant promotional pitch, people become annoyed—even disgusted.

On the other hand, if you present information of genuine value, attendees will think well of your firm and be more inclined to do business with you.

Attendees know they will be sold but want to learn something too. They realize they cannot master a complex subject in a two- or three-hour seminar, but if you can present them with one or two new ideas, or a few practical how-to tips or techniques, you'll dazzle them. They'll walk away delighted with the seminar and will become "fans" of your firm—a desirable result.

SETTING THE SEMINAR FEE

One early consideration is: Should you charge for your seminars or give them for free?

As a rule, seminars designed primarily to sell a product or service should be free. Every activity in business—promotional or otherwise—should have one primary goal and be wholly directed toward achieving that goal. Therefore, if your goal is to sell product and not generate revenue, the seminar should be free so that you maximize attendance to get the largest number of prospects in the room to hear your message and feel free to do at least some product selling.

Attendees at free seminars expect to get *some* sell and find it acceptable if not overdone. But if people have paid $295 to attend a one-day "Relational Databases" session, they want to learn how to manage, choose, or design relational databases. They don't want to hear what amounts to a reading of your sales brochure—and if they do get that, they will feel cheated.

Some companies break this rule successfully, charging large fees for their seminars and still managing to generate both sales and immediate revenue at the same time. But they are the exception. If your goal is to sell, give free seminars and treat them as promotion, not profit centers.

Some companies seek a happy compromise by charging a nominal fee—say, $10 or $25. The idea is to qualify attendees. The reasoning is: "Someone who pays $10 or $25 must really be interested, and someone not willing to pay it is not a good prospect."

This sounds sensible, but I don't agree with the strategy. I feel free offers should be free. I don't think you impress prospects or make the seminar seem more valuable by charging a nominal fee.

What's more, if you charge the same fee as *regular* paid seminars ($50 to $125 for the general public and $100 to $300 per day for business seminars), then it would be inappropriate to do *any* selling, and the presentation would have to be 100 percent educational—which isn't your goal. If your purpose is to sell a product, make the seminar free.

TYPICAL RESPONSE RATES TO SEMINAR PROMOTIONS

Most companies invite attendees to free seminars using direct mail. Response rates for free seminars in fields where the free seminar offer is common (software, computers, telecommunications) are generally not much higher than for paid seminars. Your response rate will probably be anywhere from ½ to 3 percent. If you assume a 1 percent response rate, and want 25 people in your seminar, you will need to mail 2,500 invitations and probably should mail 5,000 to be safe.

Free seminars on a topic not usually presented in such forums often get a higher response. Gary Blake, a management consultant specializing in writing seminars, recently gave a free three-hour seminar entitled "Effective Business Writing" and got a 10 percent response.

As already noted, another way to increase response is to have a celebrity as your featured speaker. This need not be a show-business celebrity, however, but preferably it is someone well known in your industry.

EXAMPLE

One software distributor recently sponsored a free lunch seminar at which Bill Gates, chairman of Microsoft, was the speaker. The seminar invitation consisted of a card listing only the location, date, and the fact that it was a lunch with Bill Gates. The banquet room was packed to overflowing with busy MIS vice presidents and DP managers—and the invitation hadn't even mentioned the topic or content.

THE BEST LENGTH AND DATE FOR
YOUR SEMINAR

Most free seminars last half a day, typically two or three hours, either in the morning or the afternoon.

What day is best? Howard Shenson, author of *How to Create and Market a Successful Seminar or Workshop* (The Consultant's Library), says that for seminars aimed at business, Wednesday or Thursday are the best days, followed by Tuesday, Friday, and Saturday. Monday and Sunday are the worst days.

For seminars aimed at consumers and the general public, Thursday and Saturday are best, followed by Wednesday, Sunday, Tuesday, and Friday. Again, Monday is not a good day.

Are some months better than others? My own experience is that the best seminar seasons are March through May and September through mid-November. Summer interferes with vacations. Winter brings the danger of cancellation due to bad weather in most regions of the United States. And from mid-November to January 1, people are concentrating on the holidays.

NAMING YOUR PROGRAM

Does it matter whether you call the event a "product demonstration," "seminar," or "workshop"? Yes. The title is very important, as it connotes value.

"Product demonstration" is least desirable and should only be used when the event is indeed a pure and straightforward demonstration of a system. "Seminar" implies that the attendee will gain useful knowledge. "Workshop" implies hands-on participation and should not be used for most free seminars.

Copywriter David Yale suggests calling the seminar a "forum" and has gotten good results doing so. I also like "briefing" for a session aimed at executives and managerial types. Programs aimed at consumers can also be "luncheons" if a light meal is served around noon or "parties" if given in a leisure atmosphere.

OBTAINING THE MAILING LIST

You will get the best results by mailing your seminar invitations to your house list or database of current and past customers, clients, and prospects. People who know you, have had dealings with you in the past, or have in the past asked for information about your product or service are much more likely to attend than people who don't know you. A seminar is an ideal forum for reawakening interest in prospects who have not taken action as well as for reactivating inactive accounts.

When renting mailing lists, select people who are the most likely prospects for the product being featured in the seminar, and be sure they live within a hundred-mile radius of the seminar site—ideally, within fifty miles.

A good source of mailing lists for seminar promotion is Hugo Dunhill Mailing Lists; for a free catalog call 212 682-8030. Also try Edith Roman Associates at 800 223-2194.

TIMING

Mail your seminar invitations third class about eight to nine weeks in advance of the seminar date if targeting a business audience. Based on a study of the seminar mailings that cross my desk, I would say that most arrive in my mailbox four to eight weeks in advance of the date.

You can probably mail on shorter notice for consumer seminars. Print ads can be placed a week or two, or even a few days, before the event to attract last-minute attendees.

Because the attendees do not pay, you don't collect money, but you still want them to register. Copy in ads and mail should read: "There is no fee to attend this seminar, but you must register in advance because attendance is limited. To reserve your seat, call [phone number] today."

And what about the mailing piece itself? There are a wide variety of formats. Some companies use self-mailers; others send personalized letters of invitation that include a circular or flier outlining the key points or benefits of attendance.

The copy doesn't have to be as long, complete, persuasive,

and hard-hitting as it is in direct-response mailings selling costly paid seminars, but you probably have to sell it 75 percent to 80 percent as hard. The copy should tell prospects what they will learn at the session and the benefits of attending.

If you offer a free gift, stress this in your letter and on the cover of your brochure or self-mailer. Free gifts have tremendous pulling power. If the gift has a retail value, say "FREE GIFT—guaranteed to be worth $35." Many people will come just to get the free gift. And if it's a sample of your product or related to your product line, that's fine.

The design of your mailing should be consistent with the event and audience. If you are inviting executives to a briefing on competing with the Japanese, the piece should be serious, somber, even urgent. If you are holding a party for expectant mothers to sell them on your diaper service, the mailing should be colorfully illustrated with pictures of babies, families, cribs, nurseries, and the like.

COPYWRITING TIPS

In your mailing, make it clear that the seminar is free—but don't make this fact your central theme or trumpet it in your headline. Write copy that makes the reader say, "This sounds wonderful. I would really love to go. How much does it cost?" Then tell him or her it's free.

Do *not* think that, just because the seminar is free, people will want to attend. "Despite being free, [free seminars] must be *sold,* just as anything else is sold," warns Herman Holtz. "The word free is one strong inducement to attend, of course, but few, if any, would attend if they were not promised a benefit they find attractive enough to merit the expenditure of their time."

EXPENDITURES

As discussed, free seminars are not a terribly expensive promotion, at least as far as incurring outside costs. If you know your product, there's no reason why your people can't develop the presentation in-house and present it themselves.

The main expense is in the mailing. Sending out 5,000 invitations will run approximately $2,000 to $3,000, depending on the format. Self-mailers generally cost much less than packages with outer envelopes, personalized letters, insert brochures, reply forms, and reply envelopes. If you use a full-scale package, you should split test a self-mailer (a mailer with no outer envelope); often you get the same response at far less cost.

You can hold the seminar at your company facilities, although a nice room in a good hotel is more pleasant and easier for attendees to find. In the suburbs, a seminar room can be rented for $100 to $300 a day; in a major city, it might run $300 to $500. The smaller your audience, the smaller the room and the lower the cost.

Food is the big expense. Coffee and tea run $1 to $2 per person per serving; soft drinks run $2 to $2.50 per can or bottle. Meals involve significantly greater expense but may be necessary if attendees expect to be fed.

Other expenses include development and reproduction of overheads, slides, handouts, and invitations. These costs can be amortized over the lifetime of the seminar. Because of the time, expense, and effort required to create an effective seminar, one-shot events do not pay off as well as repeats. So to maximize the benefit of the seminar, plan on giving it at least three or four times during the year in several different locations.

To develop a product seminar and give it once, a budget of $5,000 should be sufficient assuming you do the work yourself and do not hire outside consultants.

HOW TO SELL—TASTEFULLY—AT THE SEMINAR

The key to making your seminar an effective promotional event is to give a good seminar—one that lives up to the promise of its brochure or mailing and delivers an interesting, useful, helpful, informative presentation prospects will appreciate. If they walk away happy and pleased, you've achieved your primary goal: to make them "fans" of your company.

To further enhance selling effectiveness, you can sell your product before, during, and after the seminar. This is acceptable (because your seminar is free, and they expect it), but only if done in a gentle, reasonable, unpressured way. Don't push your product on people or mention it every minute. When people ask questions, don't answer every one by saying "Buying our product solves it!" Instead, give them an answer that helps them regardless of whether they become customers.

MORE TIPS ON MAXIMIZING THE SALES EFFECTIVENESS OF PRODUCT SEMINARS

In Advance of the Seminar . . .

- Mail a questionnaire asking prospects what topics they want addressed during the seminar. Ask them to return the questionnaire. Answer those topics at the seminar.
- Put them on your mailing list so they get at least one promotional mailing from your company before the seminar.

- Put them on the subscription list to receive your free company promotional newsletter.
- Send a confirmation letter acknowledging registration. Include easy-to-follow directions to the seminar site—both by mass transit and car.
- Call them to confirm that they are coming.

Before the Seminar Starts . . .

- Serve coffee and tea.
- Meet and shake hands with attendees. Welcome them to the seminar. Engage them in conversation to learn more about them.
- Leave product literature on a table at the back of the room and put one copy of your catalog or brochure on each chair in the room.
- Distribute an article reprint or other interesting piece for people to read before the seminar starts. Some people come early; others come late; and you want to give the early people something to do.
- Have an unannounced door prize to create additional interest and excitement. Hold the drawing at the first break. (This prevents people from walking out.)
- Give them a simple survey or questionnaire to complete while they wait for the session to start. This will be a useful tool in planning your sales approach to these people. If possible, address some of the concerns expressed on the questionnaires during your talk. (Don't identify the people asking the question unless they volunteer their identities.)
- Use name tags so attendees feel comfortable mingling. The session will be more meaningful and enjoyable if attendees can network with their peers.

During the Seminar . . .

- Work your product into your presentation and mention it briefly two or three times each hour. But only for a sentence or two. And don't overdo it. Let common sense be your guide.
- At the end, it's okay to give a five-minute pitch from the podium. After all, the audience expects it. A good lead-in is "Okay, some of you have been sitting here for three hours and wondering 'Where's the product pitch?' Well, I don't want to disappoint you, so here it is. . . ."
- At the end of the pitch say, "You've been a great audience. Thanks for your attention." Then name the company salespeople in the room and ask them to identify themselves by standing or raising their hands. Then say, "Rick, Sue, and I [or whoever the salespeople are] will stay around awhile to talk to you if you have more questions about [topic of seminar] or want more information on [name of product]. We welcome your questions and comments."
- Let people come to you. Don't have salespeople descend like hawks to "capture" prospects or put on the hard-sell. If people want to leave, let them. But be sure they have your catalog or brochure and business card before they go.

After the Seminar . . .

- Send a follow-up note thanking them for coming along with a form they can use to place an order or request more information.
- Follow-up on any specific inquiries or concerns expressed to salespeople or on questionnaires.

- Place all prospects on your in-house data base list to receive future mailings.
- Do not forget to deliver any free gifts you promised to distribute if they were not handed out at the seminar.
- When giving out a free product or sample or literature, include price-off coupons the attendees can use to purchase your products at a discount at retail outlets.
- Did the mailing piece generate the desired attendance? If not, why not? Are you using the wrong lists, or is the piece itself ineffective? Maybe your topic does not appeal to your intended audience.
- Did the right people attend for the right reasons? Did you get a room full of eager prospects who showed interest and enthusiasm in your proposition? Or were you talking to the wrong people, or prospects who just wanted the free doughnuts and couldn't care less about your widgets?
- Did the seminar itself generate the desired sales results? That is, did prospects show interest, become involved, approach salespeople, and take the next step in the buying process?
- What percentage of attendees were genuine prospects? What percentage demonstrated real interest in your product? What percentage eventually became customers or clients?
- If the results were not satisfactory, is there anything you can do to improve attendance or the quality of the presentation? Or is it possible that free seminars simply don't work for your type of offer?

SPECIAL EVENTS

Special events—grand openings, pony rides for children, barbecues and square dances, picnics, Halloween parties, and other events—are effective publicity vehicles in two ways.

First, they help market your company, product, or service to the public. People attend the event, come to your store for the free hot dogs or ice cream, then, while they are there, browse and buy.

Second, they are promotable and can get you a lot of press coverage. Editors like special events and will give them coverage.

If the event involves free food, gifts, rides, or other give-aways, editors will at least announce it in their papers, typically in a schedule of events or things-to-do-this-week column.

If the event is based on a clever gimmick or angle, editors will not only put it in the calendar but may give it broader feature coverage, both as a preview as well as a postevent write-up. This "leverages" the time and effort spent putting on the event, because you not only promote yourself to those who attend, but, through the publicity, you reach thousands of additional prospects who did not come.

It's important to maximize the selling opportunity at special events. For example, a local department store advertised that Spiderman would be at the store's grand opening to take photos with the kiddies and give away autographed comic books. When we got there, the line of parents with children to see Spiderman went around the store, with a fifty-minute wait.

Spiderman stood in front of the toy department, where he shook hands and posed with young fans. To my amazement, there were no Spiderman or other superhero toys or comic books displayed near him! In fact, there was no such display anywhere in the toy department! The store blew an opportunity to sell thousands of dollars' worth of Spiderman and superhero action figures, dolls, costumes, and other comic-book paraphernalia. Don't you make this same mistake.

Also, the only announcement of Spiderman's appearance

came in free-standing newspaper inserts and ads—the store
didn't drum up any free publicity.

You might say, "What do you expect? It's just a guy
dressed up in a Spiderman costume. No news there."

Here's where being creative and clever could have made
the difference. What about writing and distributing a press
release in the form of a tongue-in-cheek question-and-answer
interview with Spiderman? Sent with some action photos of
Spidey striking a dramatic pose or shooting a web, I guarantee at least one local editor would have enjoyed and run this
release as a feature article . . . generating publicity for
the store.

Here are some suggestions for creating special events that
not only draw big crowds but also gain publicity:

1. Tie the special event into current events or news. For
    instance, a store selling 1950s and other nostalgia
    items could have had an Elvis Presley memorabilia sale
    tied into the U.S. Postal Service's widely publicized in-
    troduction of the new Elvis stamp.

2. Tie the special event in to a holiday, anniversary, or
    other "calendar day." Virtually every day is the anni-
    versary of some famous person's birth or death; the an-
    niversary of some important event; or a holiday,
    commemorative day, or day of recognition. For ex-
    ample, you might give 25 percent off any item in your
    store to left-handed people on "National Lefty Day."

3. Involve local celebrities—have the DJ from a popular
    local radio station on hand as the master of ceremonies
    and to sign autographs. Celebrities draw crowds and
    generate press coverage.

4. Feature an unusual, interesting, or creative event as
    part of the day. For example, to promote your pizza
    parlor, you can truck in ingredients and attempt to get
    everyone present into the *Guinness Book of World Re-*

cords—by having them help you make the world's largest pizza.

An excellent reference for planning memorable special events is *The Promotional Sourcebook* (Asher Gallant Press, 516 254-2000). Especially valuable is the complete calendar of "special days," which gives you a tie-in anniversary, event, or theme for nearly every calendar day of the year.

CHAPTER 9

NEWSLETTERS: KEEPING IN TOUCH WITH CLIENTS AND CUSTOMERS

WHERE ONE-SHOT PR FAILS

Throughout this book I've been stressing the benefits of Targeted Public Relations: low cost, high credibility, ease of implementation, and fantastic results.

But I haven't told you about Targeted Public Relations' major weakness: namely, that it doesn't assure the consistent, frequent repetition of your message that is needed to get people to remember you and motivate them to buy from you.

In today's society, consumers are drowning in information. Therefore, every communication has less impact on your audience than it would have had years ago, every contact is less memorable.

For example, I once read that when Charles Dickens completed a new chapter of a book (in those days, the chapters were sometimes printed as separate booklets and sold as a series), people would crowd around the docks and hold their arms out as boxes of booklets were lowered from the ship.

(The booklets were printed in England and sent to the United States via steamship.) Today, however, the publication of most books is a nonevent, since more than 50,000 new books are written and published each year.

A targeted PR placement, while effective, is still a one-shot communication, and with so many magazines, newspapers, articles, TV shows, movies, software, and video games competing for the consumer's attention, your article or PR placement gets noticed less, has less impact.

Even a regular, frequent *program* of Targeted Public Relations cannot guarantee consistent exposure of the target audience to your key messages, since not every effort is certain to yield equal results, you cannot control the exact timing and placement of PR pickups, and the media outlets are widely dispersed and read by different people, so not every prospect will see every pickup.

However, there is a solution, one marketing communications tool that can be used to assure regular, repeat, consistent exposure to your company name, message, and information: the promotional newsletter.

USING NEWSLETTERS TO REINFORCE TARGETED PR CAMPAIGNS

In today's age of specialized information, newsletters are popular. Sources estimate that there are more than 10,000 newsletters published in the United States. And these are paid subscription newsletters, sold for profit by entrepreneurs for whom the newsletter is their primary source of income.

In this chapter we deal with another kind of newsletter—the promotional newsletter, also called the company newsletter or "house organ." These newsletters, magazines, tabloids, or other regular publications are published primarily as promotional tools. They range from simple sheets published in-house to elaborate, four-color company magazines with photography and professional writing rivaling the quality of newstand magazines.

The main purpose of such a newsletter is to establish your image and build your credibility with a select audience (the people who receive the newsletter) over an extended period of time.

Instinctively, most marketers recognize that they should be in touch with their customers and prospects far more often than they actually are. You know, for instance, that there are many people in your life—business and social—whom you don't think about, see, or talk to for long periods of time simply because you are busy and not thinking of them.

Well, your customers and prospects are busy too. And while you may be agonizing over why Joe hasn't placed an order from you recently or called your firm to handle a project, Joe isn't even thinking about you . . . because he has so much else on his mind.

You know you should be doing something to keep your name in front of Joe and remind him of your existence. But how? You may want to call or send a letter, but you think this is too pushy . . . and besides, there's no real *reason* to call, and you don't want to seem begging for business.

The newsletter solves this problem. It regularly places your name and activities in front of your customers and prospects, reminding them of your existence, products, and services on a regular basis. And you need no "excuse" to make this contact, because the prospect *expects* to receive a newsletter on a regular basis. The newsletter increases the frequency of message repetition and supplements other forms of communication such as catalogs, print ads, and sales letters.

SIZE AND FREQUENCY

How long should your newsletter be? How often should it be published?

In my opinion, four to eight pages is the ideal length for a promotional newsletter. More than that is too much reading, and two pages seems insubstantial—more like a flier or circular (which is perceived as "junk mail") than a newsletter (which is perceived as a useful publication).

As for frequency, four times a year—once every three months—is ideal. Publish fewer issues, and people aren't aware you are sending them a newsletter per se; they perceive that they're just getting a piece of mail from time to time. Four times per year is enough to establish credibility and awareness. Publishing six times or more per year is unnecessary, because some months you may prefer to make contact with your prospects using other media, such as the telephone or direct mail or catalogs.

What's more, my experience indicates that most companies don't have enough news to fill six or more issues each year. If your schedule is too frequent, you may find yourself putting unnecessary fluff and filler in the newsletter just to get something in the mail. Your readers will be turned off by the lack of quality and poor content, so this would hurt you rather than help.

BUILDING YOUR SUBSCRIBER LIST

Who should get your newsletter? Basically, it should go to anyone with whom you want to establish a regular relationship. These people can include:

- Current customers.
- Past customers.

- Current prospects.
- Past prospects.
- Expired accounts (past subscribers, "expires," and so on).
- Employees.
- Vendors.
- Colleagues.
- Consultants, gurus, and other prominent members of your industry.
- Referral sources (influential people who can refer business to you).
- Trade publication editors, business columnists, and other members of the press who might possibly use material in your newsletter in their own writings.

"All your current clients should receive your client newsletter," says Steve Klinghoffer, president of WPI Communications. "The newsletter is an important vehicle for keeping in touch on a regular and predictable basis. It confers automatic high visibility and does so in the best possible way: by reflecting you as a professional, knowledgeable and competent. This not only builds your image, but also helps to insure that current clients will remain responsive to your recommendations."

Adds Klinghoffer, "Do not neglect to send the newsletter to clients who use your services or products in a very limited manner, or whom you have not visited with recently. You may not think of them as current clients, but of course, they are. What's more, rather than drifting away from you, the newsletter offers the kind of visibility that prompts many 'limited clients' to expand their use of your products and services."

Here is how you build the subscriber list:

1. First, put all current and past prospects and customers on the list. But don't use names that are too old. For past prospects and customers, for example, you might go back two or three years—but no more than that.

2. Next, get your salespeople to give you all the names of
    the people they call on regularly. Salespeople have
    their own favorite prospects, and these people may not
    be in the advertising inquiry files. So get them to give
    you names of people who should get the newsletter.
    You essentially want to convert the dozens of individ-
    ual Rolodex™ files kept by various salespeople and
    sales reps into a single, integrated subscriber list for
    your newsletter.

3. Go to your PR department or agency and add its media
    list. Get the names of all editors who should receive the
    newsletter.

4. Make sure all new inquiries and new customers are
    added automatically to the subscription list. This in-
    cludes every response, every sales lead generated by
    your Targeted Public Relations campaigns.

5. For trade shows, create a subscription application form
    and offer a free one-year subscription to anyone who
    stops by your booth and completes the form.

6. Make sure the subscriber lists contain the names of
    your immediate supervisors, your product and brand
    managers, your sales and marketing managers, your
    CEO, and any other key personnel whose support you
    need to run an effective advertising department. Com-
    pany managers enjoy getting the newsletter and often
    will offer ideas for articles and stories you can use. You
    might also approach your most important colleague
    and ask him or her to contribute a regular column.

PROMOTING THE NEWSLETTER

In addition to compiling the list in this manner, you can do a
number of things to promote the newsletter (and to use the
newsletter offer as a promotion):

1. You can offer the newsletter as an extra incentive to
    people who respond to your direct mail. This can be as
    simple as adding a line to your reply cards with a box
    that says, "[ ] Check here if you would like a free
    1-year subscription to our quarterly newsletter, [title
    of newsletter]." You could also stress the newsletter
    offer in the P.S. of your sales letter.

2. You can offer the newsletter as an extra incentive for
    responding to your space ads. Again, add an option to
    the response coupon that says "[ ] Check here for a
    free 1-year subscription to our newsletter, [title of
    newsletter]."

3. At speeches, seminars, and presentations, your com-
    pany representatives can use the newsletter offer to
    get listeners involved in conversations with them. At
    the end of the talk, the presenter says, "Our quarterly
    newsletter, [title of newsletter], will give you more in-
    formation on this topic. Just give me your business
    card and I'll see to it you get a free one-year subscrip-
    tion to it." This way, the presenter will collect many
    business cards for follow-up—far more than he or she
    would get if there was no newsletter offer.

4. You could rent a list of names and send them the news-
    letter for free two or three times. The third or fourth
    time, you send it with a cover letter that says "We hope
    you find [title of newsletter] informative and helpful,
    and we would be happy to continue sending it at no
    cost. To continue your free subscription, just complete
    and mail the reply card enclosed." Then you continue
    sending the newsletter only to those who return the
    reply card, which eliminates the cost of continually
    renting names.

5. Send out a press release offering a free sample copy of
    the newsletter to people in your industry.

6. Run small space ads with a picture of the newsletter. Offer a free sample copy to anyone who responds.

DESIGNING YOUR NEWSLETTER

Newsletters do not have to be elaborate. But the design should be consistent from issue to issue, in order to build recognition and awareness. After a time, many recipients will come to welcome your newsletter, even seek it out from among the pile of mail in their in-basket. But this can happen only if the newsletter has a distinctive, recognizable, and consistent design.

Although many paid subscription newsletters are typewritten, you probably want a design that is a little slicker, so as to enhance your image. Text is generally typeset or desktop-published in two or three columns. Paper stock may be white or colored, and the newsletter is usually printed in one or two colors of ink. The key to the design is a distinctive masthead highlighting the name of the publication.

The look, content, and "feel" of the newsletter are usually arrived at after a couple of issues. By the third issue, you know the approximate length of copy, the type of visuals needed, the technical depth of the content, and the types of articles to be featured.

For instance, you might decide that each issue will contain two feature articles, one biographical profile, a regular question-and-answer column on technical issues, one product-related story, three or four short news tidbits, and a box with short previews of the next issue. Your newsletter may be different, of course, but the point is, you'll eventually find a formula that works and stick with it from issue to issue.

Readers like this consistency of format because they know what to look for in each issue. For instance, some people opening the Sunday paper turn to sports first; some go to the comics; others read "Dear Abby" first. In the same way, some readers might check your "technical tips" column first, while others will read the profile. Make these features look and read the same in each issue (even position them in the same spot) so readers gain a comfortable familiarity with your publication.

CHARGING A FEE FOR YOUR NEWSLETTER

One common question is "Since so many newsletters charge hefty subscription fees, what about charging a fee for my newsletter?" Don't do it. A promotional newsletter is *not* the same as a paid subscription newsletter.

The paid subscription newsletter must deliver unique and valuable editorial material to the readers—otherwise, they will not continue to pay a hefty price for it month after month. This material must be useful, informative, new, and special. In short, it must be material the reader cannot get easily elsewhere. The newsletter's purpose is to be the reader's source of critical information in the area covered by the publication.

The promotional newsletter is quite different. Although it should contain helpful and interesting information, readers expect less from a promotional newsletter than from one they pay to receive. As a result, they will accept a blend of how-to and technical information mixed with production information, company news, and sales talk. And this is the mix you want to give them. Remember, the ultimate goal of the newsletter is not to educate readers (you are not in the business of educating people for free) but to get them to do business with your firm and buy your products.

Because your newsletter is free, you're entitled to make some subtle (and not-so-subtle) sales pitches. But if you were charging, readers would not accept this. Another reason not to charge is that paid newsletters typically capture only a small percentage of any market as subscribers. If you want to reach a broader base of prospects, you must offer your newsletter free.

PUTTING YOUR NEWSLETTER TOGETHER

Putting your newsletter together is not terribly difficult. The first step is to make a list of possible story ideas. (Later in this chapter I provide a checklist of twenty-nine such ideas).

KEY POINT

The material in your promotional newsletter does not have to be original, nor must it be created solely for the newsletter. In fact, a company newsletter is an ideal medium for recycling other promotional and publicity material created by your company—speeches, articles, press releases, annual reports, presentations, and so on.

This fact helps you get maximum use out of material you've already created while minimizing the time and expense of writing and producing the newsletter.

The second step is to review your story ideas and select the ones to be featured in the next issue. If you are unsure as to how much room you have, it's better to select one or two extra ideas than one or two too few. You can always use the extra material in a future edition.

The third step is to create a file folder for each article and collect the information that will serve as background material for the person who writes the story. This background material typically includes sales brochures (for product stories), press releases (which are edited into short news stories), and reprints of published trade journal articles on a particular topic (which are often combined and compiled into a new article on a similar topic).

The fourth step is to write each story based on this material. Many advertising managers hire freelance writers to write and edit their company newsletters. A few hire their ad agency to do it. Using freelancers is usually more cost-effective. Besides, while most freelancers relish such assignments, most ad agencies don't like doing company newsletters, because they find them unprofitable.

Some articles may require more information than is contained in the background material. In this case, supply the writer with the names and phone numbers of people within your company whom he or she can interview to gather the additional information. Notify these people ahead of time that a freelance writer will be calling them to an interview for the newsletter. If they object, find substitutes.

Once you get the copy, the fifth step is to edit it, send it through for review, and make any final changes. The sixth step is to give the final copy to your graphic artist or printer, who will create a mechanical. This should be carefully proofread and reviewed before it is printed. Many companies nowadays use desktop publishing systems in-house or hire outside desktop publishing services for newsletter layout and creation.

Once the mechanical is completed and approved, you print the newsletter. If subscribers perceive it as valuable, you can periodically offer back issues as a bait piece in your ads and mailings.

If your subscriber list is small—say, only a few hundred names—you can have your computer generate gummed mailing labels and affix them in-house. Once you have a thousand or more subscribers, you might want to use a letter shop, fulfillment house, or similar mailing service to handle the mailing and distribution on a regular basis. This will not be terribly expensive.

TWENTY-NINE NEWSLETTER STORY IDEAS

1. *Product stories:* New products; improvements to existing products; new models; new accessories; new options; and new applications.
2. *News:* Joint ventures; mergers and acquisitions; new divisions formed; new departments; other company news. Also, industry news and analyses of events and trends.
3. *Tips:* Tips on product selection, installation, maintenance, repair, and troubleshooting.
4. *How-to articles:* Similar to tips, but with more detailed instructions. Examples: How to use the product; how to design a system; how to select the right type or model.
5. *Previews and reports:* Write-ups of special events such as trade shows, conferences, sales meetings, seminars, presentations, and press conferences.
6. *Case histories:* Either in-depth or brief, reporting product applications, customer success stories, or examples of outstanding service or support.
7. *People:* Company promotions, new hires, transfers, awards, anniversaries, employee profiles, human interest stories (unusual jobs, hobbies, and so on).
8. *Milestones:* "1,000th unit shipped," "sales reach $1 million mark," "division celebrates 10th anniversary," and so on.
9. *Sales news:* New customers; bids accepted; contracts renewed; satisfied customer reports.
10. *Research and development:* New products; new technol-

ogies; new patents; technology awards; inventions; innovations; and breakthroughs.

11. *Publications:* New brochures available; new ad campaigns; technical papers presented; reprints available; new or updated manuals; announcements of other recently published literature or audiovisual materials.

12. *Explanatory articles:* How a product works; industry overviews; background information on applications and technologies.

13. *Customer stories:* Interviews with customers; photos; customer news and profiles; guest articles by customers about their industries, applications, and positive experiences with the vendor's product or service.

14. *Financial news:* Quarterly and annual report highlights; presentations to financial analysts; earnings and dividend news; reported sales and profits; etc.

15. *Photos with captions:* People; facilities; products; events.

16. *Columns:* President's letter; letters to the editor; guest columns; regular features such as "Q&A" or "Tech Talk."

17. *Excerpts, reprints, or condensed versions of:* Press releases; executive speeches; journal articles; technical papers; company seminars; and so on.

18. *Quality control stories:* Quality circles; employee suggestion programs; new quality assurance methods; success rates; case histories.

19. *Productivity stories:* New programs; methods and systems to cut waste and boost efficiency.

20. *Manufacturing stories:* SPC/SQC (statistical process control/statistical quality control) stories; CIM (computer-integrated manufacturing) stories; new techniques; new equipment; raw materials; production line successes; detailed explanations of manufacturing processes; etc.

21. *Community affairs:* Fund-raisers; special events; support for the arts; scholarship programs; social responsibility programs; environmental programs; employee and corporate participation in local/regional/national events.

22. *Data processing stories:* New computer hardware and software systems; improved data processing and its benefits to customers; new data procession applications; explanations of how systems serve customers.

23. *Overseas activities:* Reports on the company's international activities; profiles of facilities, subsidiaries, branches, people, markets, and so on.

24. *Service:* Background on company service facilities; case histories of outstanding service activities; new services for customers; customer support hotlines; and the like.

25. *History:* Articles of company, industry, product, community history.

26. *Human resources:* Company benefit programs; announcement of new benefits and training and how they improve service to customers; explanations of company policies.

27. *Interviews:* With company key employees, engineers, service personnel, and so on; with customers; with suppliers (to illustrate the quality of materials going into your company's products).

28. *Forums:* Top managers answer customer complaints and concerns; service managers discuss customer needs; customers share their favorable experiences with company products and services.

29. *Gimmicks:* Contents; quizzes; trivia; puzzles; games; cartoons; recipes; computer programs; and the like.

"Make sure your newsletters contain timely, provocative information and advice that will be of specific interest to your targeted audience," recommends Klinghoffer. "The writing in your newsletters can make or break your newsletter marketing program. So make sure your newsletters feature solid information and advice framed in easy-to-read, action-oriented copy."

WHAT WILL IT COST?

The cost for producing and distributing a promotional newsletter can vary tremendously. Factors that determine cost include:

- Length (number of pages, amount of text)
- Paper stock and color (one color versus two color)
- Number to be printed and mailed

With desktop publishing, you could, if you choose, write, design, and produce camera-ready pages for your newsletter on your desktop PC or Macintosh. The only cost, aside from printing and postage, is your time and labor.

What will it cost to have an outside firm produce your newsletter? A local graphic arts firm quoted me the following fee for producing 28,000 copies of an eight-page, two-color newsletter:

One-time fee to design newsletter masthead and format (for first issue only)	$850
Production of 8-page newsletter (design, layout, mechanicals, type)	$1,675
Printing of 28,000 eight-page, 2-color newsletters	$6,500

These are 1992 prices for northern New Jersey, but at least they give you a feel for what's involved.

As for writing the newsletter, freelance writers will probably charge by the page (newsletter page, not manuscript page). The fee varies, and the range seems to be $350 to $750 per page.

Newsletters can be mailed in envelopes or without. If you mail in an envelope, consider using a 9-by-12-inch one so the newsletter can be mailed flat. A regular #10 envelope forces you to fold it, and it doesn't look as good. If you mail with no envelope, you must leave a blank space on the outer back cover for the mailing label, and your mailing indicia must also appear. You could affix postage, but that is unnecessary and labor-intensive.)

Mailing costs depend on quantity and weight. Klinghoffer advises companies to consult their local post office for details on third-class bulk rate mail if they plan to mail at least 200 newsletters at a time. Bulk rates can save almost $100 per thousand newsletters mailed.

If your newsletter contains valuable information, you might provide those who get it with a three-ring notebook or binder for storing issues. Store any extra issues left over from each printing, so you can fulfill requests for back issues if you get them or have extras to hand out at trade shows, speaking engagements, or seminars.

CHAPTER 10

RADIO AND TV PUBLICITY: HOW TO GET FAMOUS QUICK

WHY RADIO? WHY TELEVISION?

Today we live in an age of electronic information, with people reading less and watching and listening more. Therefore, getting on radio and TV enables you to reach additional prospects who may not read the newspaper or magazines.

But there are many other reasons why radio and TV publicity is so desirable.

"Radio and television are intimate media," says Dr. Jeffrey Lant on his audiocassette tape *How to Get Free Time on Radio and TV* (JLA Publications, 617 547-6372). "You have the chance to lower the buyer's anxieties about you and get them enthusiastic. Properly handled, your appearance on the media enables you to come across as a friend, even as a benefactor to your prospects. You can speak to them honestly, directly, sincerely, and get them genuinely enthusiastic about your offer. No paid ad is ever as direct and warm as a media appearance, and ads don't make you famous, while media appearances do."

Note that you do not have to be a celebrity to be a guest on radio or television. The media directories in the appendix list thousands of radio, broadcast, and cable shows in need of interesting, informative guests. While celebrities do get lots of airtime, at least as much airtime is given to people who, like you, have knowledge of a specialized subject of interest to a particular audience, and can communicate this knowledge in an interesting, enjoyable, clear way.

"Talk and interview shows are a great way to get your message to the world, since talk shows are always looking for interesting guests," says David Yale, author of *The Publicity Handbook* (NTC Business Books). According to Yale, 30 percent of radio and TV producers say they are interested in booking guests who speak on topical issues, 16 percent are interested in having people speak about new products, and 12 percent like to book authors.

WHOM TO CONTACT

The appendix lists several directories of radio and TV talk shows and their personnel, including the producer, receptionist, program manager, and host.

Al Parinello, in his book *On the Air: How to Get on Radio and TV Talk Shows and What to Do When You Get There* (Career Press, 800 CAREER-1), says that to get on a radio or TV talk show, you must begin by contacting the producer, because the producer—not the host—decides who will be the guests on the show.

According to Lant, this is true at larger radio stations. At many smaller stations hosts are often their own producers and are therefore the ones you should contact.

Parinello recommends the following steps for contacting producers to get yourself as a guest on their radio or TV show:

1. Look up the producer in the media directory and call him or her.

2. Be brief. As in any sales call, you must immediately say who you are, why you are calling, and give reasons why the person should listen to you—why he or she should consider having you as a guest on the show.

3. Do not pretend to be a publicist. If you are calling for yourself, say so. Do not try to overimpress or exaggerate, and don't lie. "Producers can tell a phony immediately," says Parinello.

4. If the producer is not interested, thank him for his time, get off the phone, and call the producer of the next show you want to get onto. Do not argue with a producer who turns you down, or try to prove that you indeed are a good potential guest; producers know what they are looking for in a guest. Do not ask producers who turn you down for a referral or recommendation to another show; they are not in business to be your publicist.

5. You are unlikely to get booked for the show over the phone. Producers who are interested will ask you to send a package of information about you and your topic.

6. What should the package include? Parinello says the media kit can include such items as press releases, a personal biography, testimonials or endorsements, reprints of articles written by or about you, a sample of your product, and a tip sheet. The latter is a list of ten to fifteen suggested questions the host might ask you about your topic. In addition, if you have made prior appearances on radio or TV, include a list of them (program names, stations, dates, and topic). I'd also recommend including an audio- or videotape of a recent media appearance if it's impressive.

Dr. Lant advocates persistent follow-up as a way to get yourself booked as a guest on radio and TV shows.

"Media people are busy," writes Lant in his self-syndicated "Sure-Fire Success" business column. "If you want to be on the show, persist. Follow up your initial letter with a phone call. A second phone call. And a note. If this still doesn't work, send another letter saying you're going to stay in touch, because the topic is important. Then stay in touch. Send clippings from print media featuring you, media releases, and articles you've written. Remember, one show can easily get you the attention of millions of people who can buy what you're selling. What you're seeking—publicity—is valuable. And you're going to have to work to get it."

BE ACCESSIBLE

A key ingredient of getting publicity in any medium, but especially on TV and radio, is to be accessible, flexible, and accommodating.

When the producer calls and says, "We got your material and are interested in having you on the *Joe Shmoe Show;* how does 10 A.M. on Thursday sound?" say yes, you can do it. Give the media first priority, and accept the first suggested time or date unless you absolutely cannot do so. If you are difficult, hard to schedule, and have a conflict with every date producers suggest, after you turn down three or four suggested dates they are going to get impatient, say "thanks anyway," and call the next candidate from the pile of hundreds of media kits they have received.

While producers generally treat guests nicely, I always behave as if they are my client: I am in business to serve their needs, not the other way around. This attitude works and gets results.

A friend has a policy of being accessible to the media twenty-four hours a day, seven days a week, and it works: He gets one media placement or interview every day of the year. He says that once he was awakened at 4 A.M. by a phone call from the producer of a late-night radio call-in show; the scheduled guest was not available, and could my friend do the interview?

"When?" my friend asked sleepily.

"Right now!" the panicked producer begged. My friend agreed and did the show from his bed, using the phone on his nightstand!

PREPARING TO GO ON THE AIR

Al Parinello provides this ten-point checklist you can use to prepare for media appearances. (I've embellished it with my own comments.)

1. Familiarize yourself with the talk show on which you are going to appear. Listen to or watch it. Know the host's name, format, manner of interviewing, and what is expected of you. Know the host's idiosyncrasies so you can avoid surprise and potential embarrassment (for example, you've written a book on liberal politics and didn't know the host was an ultra-conservative).

2. Know who the audience is—who listens to or watches the show.

3. Take advantage of every opportunity to promote your appearance. For example, if you are going to be on a popular radio show broadcast in the Washington,

D.C., area, you might call and let your Washington-based clients know it.

4. Rehearse answering all possible questions that may be asked of you. Not just the ones on your tip sheet, but any the interviewer is likely to ask.

5. Know in advance the major points you want to make, the messages you want to get across. Practice saying them in short phrases you can "slip into" the conversation in case the host doesn't ask questions whose answers help make your point.

6. If you are on a call-in show, arrange for two or three friends to call in with prepared questions. This can get things going, save you the embarrassment of a quiet phone line (if people are not calling), and ensure that you get to answer the two or three questions you most wanted to talk about.

7. Have your 800 or local telephone number and mailing address ready.

8. Take with you any materials you might need to refer to. If you're an author doing a call-in radio show, for example, have a copy of your book with you. If you want to support your opinions with facts and statistics but your memory is not great, jot the key facts on index cards and have them handy.

9. Have a free tip sheet, special report, booklet, or reprint you can offer callers or viewers as a give-away. This bait piece contains information that expands on and gives more detail about one or more of the topics you are discussing on the show. According to Parinello, having such a bait piece can make the difference between tremendous versus minimal lead generation from a TV or radio appearance. (You can use the bait piece you created using the guidelines in chapter 4.)

10. Work on a definition of what you do and boil it down
     to a single brief sentence you can say on TV or radio.
     For example, "My company, CTC, helps business-
     people improve their writing skills."

Here are some additional preparation tips:

• For television appearances, make sure you look your
  best. This sounds silly, but have you ever, five minutes
  before you had to leave for a job interview or other important meeting, discovered that you had no clean shirts,
  no razor blades for a shave, dirty shoes that need polishing, or that you really should have washed your hair and
  showered more recently?
     Don't get caught in a frantic rush to look good for
  your TV appearance. A few days in advance, have your
  hair cut or styled, get your suit dry cleaned and your
  shirts or blouses laundered, make sure the shoes are polished and that the clothes you want to wear are all ready
  to go.
• What to wear on TV? The National Association of Broadcasters advises: "Wear medium tones of gray, brown, or
  blue in a style in which you feel most comfortable. Avoid
  distracting stripes, pronounced checks, or sharply con-
  trasted patterns. Off-white or pastel shades for shirts
  and blouses is best. If you wear glasses, wear them on
  the air; the studio crew will arrange the light to avoid
  any glare or reflections." (Source: *The Publicity Handbook*,
  NTC Business Books, pp. 243–244).
• For television and in-studio radio shows, leave for the
  interview early. This is one interview for which you absolutely cannot be late: A client or recruiter can always
  wait, but an 11 A.M. show must start at 11 whether you
  are there or not. If the show starts at 11 A.M. and you

were told to be there at 10 A.M., and it takes an hour to drive in normal traffic, you might think you should leave at 9 A.M. I would recommend you leave at 8 or 8:15 the latest . . . just in case. There is nothing as uncomfortable as being stuck in traffic at 10:45 for an 11 A.M. radio appearance. Trust me—I know from experience.

- For call-in radio shows that interview you by phone from your home or office, arrange for absolute silence and no interruptions during the interview. This is *very* important. Being interrupted is unprofessional, annoying to host and listeners, will ensure that you are never invited back, and can make you lose your composure and throw you off track.

Put a DO NOT DISTURB sign on the door—a big one, in large bold letters. Let others know you will be doing a radio show via phone and cannot be disturbed for any reason.

If possible, do the interview without other people around. If you're doing it from home, ask your spouse to take the kids for ice cream and put the dog in the dog run.

Do you have call-waiting on your phone? Use a call-blocking feature to shut off the call waiting, or have someone call you to tie up your second line, to prevent your phone interview from being interrupted by the annoying call-waiting click signal. If there are other phones in the home or office that can ring within earshot of your phone, take them off the hook.

Also, turn off your radio. You cannot talk on the phone to a radio show and listen to it at the same time.

Make sure you have a glass of water handy and that the air conditioner or heat is not turned up too high. You want to be comfortable, as you will not be able to get up and change the thermostat once the interview begins.

KNOW YOUR TOPIC

Spend some time boning up on your topic before you go on the show. A radio or TV appearance is the ultimate think-on-your-feet challenge. No matter how well you prepare, callers and hosts will ask some questions on highly specific situations that require you to work out an answer instantly, on the spot, then present it in a clear manner, without hesitation, in thirty to sixty seconds.

Spend an evening reading through your press releases, press kit, book, article clippings, brochure, annual report, or whatever source material is the basis for your topic. Take notes on some interesting highlights, and jot these key facts and figures on a few index cards or sheet of paper. Take this material with you. You can study it while you wait to go on the air and, on radio, refer to it without the audience knowing you are using a crib sheet.

The listener and host expect you to be an expert in your topic; that's why you are there. However, part of being an expert is to know how far your expertise extends and where it ends. This honesty impresses hosts and viewers, rather than turning them off. I have two specific strategies for handling questions that throw me off balance and to which I don't have a good answer (or can't come up with one on the spot).

The first is to decline to answer based on limits of expertise. For instance, on a recent radio appearance where I was talking about how to be a more effective salesperson, a caller asked about managing a sales force and specifically about whether I knew compensation schemes that would reward salespeople for getting repeat business from existing accounts. I immediately answered, "Michael, I'm sorry, but my expertise is selling techniques, not management of sales-people. I know nothing about management and have no idea how to compensate a sales force. You might try asking colleagues who are sales managers at other companies in your industry."

The second strategy is to say "I don't know the answer to that question, George, but if you call me at my office tomorrow we can discuss it further; I will then research it and get the answer for you or put you in touch with someone who knows. Mr. Host, may I give George my office number?" This demonstrates that you are a helpful source of information and gets you off the hook of having to know it all.

The late Isaac Asimov, prolific author of more than 400 books on science, history, science fiction, literature, and other topics, tells an amusing story about the media's expectations of an "expert."

He was booked on a radio talk show by his publisher to promote his latest book, *The Human Brain*. When the interviewer asked him a question about the brain, he answered, "I don't know."

"What do you mean you don't know?" asked the interviewer. "You wrote a book on the human brain!"

"Yes," Asimov replied, "but I've written hundreds of books on dozens of topics, and I can't be an expert on all of them. I only know what's in the book, and in fact, I can't even remember all of that!"

Exasperated, the interviewer said, "So you're not an expert on anything?"

"Oh, I'm an expert on one thing," said Asimov.

"On what?" asked the host.

"On being an expert," Asimov replied. "Do you want to talk about that?"

The host declined.

HANDLE SHOCKS GRACEFULLY

Being a guest on a radio or TV talk show is not always a winning situation.

It takes lot of effort and time to get on the show, prepare, and do the actual interview. For us small businesspeople, time is money. So, unlike many people, we don't do it for the fun or glory or to feed our ego. We do it for the sole purpose of publicizing our product or service, generating leads, enhancing our visibility and reputation, and making more sales and profits. (At least, that's my motivation.)

So when we go to all this trouble and the media appearance doesn't work out, the tendency is to get upset and angry. But don't let it show. Instead, handle the situation gracefully, never yell or scream or complain, and always leave people thinking well of you. This positive behavior increases your chances of getting more and better media opportunities; negative behavior will give you a reputation as a difficult person and make media people want to avoid you.

Most media appearances do go well, but there are horror stories. One friend recalls driving two hours in torrential rains to keep an appointment to appear on a radio show. When he arrived, another guest was sitting down in the interviewee's chair. "Whoops," the assistant program manager told him. "I must have forgotten to make a note after we talked, and I guess I forgot to schedule you in. Can you come back next week?"

And of course, we've all heard about the authors and other "last guests" on the *Tonight Show* who *know* they're going to get bumped if the celebrity on before them has a big mouth and is in a talkative mood. Can you imagine being in Burbank ready to appear on the *Tonight Show*, then watch the final minutes of the show tick by as Madonna or Charo keeps yakking? That's media hell.

Another "horror story" happened to my friend Richard Armstrong. He was thrilled when his publisher booked him on the Bob Grant show, a top-rated talk show in the New York City market, to discuss his new book on politics, *The Next Hurrah*.

Unfortunately, when he got there, he discovered that he was *not* the sole guest but that another author would be on at the same time. The author was celebrity George Plimpton. Worse, Plimpton had just written a book on baseball, and wanted to discuss baseball, not politics. The show made absolutely no sense, with Plimpton talking about baseball and Bob and Richard discussing politics (with Plimpton also commenting on politics but obviously disinterested in doing so), but Richard performed like a pro and did well.

DON'T PROMOTE YOUR PRODUCT, SOLVE YOUR PROSPECT'S PROBLEMS

Most experts tell you, "Plug your product or service when on the air." I disagree. People don't want to hear about your book or video or accounting firm; they want to get solutions to their most pressing problems. So rather than talk about you, your product, your service, or what you know, focus on the listeners—what they need, what they want, their problems and concerns.

Example: I recently was a guest on a number of call-in radio shows to promote my book *Selling Your Services: Proven Strategies for Getting Clients to Hire You (or Your Firm)* (Henry Holt). Repeatedly the hosts would ask, "Tell us about your book, Bob."

I'd answer, "I'd be happy to talk about the book, Mr. Host. But what I'd *really* like to do is to help your listeners overcome their fear of making cold calls, overcome all the objections they are getting from prospects, and feel more confident about selling and get better results. So, those of you listening out there, when you call, we'll go through your particular selling situation and *solve the problem* right over the phone!"

The hosts were delighted with this approach, as were the listeners. I created a much more interesting, useful show by working with the listeners as if they were clients, rather than saying "my book this" and "my book that," as 99 percent of authors do. And what about promoting the book? No problem: The host did that for me, because he was enthusiastic about my information and wanted to help listeners get more of it.

Benefits were twofold. First, I came across as a credible, respectable expert, not a self-interested author trying to get the listeners to buy a book. Second, the promotion of the book by the host was more effective than me saying it, since it amounts to a third-party endorsement: the host saying the book was great and telling his listeners they should order it.

Notes Lant, "Radio and television are warm and intimate. Thus, you must personalize what you know, reach out and talk directly to your prospects as a friend, entirely honestly, as if you are having a conversation. The fact that you can't see the person you are talking to is irrelevant. That person must feel the force of your personality."

DOTTIE WALTERS'S TIPS FOR BEING INTERVIEWED ON RADIO

Dottie Walters, publisher of the newsletter *Sharing Ideas*, offers the following tips for being interviewed on radio:

- *Prepare.* Write out the fifteen most likely questions you'll be asked. Develop your answers and practice answering them.
- *Restate the question before giving your answer.*
- *Be brief.* After twenty to thirty seconds, you're probably overanswering. If an answer goes beyond that, summarize it.
- *Use humor.* But don't tell jokes. Short anecdotes are effective.

- *Demonstrate you're an authority.* Use facts, enumerating your points. Use dramatic startling statistics and findings.
- *Elaborate beyond yes or no.* Make specific points. Use examples to bring home each point. Give reasons.
- *Talk personally, concretely, and colorfully.* Look at the interviewer when you talk. Use names—the person interviewing you, the people calling into the show. Later in the show, refer by name to people who have called in.
- *Be positive and show energy through enthusiasm and conviction.* Don't repeat or paraphrase a caller's damaging question. It's okay to interrupt a question based on a false fact or premise. End each segment with an upbeat, summarizing benefit.

GET A TAPE OF YOUR GUEST APPEARANCE

Whenever possible, get a tape of each radio and TV appearance you make. The tapes have a number of uses:

1. You can use them to convince producers of other radio and TV shows that you are a good guest, entertaining, pleasant, bright, and informative, with information relevant to their audience.

   Producers are somewhat reluctant to book guests who are experts but have no or little experience in broadcast media. An audio- or videotape of a good performance eliminates that reluctance.
2. Listening to the tapes help you improve your performance so you are better next time.
3. You can use the tapes as marketing communications tools. For example, if you are a consultant specializing

in quality, and you were on a cable TV business show discussing quality, make copies of the video and send it to clients and prospects.

4. Give copies of the tapes to your mom and dad. They'll be thrilled. (The extra copies are for mailing to Uncle Ned and Grandma Nellie.)

How do you get a tape? Before my scheduled interview, I call up the producer, say who I am and when I am scheduled to be on the show, then say, "May I ask a favor? I would love to get an audiotape of the broadcast. If I send you payment, would you be willing to tape the show and mail the tape to me? If not, no problem, of course."

Most will agree and, further, not charge you for it (but you should always offer payment). Others might ask for a nominal sum to cover the cost of duplication and mailing—$5 or $10 for an audiotape of a radio show, $50 to $75 for a videotape of a half-hour TV show.

While it's best to get an original tape from the studio (because originals give the best-quality duplications), you can, of course, arrange to tape your appearance yourself. If you are on TV, you can program your VCR to tape you while you're on the air. If you are on radio, some stereo systems allow direct recording from the radio to the blank cassette. Putting a cassette recorder near a radio and picking up the sound from the speaker usually results in a poor-quality recording not good enough for duplication.

CHAPTER 11

PREPARING YOUR MEDIA KIT

A media kit is a package of PR materials you have prepared for a variety of uses. It consists of a number of different documents that are prewritten, standardized, and can be pulled off the shelf at a moment's notice to fulfill a request for information.

While putting together a media kit seems like a daunting task, it actually saves you lots of time when handling PR programs and media requests for information. Without a kit or file of prepared press materials, you must write a letter or a blurb to fulfill each request from a reporter, editor, investor, or other information seeker.

With a set of prepared media documents at the ready, you simply pull and mail or fax the appropriate piece to your media source. This not only saves time and effort, but it lets you respond to the request faster . . . and the speed of response to a media request often makes the difference as to whether you get the coverage.

FORMAT FOR MEDIA MATERIALS

The two format choices are to print quantities of each piece to have on hand, or else to keep your media kit documents stored in your PC on hard disk and print copies of the documents when needed.

The advantage of having pieces printed and on file is that they can be pulled more easily, and you save wear and tear on your printer. The advantage of having the pieces stored on floppy disk is that you can easily keep the documents updated; whenever there is a change, just open the file and make the change. When you get a request and print that document file, you are assured of giving your media source the latest information.

Another advantage of keeping media kits on computer is that you can easily custom-tailor materials for different editors. Just make a duplicate of the file, then edit the duplicate to customize it to a particular publication or editor.

ELEMENTS OF THE MEDIA KIT

Although the variety of elements that can go into a media kit is almost limitless, the most common items are:

- Media kit cover
- Company bio or backgrounder
- Individual bios
- Product releases
- Tip sheets or fact sheets
- Kudos sheet
- Photos
- Article reprints
- Brochures, catalogs, data sheets, and other product literature

Let's take a quick look at each element.

Media Kit Cover

The media kit cover is a pocket folder, typically printed in one or two colors on a glossy stock. The front cover usually consists of an imprint of the company logo; this can be embossed for visual effect. The inside of the folder has a pocket on either side. The back cover is usually blank.

Most companies prefer this subtle, laid-back design, making their press kit covers attractive and impressive, not promotional. Some PR practitioners, such as Steve Davis, head of his own NYC-based PR firm, feel the cover should be more promotional.

"Put some sales sizzle on the cover," writes Davis in *Playthings* (February 1988). "Since the focus is on what's new, a couple of eye-catching headlines would at least convey some semblance of excitement and information. Media people have specific wants and needs. Pressroom material must reach out and immediately attract the attention of the editor. And once in hand, the information must be persuasive."

For example, if you manufacture semiconductors, you might put in big, bold letters on the front cover of your media kit the headline NEWS ABOUT NEW DEVELOPMENTS IN SEMICONDUCTOR TECHNOLOGY. Or something like that.

What about size? Make the kit cover 9 by 12 inches. People often dump oversize press folders that don't fit into a standard file cabinet. Yet the folder must be large enough so the pocket can contain 8 ½-by-11-inch papers.

Company Bio or Backgrounder

The company bio or backgrounder is a press release, typically two to five pages, that presents an overview of the company—

its history, markets, products, services, and capabilities.

The company bio or backgrounder communicates the same information to editors that capabilities brochures are designed to communicate to customers and prospects. It is designed to tell the editor quickly who you are, what you do, and what makes your company special.

Unlike the capabilities brochure, which tends to dramatize the company story, the backgrounder should be straightforward and factual. Editors will not run it as a story; instead, they will use it as a reference when seeking specific facts about your company to incorporate into articles they are preparing.

Having a press backgrounder eliminates the need to include an "about the company" section in other press releases used in the media kit.

Here are some of the topics that may be included in the backgrounder:

- Full name of the company
- Type of business
- Corporate structure (divisions, departments, subsidiaries, branch and regional offices)
- Company mission statement or business philosophy
- Company history
- Plants and other key facilities
- Major markets served
- Distribution system
- Sales
- Ranking in its field relative to competition or market share
- Financial information
- Number of employees
- Employee benefits programs
- Noteworthy employees

- Inventions, patents, industry firsts
- Key achievements or accomplishments
- Research and development activities
- Quality control practices
- Community relations
- Environmental activities
- Awards
- Policies
- Objectives, goals, plans

Individual Bios

Brief biographies of key individuals, especially those likely to be quoted in news releases or interviewed by the press, may be included in the media kit. These can be typewritten in press release or any other format, and are typically one-half to one page in length.

Individual employee biographies are used more frequently by service firms, especially smaller ones, rather than manufacturers. Reason: The noteworthiness of smaller firms is often tied to the credentials and accomplishments of the owner or other key employees.

Biographies of individuals typically include:

- Person's full name
- Job title
- Job responsibilities
- Degrees earned and schools attended (high school and colleges)
- Job history (other positions at this company plus previous employment history)
- Family information (spouse, children, town of residence)
- Community involvement
- Key accomplishments, both personal and corporate

- Publications, patents, awards, and other industry, professional, or personal recognition
- Memberships in professional societies and other organizations

"Keep in mind that biographical details are not there for your greater glorification but to motivate a prospect to take immediate action," writes Dr. Jeffrey Lant in one of his columns. "Thus, even the biographical features of your life must be transformed into benefits the prospect wishes to achieve and which he understands he can get only with your help."

Product Releases

The press kit typically contains a separate product release for every major product or product line you manufacture or every key service your firm provides. Product releases should be one to three pages each. See chapter 5 for instructions on how to write product releases.

Tip Sheets or Fact Sheets

Fact sheets are one- or two-page summaries or listings of key facts of interest to the media. The facts may be about a product, technology, activity, service, or anything else you want to promote. A fact sheet in a media kit for a new restaurant, for example, might contain recipes of four or five of the chef's most popular dishes.

Fact sheets are written in list format, using bullets, numbers, tables, and the like, rather than in narrative format. They are meant to be used as references, not reprinted as is. A chemical manufacturer, for example, might put the specifications (chemical formula, specific gravity, boiling point, dew point, and so on) for each chemical it sells on a separate fact sheet.

Kudos Sheet

A kudos sheet is included to show editors and other reviewers that your company is successful because you have many customers, users, or clients who like you and your product.

The kudos sheet can consist of a list of customer names, a referral list (customer names with addresses and phone numbers editors can call), testimonials (quotations from satisfied customers), or any combination of the three. Kudos sheets are typically one or two typewritten pages.

Photos

Include photos of key individuals, products, facilities, and anything else of interest that can be used to accompany articles based on the releases included in the kit. Photos should be black and white, 5 by 7 inches or larger. Captions should be typed on paper, then affixed to the back of the photos using invisible cellophane tape.

Do not type or write with a ballpoint pen directly on the back of the photo; this could damage the photo. Do not paper clip photos. Just insert them into the pockets of your press kit.

Article Reprints

You may want to include full-length reprints of one, two, or three major articles written about your company or product. This shows editors that your company or product has been found newsworthy by other editors or writers, and also gives them a model or "sample" article they can follow in doing their own stories.

Another technique is to do a collage or paste-up of a group of short news clips about your company or product, then reprint them on one or two sheets of paper. The purpose is not to provide text other editors can copy but to show that you have received extensive coverage and many placements in a wide range of publications—an indication that your press releases are newsworthy and of value.

Brochures and Other Product Literature

Do not stuff your press kit full of every product brochure and spec sheet you can find, simply to fill it up. Notes Steve Davis, "Editors use literature as reference material, not prime source information."

Editors prefer to work from press releases rather than ad reprints or promotional brochures, so you should take all key information necessary for the editors to write stories about you from your brochures and put it into press releases . . . even though you think your brochures already do a good job of telling the story. The media kit should contain these press releases, not your brochures.

HOW MUCH MATERIAL SHOULD YOU INCLUDE IN THE MEDIA KIT?

"If a kit is stuffed with every brochure or manual produced in the last year, the sheer weight is an impediment," writes Davis. "Too often I've seen editors pick up a press kit and grunt. Some won't even take a heavy kit with them unless it's a high priority. Lean and mean should be the concept."

If you have too many product press releases, for example,

maybe you should have one release per product *line* rather than one release per product.

Or you might include press releases only for one of your three or four most important products, then combine short descriptions (one or two paragraphs each) of all of your other products in a separate release of two or three pages.

One firm had so many PR materials that it didn't know what to include in their media kit—and what to leave out. The solution?

It put in only three or four of their most important items plus a "bibliography"—a four-page listing of other press materials it had available but that were not included in the kit. The bibliography included a short message urging editors to request any of the other materials they wanted to review. The request could be made via phone or by checking the items desired and faxing the list back to the publicist.

HOW TO WRITE CLEARER, MORE EFFECTIVE PR MATERIALS

Quill Communications, a marketing communications agency based in Encinitas, California, offers the following checklist for businesspeople planning to write their own PR materials and related marketing documents:

1. *Review your past successes and failures.* Why are your customers customers? What did you do to turn them into customers? What didn't work in the past? Detail the steps you took and the information provided. Remember, the PR documents must have strong RSI (appeal to reader/customer/prospect self-interest) as well as ESI (editor self-interest).

2. *Profile your audience.* What characteristics do they

have in common? Why would the editors and their readers be interested in your story? List their needs, interests, and wants.

3. *Determine when the audience will be reading the material.* The tone and content can change depending on when audience members will be reading it. Are they going to receive the material at a trade show? after a press conference? in the mail?

4. *Set your objectives.* No matter how well written, the PR materials will be ineffective if you don't know what you're trying to accomplish.

   Are you trying to convince the public that your hair replacement technique is superior to others? Or is your goal to get people to request your free "Baldness Prevention Booklet"? Or to position yourself as an expert in fashion, health, and beauty whom writers can call on as a source for stories on hair loss and hair grooming?

5. *Determine the key idea or theme of the piece.* What is the single most important idea that needs to be conveyed to the reader?

6. *Make a list of benefits and features.* Editors like and use press materials with specifics—benefits, features, facts that support the key selling idea; they dislike and usually discard materials that talk in generalities and don't give the specific facts.

7. *Establish priorities and objectives.* Not every facet of your product, organization, or story can be told in a single piece of literature. What is the key theme of each particular piece in the media kit? Which points and facts must be included in this document, and which ones are more appropriate for other documents in the media kit?

8. *Determine the tone.* How you say something is as impor-

tant as what you say. Use a tone and language appropriate to the audience. Chiropractors, for example, are not the same as neurosurgeons.

9. *Develop a schedule, with priorities.* Plan your writing schedule. Which PR document is most essential? Which must be produced first, second, third? Allow plenty of time to review the copy after the first and second drafts.

10. *Organize your material.* Write each point you want to make on a 3-by-5-inch index card, or use an outliner software program. How you organize depends on the objective, idea, and content of your materials.

11. *Write about 20 percent more copy than you need, then edit back.* Editing boils your copy down to the essentials, but first you need some raw material to work with.

12. *Use simple words.* The purpose is to inform and interest, not prove how smart you are.

13. *Read your copy aloud.* Did you stumble on any words or sentences? Rewrite what sounds awkward or unclear.

14. *Select your technical terms carefully.* Be sensitive to the technical knowledge and backgrounds of your audiences—editors as well as their readers.

15. *Avoid overused terms.* So many companies have used the terms state of the art, cutting edge, and innovative to describe their products, these terms have become trite.

16. *Use one tense.* As a rule, do not mix the tenses of verbs in the same sentence.

17. *Rewrite and revise your copy.* Writing is rewriting and rewriting until you run out of time.

18. *Trim the fat.* Cross out any word, sentence, or paragraph that doesn't support the point you want to make.

19. *Save the trimmings.* As you edit, save discarded sentences and paragraphs to use in your captions or in other materials.

20. *Check the details.* It's easy to skip over the product and company names, phone numbers, trademarks, fax numbers, specifications, numbers, units of measure, dates, and other details. Take the time to make sure they are correct and complete.

USING TECHNOLOGY TO DISTRIBUTE MEDIA MATERIALS

In today's fast-paced electronic society, PR professionals and other marketers are looking for a way to get the jump on the competition and get their materials to editors faster.

Editors and publishers are showing interest in the use of electronic technology in reporting and journalism. For example, I have seen several publications run voice-mail reader surveys on industry issues. The survey questions are printed as a short article or sidebar in the magazine, and the reader is given a phone number to call to answer the questions. The phone number is connected to a voice mail system that automatically asks the questions in sequence and records the response.

The advantage? More readers respond, because it's easier to pick up the phone and call than pick up a pen and fill in a questionnaire or write out lengthy answers to open-ended survey questions.

PR professionals also seek to use technology to communicate PR information to editors. In the 1990s, using the fax to transmit PR materials has become the rage. The reasoning is that a fax stands out from the dozens of printed releases received in the mail each day and the fax also allows timely material to be received more quickly.

Personally, I'm not a big fan of using the fax for an initial press release mailing, unless the story is extremely critical and time-sensitive. For 99 percent of the releases you will send, the publication does not perceive the information as urgent or high priority. The decision to run it will be based on whether the item is interesting and newsworthy, and there will usually be no particular deadline or publication schedule for using it—the editor will run it when space is available.

Therefore, using a fax to send a nonessential communication is, to me, inappropriate. Editors aren't going to pay more attention or be more likely to use your material because it's a fax rather than a printed release. In fact, some may even resent your taking up their time and fax paper with inessential messages.

I would use a fax only in two cases. The first case is when the news is so timely and critical that the delay of printing and mailing releases would mean a lost media opportunity: By the time the printed release arrived, the event would be over, and it would be too late to run the story. In such a case, by all means send a fax.

The second good use of a fax in PR is to follow up with editors. For example, if an editor is interested but calls you asking for more information, fax the additional details to help her put her story together faster and meet her deadline. She'll appreciate prompt and timely response.

A fax is also good if you call to follow-up a mailing of a press release and the editor says he didn't get it or doesn't remember it. You can briefly explain the story and, if he shows interest, fax another copy over to him right away. Since he just spoke to you about it and knows your fax is coming, he'll at least read it over.

Media Distribution Services (MDS), 307 West 36th Street, New York, NY 10018, 212 279-4800, is one service that can fax your media materials en masse to multiple media outlets. MDS has a database containing the fax numbers of 150,000 reporters, editors, and broadcasters at more than 40,000 print and broadcast media in the United States and Canada. You can select from the database by more than 2,500 classifications of editorial interest. MDS can fax your release to any number of media, from one to one thousand or more, simultaneously.

CHAPTER 12

INTEGRATING TARGETED PUBLIC RELATIONS WITH OTHER PROMOTIONS

INTEGRATING TARGETED PR WITH OTHER MARKETING COMMUNICATIONS

Public relations will generate coverage and many leads and media placements for your product or service, even when it is your sole marketing tool. But the key to getting the most out of every dollar spent on PR is to integrate PR with other marketing communications activities—to recycle and reuse the material so it gets maximum exposure. Doing so not only saves money by eliminating the need to "reinvent the wheel" for every promotion, but it also exposes your prospects repeatedly to the same message—important in building "top-of-mind" awareness.

Here are just some of the ways in which PR, advertising, direct mail, and other marketing activities can be integrated, and how materials created for one purpose can be used in many other applications effectively and profitably:

1. Reprint articles and news blurbs generated by PR placements. Use the article reprints as supplementary sales literature in inquiry fulfillment kits.

2. Have a library of article reprints salespeople can use to reinforce the sales message. For example, when a customer isn't buying because of a quality concern, it would help if the salesperson could reach into a file, pull a published article about the quality awards your company has won, and fax that to the prospect as they are talking on the phone. Or mail it with a follow-up letter.

3. Turn feature-length article manuscripts, published and unpublished, into special reports, booklets, or other information premiums. These can be offered as bait pieces in press releases, ads, and direct mail.

4. Use article reprints instead of product literature to accompany sales letters in direct-mail campaigns. Often the article reprint is more interesting and credible to the prospect than a slick brochure.

5. Turn the article into a self-mailer. Reprint the article on the inside panels; use teaser copy and other sales messages to get the prospect into the piece. Print in two or three colors, with yellow highlights or red circles and underlines drawing the reader's attention to key points in the article.

6. Offer bait pieces developed for PR releases in direct-mail packages. Have sales letters stress or at least mention the offer of the free report or booklet. This will significantly increase response.

7. Offer the bait piece in print ads. Show a photo of the booklet or report cover in your ad. Highlight the offer in copy. Stress that it is free. Provide a toll-free telephone number and coupon for response.

8. Condense articles and press releases and reprint the

stories in abbreviated form in your company newsletter or house organ.

9. Make audio or video recordings of speeches and seminars given by company executives. Offer the audio- or videocassettes as bait pieces in ads and mailings. Or include them in the outgoing direct-mail package or in inquiry fulfillment packages.

10. Enter the names, addresses, phone, and fax of all leads generated through PR into your database for future follow-up and promotions.

11. Incorporate PR activities into your advertising or marketing plan. You'll find they make it possible for you to get many more opportunities to reach your target audience with minimal additional expense.

12. Support more expensive marketing activities—direct mail, print ads, catalogs, brochures—with PR. For example, if you create a special report for a direct-mail offer, do a press release offering the report. If you produce a new catalog, send out a release announcing its publication. If you conduct a market research survey, announce the most significant results by mailing a release to appropriate media.

TAKE ADVANTAGE OF OPPORTUNITIES AS THEY ARISE

While I'm all for planning communications activities, there's a danger of being locked into a plan so tightly that you proceed like a horse with blinders on: You follow the course you've set, but deny yourself excursions along profitable sidepaths.

Be flexible. If a great PR opportunity arises, take advantage of it. Even if it's not in the marketing plan. Even if it's not in the budget. If there's a good chance of making profit from it, take the risk and make the investment.

MONITORING AND MEASURING RESULTS

Establish goals and objectives for your PR efforts.

The goal could be to generate a certain number of leads, close a certain number of deals, get so many new customers or accounts, generate a specific dollar volume in revenue, or sell so many units of the product. Some people measure the PR effort's success by number of article placements generated, or even by the number of column inches or pages of coverage generated.

You can certainly make "gaining visibility" or "building image" one of your goals, but in addition you should also have a measurable objective, such as leads, sales, or placements. This makes it easier to determine the success of the PR program and the return on investment.

Whenever possible, key code PR materials (for example, add extensions to telephone numbers and department numbers to addresses) so you know which leads are PR-generated. Since the source of many leads is not apparent, get in the habit of asking prospects where they got your name.

Keep records in a notebook or on computer. Records let you know how well you've done.

Measuring results by placements or column inches is more difficult than counting leads or inquiries, because often you don't know it when a publication picks up your material. You can scan all pertinent publications yourself, looking for placements, but this is enormously time consuming.

Approximately 99 percent of publications will *not* notify you that they've used your material or send you a copy of the story. So when you see placements of your release, you're probably only seeing a small fraction of the results.

One solution is to hire a clipping service that will send you clippings of your placements. Some of the larger PR clipping services include Bacon's (800 621-0561), Burrelle's Press Clipping Service (201 992-6600), and Luce Press Clipping Service (800 528-8226). Call for information and a brochure.

Cetex Corporation, of Medford, New Jersey, offers a PC software product, Cliptrak, that supports tracking and analysis of news clippings. Cliptrak lets you track press coverage by product, subject, organization, competition, region, author, client, type of coverage, and twenty-one other categories. It also computes the total media coverage in column inches and translates this into ad space equivalents (what the free coverage would have cost if run as a paid ad in the same amount of space). For information call 609 953-1406.

ENHANCE YOUR PR KNOWLEDGE

If PR is your full-time responsibility, or if you're serious about improving your skills and abilities as a PR professional, you'll want to investigate membership in the Public Relations Society of America (PRSA)—the largest national organization for PR professionals. PRSA offers regional seminars, a national conference, publications, accreditation, awards, a job hotline, and more. For information contact PRSA, 33 Irving Place, New York, NY 10003, 212 995-2230.

Another way to improve your PR expertise is to read some of the periodicals and books listed in the appendix.

TWO CASE STUDIES

How do successful PR practitioners plan and manage PR programs for real-life clients? Here are two case studies* that give a brief look into how it was done for two different com-

*Reprinted with permission of Renee Sall Associates.

panies. Both were clients of Renee Sall Associates, a New York City–based PR firm.

Positioning a NY Attorney as an Expert

A successful New York matrimonial attorney was interested in enhancing his image and developing a strong profile as one of the nation's top authorities. The strategy was to position the attorney as an expert in all areas of family law.

Since principals in major cases are inundated by requests for interviews from the media, an outside expert who can provide thoughtful and insightful commentary on legal issues of the day is a valuable commodity to a journalist or reporter.

The PR strategy? When a high-profile trial (the Trump divorce) was covered in the press, pitch letters were prepared featuring the attorney's observations on that particular issue, suggesting that journalists use him as a source of "expert legal opinion" in stories they were preparing about the case.

This resulted in a steady flow of publicity as the press became aware of his credentials and began to rely on his expert commentary. The placements ranged from ABC-TV's *Primetime Live* to WNEW Radio's nationally syndicated *Larry King Live* to articles in *Harper's Bazaar* and *Manhattan Inc.*

In addition, the attorney was booked by his PR agency as a regular lecturer for an adult seminar entitled "The Legality of Love." With this newfound publicity and notoriety, even a British journalist took note of all the media attention this attorney was receiving and featured him as the subject of a major story in the London *Daily Mail.*

This exposure became an invaluable addition to the attorney's business and following. Calls for consultations poured into his office and, over the course of a year, led to a substantial increase in his total client base.

After a year of PR efforts, the attorney and his PR firm are now contacted daily by television producers, magazine editors, and radio commentators for ideas regarding upcoming feature stories and scheduled programs.

Courier Service

At the time the PR program began, this company was a messenger service in the process of expansion via the acquisition of other messenger companies. The problem was that the industry was suffering from the rapidly increasing popularity of fax machines.

In the past, a time-sensitive document would have required expeditious hand delivery. Now, due to facsimile machines and almost instant transmission, they can be sent and received at a fraction of the cost of using a messenger.

Realizing that the messenger industry would never return to its "pre-fax" status, the company wanted to publicize a new service, "facilities management," which is the business of taking over a major corporation's entire support center (mailrooms, messenger services, and in-house copy centers) as a way to reduce staff and overhead and thereby lower operating costs.

The entire PR campaign focused on facilities management as being the wave of the future as corporate America seeks leaner, highly cost-effective methods to maintain operations.

The courier company's role in this new management strategy was highlighted in numerous pitch letters and press releases directed to media outlets catering to the target market: chief executive officers and upper-echelon management. Media materials also included several articles about facilities management with the client's name featured in the byline.

Leader's magazine, a publication whose controlled circulation is comprised exclusively of CEOs of top corporations, was one of many publications that accepted the articles. The PR effort also got the client (the CEO of the courier company) on *Financial News Network* as well as *Business News Network*, a well-received syndicated radio program.

In addition, several business publications, including *Fortune* and *Forbes*, have run stories on facilities management in which the client was prominently featured and quoted.

PUBLIC RELATIONS IN A RECESSION

In a recession, advertising is one of the first things to be cut.

When the economy is slow and business is poor, money becomes tight. Businesses can't stop paying the electric bill or the phone bill, and they have to keep buying raw materials or the product can't be made.

However, management sees that the business will continue to run tomorrow without advertising, so marketing activities are reduced.

This is understandable but dangerous. Stopping your marketing may have no immediate effect, but six months from now, you may come into work to find that you have no new jobs, no new customers, no new sales, and no leads or prospects for getting more business. That's because the marketing cuts you made have finally caught up with you: Not generating leads and interest for future business through marketing done today means no sales and business tomorrow.

Stopping marketing when things are very bad (when you

have no money) or very good (when you have more business than you can handle) is a natural tendency. But it will result in the number of leads and sales being uneven throughout the year. Sales go up, you stop marketing, leads dry up, sales go down. So you start marketing, get leads, rebuild your business. Then you get comfortable, stop marketing, and the cycle continues.

Doing steady marketing all year long will ensure a continuous flow of new business leads and sales throughout the year, eliminating slow and lean periods.

But, you may object, if we're in a recession we just won't have the money.

The solution is not to cut marketing, but to shift the emphasis from expensive marketing methods, such as paid advertising, to less expensive methods, such as low-cost publicity, postcard decks, and sales promotion.

Publicity is an extremely cost-effective means of marketing your product or service. In a robust economy, a Targeted Public Relations campaign can complement your expensive advertising and promotion programs. Synergy is achieved, and the results generated by an integrated communications program are generally greater than the response PR or ads or telemarketing would have generated by themselves.

In a recession, you can use low-cost PR to augment or even replace advertising and other marketing programs. If you can't afford an ad, send a press release. If you can't afford a big booth at the trade show, hold you own seminar locally.

According to Renee Sall, president of Renee Sall Associates, "In a depressed economy, maintaining your company's visibility will become more important to economic survival than ever before. One major dilemma is that the urgent need to increase public awareness is being met head on by a sharp decrease in the available dollars required to support such an effort. Generating and increasing public awareness for a product or service has traditionally been accomplished through advertising. While the media often extend discounts or cut advertising rates to stimulate advertiser interest in their magazine or paper during a weak market, you will usually find that these 'bargains' rarely compensate for the overall loss in business that you are experiencing.

"The scenario does not have to be as bleak as it seems. Just when advertising begins to falter, a professionally administered public relations program can pick up the slack. A comprehensive PR campaign can cost as little as one-fourth of a comparable advertising effort, and can yield results that will turn your company's shrinking bottom line around in dramatic fashion.

"At first glance, there is an understandable hesitancy to invest in any form of sales promotion while a recession looms so large. A downturn in the economy is often met by an implementation of cost-cutting measures, especially the reduction of intangibles such as publicity and promotion. This play-it-safe philosophy is quite often the first step companies adopt to limit spending.

"Unfortunately, the only result this practice guarantees is stagnant sales. Your sales are already down; the last thing you want to do is keep them at this level. You need to revise your promotional budget and use it more effectively, not eliminate it. A sound public relations program can boost visibility and sales at a time when every sector is cutting back. With fewer companies actively promoting themselves, your message will stand out, affording you the best opportunity to get an edge on the competition.

"In addition, there is an unspoken message communicated about your company through PR done in a recession. That message is 'We are doing well, we are surviving and are here for you, because we have a product or service that is in demand, even during a recession!'

"With careful evaluation, detailed research, and a creative approach, you can get your message across and balance your budget as well. And in a recession, that's good news."

MORE TIPS ON PUBLICIZING AND PROMOTING YOUR PRODUCT IN A RECESSION

Don Levin, president of Levin Public Relations & Marketing of White Plains, New York, offers these tips for increasing sales in a slow economy:

1. *Rethink what business you're really in.* Link your product lines with specific target markets. Determine the most cost-effective marketing steps that will put your product lines before the buying influences and decision makers. The most profitable companies keep examining and refining their fundamentals.
2. *Refine your unique selling proposition* (USP). Your unique selling proposition is the one most powerful reason for prospects to choose your company or your product. If you can't explain your USP in twenty words, you need to define it better.
3. *Expand your domain.* Don't leap to the unknown. Rather, edge outward to new geography, products, services, personnel, and service methodologies. If possible, extend your business to growth locations—those regions of the country least affected by the recession.
4. *Keep after the buyer.* Keep reminding your prospects and customers why you're more cost-effective than your competitors. Update your database. Call old prospects.

5. *Overcome objections and barriers to making the sale.* List the top ten reasons why prospects don't say yes. Study their concerns so you can combat them.

6. *Move toward number one.* Drive toward industry leadership. Do things that would be expected of the leader. Assume a greater role than your competitors.

   Leaders set the business standards. They become keynote speakers at major conferences to propose resolutions to business issues. Every November they forecast the next year in their markets, so editors include their quotes in December outlook articles. Their comments regularly appear in business publications because reporters learn that they answer questions quickly and with substance.

7. *Upgrade your staff.* Train, educate, let them grow. Trust them. Involve them in your increasingly important issues.

8. *Try different approaches.* Do market research even if you feel you know the market. Find the big idea that will make a difference to your prospect. If you have been relying on advertising to bring in sales leads, try adding a layer of professional publicity and sales promotion.

9. *Gather your allies.* Identify companies and individuals with a stake in your success. Nurture them. Give them the tools to support your growth program.

10. *Communicate more effectively.* Exploit the tools of publicity, presentations, direct mail, seminars, advertising. Use outside help judiciously. Question your own assumptions. Evaluate competitive strength and weakness in this area, then leapfrog to prominence.

    For example, if you've published articles, it may be time for a book. If you have multiple sales sheets, it may be time for a brochure. Is your company name, motto, address, phone, and fax on every single page that a customer or prospect might see?

GETTING HELP

Firms handling their own public relations sometimes reach a point where they can no longer do everything in-house and turn to outside sources for help.

The type of help they seek generally falls into four categories:

1. Administrative detail—primarily distributing press releases
2. Planning, media contact, and other PR services
3. Writing
4. Graphic design, including desktop publishing, photography, and production of printed materials

Let's take a brief look at who can help and how you can find them.

Administrative Details

The most logical thing to farm out is distribution of press releases. Many fine distribution services available charge low fees. It is often more cost-effective to have such a service handle press release mailings than to rent the names, affix the labels, print and collate the press releases, stuff them in envelopes, and take them to the post office yourself.

Two of the largest press release distribution services, discussed elsewhere in this book, are Bacon's Publicity Distribution Service (800 621-0561) and Media Distribution Services, Inc. (212 247-4800). MDS can send your release out via first-class mail or fax; Bacon's uses mail only.

Another well-known press release distribution service is PR Newswire, 150 E. 58th Street, New York, NY 10155, 212 832-9400. It sends press releases electronically via wire, and publications receive them on the same Teletype machines and computer terminals over which they get stories from Associated Press and UPI. PR Newswire can also fax or mail press materials, if desired.

Planning, Media Contact, Follow-up, and Other PR Services

Some of the labor-intensive aspects of running a PR campaign include planning your PR strategy, selecting appropriate media outlets, making contact with the media, and following up on PR opportunities. Public relations firms can provide these services; some freelancers and independent PR consultants and counselors also do this type of work.

PR agencies generally charge an hourly rate, ranging from $100 to $150 an hour and up, and require a monthly retainer with a minimum commitment of three to six months' service or more. Retainers are usually $1,000 to $2,000 per month or more.

Work performed for the client is billed at the hourly rate against the retainer. For example, if your PR agency charges $125 an hour and the monthly retainer is $1,000, you would be entitled to eight hours of service per month.

PR agencies are listed in the Yellow Pages under "Public Relations Firms." A better way to find a PR firm is by getting recommendations from colleagues.

Or you can contact PR firms listed in *O'Dwyers Directory of PR Firms*, a directory listing more than 1,200 PR firms nationwide. Ask your library's reference librarian or contact the publisher, J. R. O'Dwyer Company, 271 Madison Avenue, New York, NY 10016, 212 679-2471.

PR Writing

If you hire a PR agency, it can handle the writing of releases, articles, and other PR materials for you. If your volume is not large enough to justify putting a PR firm on monthly retainer, however, freelance copywriters are available who write PR materials and other marketing documents on a per-project basis. This might be the solution for you.

Writers charge by the project or by the hour, with a wide range of fees. Hourly fees for PR writers range from $50 to $150 and up. The fee for having a press release written can range from $100 to $800, depending on length, complexity, and the experience of the writer.

Having a writer ghostwrite a feature article might run anywhere from $800 to $3,000 or more, depending on length. A good rule of thumb is a dollar per word, although that gives a rough estimate only. Other factors, including degree of difficulty and amount of work required, could result in a higher or lower fee.

To find a writer, look in the Yellow Pages under "Writers" or ask colleagues for names of writers they have used. Local ad agencies and PR firms may also know of freelance writers you can hire. Some writers advertise their services in the classified ad sections of marketing, PR, and advertising trade publications, such as *Adweek* and *Direct*.

Graphics

You may need the help of an outside vendor to put together printed materials such as press kit covers, brochures, newsletters, and booklets and special report bait pieces.

Desktop publishing services can more than adequately handle simple tasks, such as one- or two-color booklets and newsletters that are mostly type (no elaborate design, photos, or illustrations). Hourly fees range from $35 to $65 an hour and up.

Freelance graphic artists or art studios have more design experience and can handle more complex pieces, such as annual reports, four-color company magazines, and brochures. Hourly rates range from $50 to $135 an hour and up.

If you need drawings, a freelance illustrator can help. The fee for a single illustration could range from $150 to $500 for something relatively simple to $1,000 and up for a complex rendering.

Freelance photographers can take pictures at events, go on location to shoot manufacturing or people photos for case history articles, and handle other black-and-white and color photography needs. Rates range from $500 to $1,000 a day for a competent PR photographer. (*Note:* Some advertising photographers specializing in fashion, annual reports, and other top-of-the-line work charge from $2,000 to $5,000 per day, but most PR applications do not require this level of sophistication.)

Again, check the Yellow Pages under the appropriate categories ("Photographers," "Illustration," "Desktop Publishing," "Graphic Artists"). Or ask colleagues at other companies. Local ad agencies and PR firms can also point you in the right direction. Also ask other vendors: For example, your PR writer is likely to know of several good graphic artists he or she can recommend to you.

MORE WAYS TO MAXIMIZE TARGETED PUBLIC RELATIONS RESULTS

The editors of *communications briefings* (700 Black Horse Pike, Suite 110, Blackwood, NJ 08012) suggest these additional tips—many of which focus on local angles—for getting results from your PR programs:

1. Take a look now at holidays and anniversaries coming up during the next twelve to eighteen months. Look for obvious promotion and event tie-ins while you have time to plan.

2. If you send speakers into the community through a speakers' bureau, remember to alert area media to significant presentations your speakers may be making. Along with reaching audiences directly, your speakers may provide the fodder for some good publicity as well.

3. Go beyond your traditional image and seek out new audiences for your products and services. You'll boost your business while doing something new and different—the very definition of making news.

   One college launched a program to help workers tired of current jobs decide on new careers—careers, of course, that the college could help them launch. A newspaper incorporated its product into junior high school reading classes. A restaurant began making home deliveries to the elderly and the disabled.

4. Consider launching a public information service aimed at educating consumers on issues you and others in your organization are experts on.

   A supermarket chain employs dietitians to appear on talk shows to talk about menu planning and smart shopping. A hospital uses nurses and doctors to talk about child care. A detergent company uses its technicians to discuss the best ways to care for furniture, clean stains, and organize housework.

5. Never miss the chance to develop a year-end wrap-up story on your organization's successes during the past twelve months. Also consider doing a look-ahead as each new year approaches.

   Focus on your organization as well as its employees and the community it serves. Show how what your

organization plans for the days ahead will affect many
different audiences.

TO SUM UP ...

Public relations has always been one of the most affordable
marketing communications tools. And now you have the techniques to make it one of the most measurable, as well. By
converting your ordinary PR efforts to Targeted Public Relations, you'll not only gain more visibility and fame, but
you'll generate highly profitable inquiries, leads, orders, and
sales, too.

These techniques have worked for hundreds of companies
nationwide, and I am confident they will work for you.

APPENDIX: SOURCES AND RESOURCES

A lot of good information is available on public relations. What follows is a sampling of some selected resources, many of which I personally use and can recommend.

PUBLICATIONS

BUSINESS MARKETING MAGAZINE
220 E. 42nd Street
New York, NY 10017
212 210-0100

Monthly magazine devoted exclusively to business-to-business marketing.

JEFF DAVIDSON
Jeffrey P. Davidson, CMC
3713 S. Geo. Mason Drive, #1216W
Falls Church, VA 22041
800 735-1994 or 703 931-1984

Davidson is the author of 1,900 articles, 17 books, and numerous audiocasettes, many of them on marketing and sales topics—and all of them excellent. Call or write for a catalog and order form.

THE LEVIN REPORT
Don Levin
Levin Public Relations
30 Glenn Street
White Plains, NY 10603–3213
914 993-0900

A newsletter presenting practical, proven public relations tips and techniques that work.

THE LIBEY LETTER
Donald R. Libey Consultancy Incorporated
1308 Keswick Avenue
Haddon Heights, NJ 08035
609 573-9448

A highly informative, wonderfully written monthly newsletter on the strategies, trends, and future direction of marketing. Highly recommended.

THE MARKETING COMMUNICATIONS REPORT
Pete Silver
4300 NW 23rd Avenue
Suite 528
Gainesville, FL 32606
904 371-2083

Short, concise, lively monthly newsletter providing marketing tips and ideas. Pete is expert in all phases of marketing communications, especially use of newsletters and toll-free 800 numbers as marketing tools.

THE PUBLIC RELATIONS JOURNAL
Public Relations Society of America
33 Irving Place
New York, NY 10003
212 995-2230

The official magazine of the Public Relations Society of America. Free to members. Excellent, informative articles. Monthly.

RADIO-TV INTERVIEW REPORT
Bradley Communications Corp.
135 E. Plumstead Avenue, Box 126
Lansdowne, PA 19050–8206
800 989-1400

This magazine, published twice a month, is circulated to more than 3,800 media professionals who book guests for TV and radio shows nationwide. To get on these shows, you run an ad in *Radio-TV Interview Report* featuring the topic, person, or issue you want to publicize. My publisher ran an ad for one of my previous books, and I was booked on several radio shows as a result—so it works.

SURE-FIRE BUSINESS SUCCESS CATALOG
Dr. Jeffrey Lant
JLA Publications
50 Follen Street
Suite 507
Cambridge, MA 02139
617 547-6372

Quarterly 16-page catalog containing more than 120 recommendations on small-business marketing and management. Call or write for free one-year subscription.

BOOKS

Barhydt, James T., *The Complete Book of Product Publicity* (New York: AMACOM, 1987), 308 pp.

This book focuses on publicizing products and is especially good for PR and product managers wishing to publicize industrial products.

Bly, Robert W., *The Copywriter's Handbook* (New York: Henry Holt & Co., 1990), 368 pp.

How to write copy for press releases, newsletters, speeches, brochures, ads, and every other type of marketing document you need to produce.

Harris, Thomas L., *Marketers Guide to PR: How America's Top Companies Are Using the New PR* (New York: John Wiley & Sons, 1991).

Reports on case studies of how well-known companies handle their PR.

Pinsdorf, Marian K., *Communicating When Your Company Is Under Siege: Surviving Public Crisis* (Lexington, MA: Lexington Books, 1987), 171 pp.

Focuses on that special aspect of PR called "crisis management." Targeted mostly toward bigger firms that get into the front pages and evening news a lot and need strategies for averting negative publicity.

GRAPHIC ARTISTS

STAN GREENFIELD
39 W. 37th Street, 14th floor
New York, NY 10018
212 768-7653

First-rate freelance graphic artist capable of producing brochures, catalogs, and other promotional materials.

RUTLEDGE & BROWN COMPANY
Steve Brown
25 West 39th Street
Suite 1101
New York, NY 10018
212 730-7959

Steve is a freelance graphic artist. He specializes in brochures and collateral but also does excellent work on press kits, PR letterhead, and other materials.

DESKTOP PUBLISHING

DESIGN ON DISK
1013 Teaneck Road
Teaneck, NJ 07666
201 837-7171

Excellent desktop publishing resource for "quickie" materials as well as higher-quality jobs.

MARTIN UNLIMITED
David Martin
2 Marine View Plaza
Hoboken, NJ 07030
201 798-0298

Quality Macintosh desktop publishing at reasonable prices.

ORGANIZATIONS

BUSINESS/PROFESSIONAL ADVERTISING ASSOCIATION
901 North Washington Street, Suite 206
Alexandria, VA 22314
703 683-2722

The only national association for professionals involved in business-to-business marketing communications. I have been a member since 1981 and recommend it highly.

PRSA
Public Relations Society of America
33 Irving Place
New York, NY 10003
212 995-2230

A national association for public relations professionals with 15,000 members and 100 chapters.

PUBLICITY DISTRIBUTION/OUTLETS

This is where you go for lists and mailing labels of magazines, newspapers, and radio and TV stations to which you mail your press releases.

BACON'S PUBLICITY CHECKER
332 S. Michigan Avenue
Chicago, IL 60604
800 621-0561

Bacon's publishes annual directories of media sources in the following categories: TV and radio, newspapers, and magazines. Bacon's will also provide pressure-sensitive mailing labels or handle the printing and mailing of your press releases for you at a reasonable rate. I use Bacon's for my clients all the time and am extremely satisfied both with the price and the results.

BRADLEY'S TOP TALK SHOWS
Bradley Communications Corp.
135 E. Plumstead Avenue, Box 126
Lansdowne, PA 19050–8206
800 989-1400

A directory of the nation's top talk shows. Gives you the name, station, address, and phone number for the chief booker at the top 700 radio and top 50 TV talk shows nationwide.

CABLE CONTACTS
BPI Media Services
PO Box 2015
Lakewood, NJ 08701
201 363-5633

This media directory focuses on the top 50 markets and contains information on 719 local cable systems in the United States and Canada, 1,245 programs, and 227 satellite networks, pay services, superstations, associations, text services, independent producers, and multiple system operators. Program listings include the names of the host and producer along with guest information and material requirements.

DIRECTORY OF WOMEN'S MEDIA
National Council for Research on Women
47–49 East 65th Street
New York, NY 10021
212 570-5001

Media directory containing descriptions of more than 1,000 print and electronic media, publishers, bookstores, libraries, distributors, archives and other media resources by, for, and about women.

EDITOR & PUBLISHER INTERNATIONAL YEARBOOK
11 W. 19th Street
New York, NY 10011
212 675-4380

Annual directory listing the publishers and editors at more than 250,000 U.S., Canadian, and foreign newspapers. Probably the most comprehensive media directory for newspapers available.

EDUCATIONAL PRESS ASSOCIATION OF AMERICA—MEMBERSHIP ROSTER
Communications Department
Glassboro State College
Glassboro, NJ 08028
609 863-7349

A small directory listing more than 800 writers, editors, and journalists who write about educational topics.

GEBBIE ALL-IN-ONE DIRECTORY
Box 1000
New Paltz, NY 12561
914 255-7560

A directory with 30,000 listings covering newspapers, magazines, radio, and TV in a single volume. Listings are also available on computer disk or mailing labels.

HUDSON'S SUBSCRIPTION NEWSLETTER DIRECTORY
The Newsletter Clearinghouse
44 W. Market Street
Rhinebeck, NY 12572–1403
914 876-2081

Annual media directory providing contact information for more than 3,000 subscription newsletters (newsletters people pay to receive versus free newsletters distributed by companies as promotions or employee communications).

MEDIAMAPS
130 The Great Road
Bedford, MA 01730
617 275-4999

MediaMaps specializes in PR coverage of the computer industry and computer industry publications. Consider MediaMaps if you use PR to promote software, hardware, peripherals, and related high-tech products and services of interest to computer users and professionals.

NATIONAL RADIO PUBLICITY OUTLETS
Public Relations Plus, Inc.
PO Box 1197
New Milford, CT 06776
203 354-9361

A comprehensive media directory featuring 6,800 radio networks and stations.

OXBRIDGE DIRECTORY OF NEWSLETTERS
Oxbridge Communications, Inc.
150 Fifth Avenue
New York, NY 10011
800 955-0231

Information on more than 20,000 U.S. and Canadian newsletters. Also available on-line.

THE POCKET MEDIA GUIDE
Media Distribution Services
307 West 36th Street
New York, NY 10018
212 279-4800 or 800 MDS-DATA

One of the largest full-service press release distribution services, MDS features a computerized database of 150,000 editors, reporters, and broadcasters at more than 40,000 media outlets in the U.S. and Canada. Call for details and a copy of the *Pocket Media Guide*.

POWER MEDIA SELECTS
Broadcast Interview Source
2233 Wisconsin Avenue NW
Suite 540

Washington, D.C.
202 333-4904

A directory with contact names, addresses, phone numbers, and profiles of more than 3,000 of the most influential print and broadcast media contacts. Updated every six months. This book is *selective* ("influential" media), compared to Bacon's, which is comprehensive.

RADIO CONTACTS
BPI Media Services
PO Box 2015
Lakewood, NJ 08701
201 363-5633

A directory listing 4,000 radio stations and 4,300 radio shows including program host and contacts.

SYNDICATED COLUMNIST CONTACTS
BPI Media Services
PO Box 2015
Lakewood, NJ 08701
201 363-5633

A complete directory of syndicated columnists in print media nationwide, with listings of more than 1,500 individual columnists organized by area of coverage (business, medical, advice, and so on).

TALK SHOW SELECTS
Broadcast Interview Source
2233 Wisconsin Avenue NW
Suite 540
Washington, DC 20007
202 333-4904

A directory with contact names, addresses, phone numbers, and profiles of over 600 of the most influential talk show hosts, producers, and programming executives in the nation. Excellent for those pursuing radio and TV PR opportunities.

TELEVISION CONTACTS
BPI Media Services
PO Box 2015
Lakewood, NJ 08701
201 363-5633

A directory covering 1,100 TV stations and more than 2,000 programs. Listings include host and contact names, show format, preferred guests, and subjects covered.

WORKING PRESS OF THE NATION: INTERNAL PUBLICATIONS
National Research Bureau (NRB)
225 W. Wacker Drive
Chicago, IL 60606–1229
800 456-4555

A media directory listing more than 2,600 "internal publications" (employee newsletters, company magazines, and house organs published by corporations for distribution to employees and customers). This complements the *Hudson Directory of Newsletters*, which is a media directory of *subscription* newsletters (newsletters you pay for).

TELEPHONE HOTLINES

THE PUBLIC RELATIONS HOTLINE
The Caruba Organization
Box 40
Maplewood, NJ 07040
201 763-6392

A hotline offering PR consultation by the hour over the telephone. Charge it to your MasterCard or Visa. Call between 9 A.M. and 5 P.M. EST, Monday through Friday.

INDEX

ABOUT THE AUTHOR

Robert W. Bly is an independent copywriter and marketing consultant. He writes public relations plans and marketing materials for such clients as Associated Air Freight, American Medical Collection Agency, Edith Roman Associates, Grumman, Sony, Timeplex, Fala Direct Marketing, JMW Consultants, Howard Lanin Productions, and The BOC Group.

Mr. Bly is the author of twenty-five books including *The Copywriter's Handbook, Secrets of a Freelance Writer*, and *Selling Your Services* (all three published by Henry Holt). Other titles include *Create the Perfect Sales Piece* (John Wiley) and *How to Promote Your Own Business* (New American Library).

A frequent speaker, Bob Bly has presented marketing seminars to such groups as the International Tile Exposition, American Marketing Association, Financial Advertising and Marketing Association, Business/Professional Advertising Association, Women's Direct Response Group, and the Publicity Club of New York. His articles have appeared in *New Jersey*

Monthly, Amtrak Express, Writer's Digest, Cosmopolitan, and
many other magazines.

Questions and comments on *Targeted Public Relations* may
be sent to:

Bob Bly
Copywriter/Consultant
22 E. Quackenbush Avenue
Dumont, NJ 07628
201 385-1220